#O.I.R.- BLACK HEARTS, TOP GUNS, AND GOING VIRAL AT WAR

By: Daniel Johnson

First Edition: January 2021

Book design by Daniel Johnson
Original news articles edited by Nathan Hoskins and Ireka Sanders.

ISBN 978-0-578-82835-0 (eBook)
ISBN 978-1-7364657-0-7 (Paperback)

TO

The personnel of the 2nd BCT, 101st Airborne Division,
And all those who have served, are serving, or will serve
our nation, Both in and out of uniform.

ABBREVIATIONS

Note: Military Ranks follow AP style guide rules

PAO	Public Affairs Officer
ISIL	Islamic State of Iraq and the Levant
ISIS	Islamic State of Iraq and Syria
PMF	Paramilitary Forces
Fed Pol	Iraqi Federal Military Police
TOC	Tactical Operations Center
HE	High Explosives
OIR	Operation Inherent Resolve
CJFLCC	Combined Joint Forces Land Component Command
CJTF-OIR	Combined Joint Task Force
IED	Improvised explosive device
VBIED	Vehicle Borne Improvised Explosive Device
HIMARS	High Mobility Artillery Rocket Systems
COIN	Counterinsurgency
TAA	Tactical Assembly Area
PAA	Position Area for Artillery
CJOC	Combined Joint Operations Center
ISF	Iraqi Security Forces
KSB	Kara Soar Base
DVIDS	Defense Visual Information Distribution Service
BOC	Baghdad Operations Command

DFAC	Dining Facility
Humvee	High Mobility Multipurpose Wheeled Vehicle
COP	Combat Outpost
FOB	Forward Operating Base
KLE	Key Leader Engagement
FDC	Fire Direction Center
ISR	Intelligence, Surveillance, and Reconnaissance

CONTENTS

Introduction-Help From Above- August 2017

A copy of "Help From Above", which hangs in the headquarters of 2nd Battalion, 327th Infantry Regiment, 101st Airborne Division (Air Assault). The photo was donated by Art Greenspon to the 101st when he was inducted as an honorary member of the 327th Infantry Regiment in 2014. Greenspon identified the names and positions of the Soldiers in the photo. Sgt. Maj Watson Baldwin stands with his hands raised signaling to a helicopter. Spc. 4 Dallas Brown lays on the ground grimacing in pain. Sgt. Tim Wintenburg, helmetless on the far right, glances back at the camera. (Photo by Daniel Johnson, Original Photo by Art Greenspon, Associated Press, April 1968.

Appalachian State's Criminal Justice program is one of the most excellent journalism schools in the country. It must be- no one else from any institution or company, including the Associated Press, had asked Tim Wintenburg about the photo in the almost 50 years since that day in Vietnam.

All of that sleeping --- I mean *reflecting* I did in Criminal Law class had finally paid off.

"I've waited a long time to talk about this," Mr. Wintenburg's words to me on the phone, a tone of relief and shock evident in his voice. His buddy Dallas Clark, also in the photo, had called him with information about a lieutenant from the 101st Airborne Division who wanted to interview the Soldiers and write a story about one of the most iconic images of the Vietnam War.

April 1968. The A Shau Valley, near the Laos border. AP photographer Art Greenspon is embedded with Soldiers from Company A, 2nd Battalion,

327th Infantry Regiment, 101st Airborne Division. A search and destroy operation, with Lt. Tom Sewell's 1st platoon in the lead. There was a pause in the patrol, and Dallas Brown was relaxing near a tree, when he noticed, in his words, a "tree moving." An ambush. A firefight through the foliage, a chaotic melee symbolic of the conflict in Vietnam.

Multiple men were wounded, and Lt. Sewell's platoon set up the hasty LZ for medical evacuation. A Soldier in the middle of the clearing spread opens his arms to guide the helicopter in.

"Help from Above." Art Greenspon shot the photo.

The subject of the photograph, Sgt. Maj. Watson Baldwin, who was a Staff Sgt. at the time and Sewell's platoon sergeant, stood with his arms outstretched in the air, signaling the incoming aircraft. On the ground lay Spc. 4 Dallas Brown, writhing in pain from a back injury. In the far right, a helmetless Soldier, Sgt. Tim Wintenburg, glanced back at the camera as he carried a wounded comrade.

Greenspon sold the photo to the AP and it quickly became one of the most iconic images of the conflict. Over the years, the photo was an inspiration for the poster of the Vietnam War movie "Platoon", graced the covers of books, and could be found on front pages of newspapers.

Still, no one ever thought to ask who the Soldiers were, to write their stories down, aside from Greenspon. Until me.

Baldwin died in 2005, his tale untold, though his figure inspired images and thoughts across the years. Tim Wintenburg, Dallas Brown, and Tom Sewell were still alive, having settled across the nation, and were willing to talk. In the intervening years, they had gone into bus driving, industry, and other work, veterans of a war that the country sometimes tried to forget. But, *they* could not forget.

"Watson Baldwin was the finest platoon sergeant I had when I was in the Army," Wintenburg continued, as he recalled the firefight. "He was a lead-by-example type of guy, always upfront leading the way and making sure we were doing the right thing. Baldwin was also very compassionate. He did two tours in Vietnam and retired as a sergeant major. After the war, he went into trucking before he died."

The conversations with Wintenburg, Brown, and Sewell filled in the details about the event and their lives afterwards. They spoke of how Wintenburg had decided to become a paratrooper because it looked athletic, how Brown and a bunch of high school friends walked down to the recruiter's office one day, and how Sewell had been working with his father when he received the draft letter in the mail.

When the photo was published by the AP in 1968, the only notification the *subjects* of the photo got at the time was a letter Sewell's mother sent him in the mail with the newspaper clipping attached. It didn't even have their names as part of the caption. The crazy thing was, no one even thought to ask, besides Art Greenspon.

"What people didn't understand back then but understand more now is that we were Soldiers doing our jobs," Wintenburg's words, a common refrain heard throughout conflicts in history, among many different nationalities. "A lot of things back in the 'world' as we called it didn't matter out there. What mattered was that it was life and death, and what mattered was keeping each other alive. The loyalty we had to each other was profound."

As I listened to the words from each of them, I knew for the story to be complete I needed the photo with them marked out and identified with each of their locations. I'm not a great photographer, but the one thing I learned-deliver the goods upfront. Draw in the reader — the proof in the pudding.

I called the Associated Press.

As soon as I informed the person who answered the phone that I had some questions about the Soldiers in Art Greenspon's photo, I found myself speaking to the head of the Nashville Bureau of the Associated Press a few minutes later.

"How did you track these guys down?" the voice of the head of the Nashville Bureau of the AP spoke to me, doubting (and I don't blame him) that my story was true.

"I asked around," my response, and a true one at that. One of the Vietnam Veterans visiting base had said that he knew where to find the guys and to give the division association a call, which I had done.

"I'm wondering if you had Mr. Greenspon's contact information," my request. Surely the AP would have it, I thought to myself?

"Maybe," the bureau head replied. He knew a scoop when he heard one. We both had something the other wanted, and it was time to negotiate a deal. "He doesn't exactly talk to a lot of people."

I would learn later that the small list didn't include the Associated Press.

"What are you planning to do with the information?" his question. The hidden one, "Are you going to try to sell this to another media organization."

"Write an article for the Army," my reply.

"Really?" his response, questioning.

"You know, the AP sometimes publishes articles written in by submission," a savvy, veteran move. They were a contracting organization. What difference was this from an AP writer sent out to get something? Even better, the story had come to *him*. Surely, I would agree, who wouldn't? This was the opportunity of a lifetime, a chance to have a story run by newspapers across the nation and world. All I had to do was say yes.

I had come a long way from April of 2016; the beginning of a confluence of events which would find me being dropped into Iraq with no idea how to take a photo or to craft a story.

But then I'd be breaking my promise to those veterans when I said I was writing the story for the United States Army first and foremost, so it could be freely accessible by all. The AP could pick it up after, I figured.

It had already happened to me before.

"Yeah, I've already had a photo run by you guys before." My reply.

"Really." Shocked. But also, the important inflection of interest piqued.

"I'll have to get back to you on that." My response, half lying. I knew this route was a dead end unless there was some give and take. I decided to talk to Dallas Brown; he had Mr. Greenspon's number, which he had always kept so, in his words, "That people will believe me when I tell them about the photo."

I thanked him and gave the digits a call.

"Hello?" a voice on the other line, a questioning tone after no doubt receiving many calls of this nature.

"Hi," my response, unsure of how to proceed. "I was given this number by a Mr. Dallas Brown. May I speak to Mr. Greenspon?"

"What organization are you with?"

"Lt. Daniel Johnson, 101st Airborne Division Public Affairs," my response. Mr. Greenspon was out at the moment, the reply. I could read between the lines- he didn't want to be bothered.

There was no way he'd want to talk to little old 1st Lt. Johnson. Who could blame him?

My phone vibrated.

I glanced down at the number --- the same one I had called.

The voice of Art Greenspon on the line as soon as I said hello.

He introduced himself, then came the kicker.

"I read your stories. I always look people up when they call," I started to coldly sweat, waiting for him to say they were garbage. "They're extremely well written; I can tell you're good at your craft."

I was shocked. Greenspon spoke about his experiences, his time in Vietnam, and how honored he was when he visited Fort Campbell a few years before.

"The photo is hanging on the wall in the 502nd battalion headquarters with all the names," he informed me. "I'm glad you're writing an article, please send me a copy when it's complete."

With the photo, I had everything I needed and the article was published. The Associated Press did a follow-up story on the Soldiers a few months later, their names hitting the national papers. Their story had finally been told to the world.

Mr. Greenspon's response when I sent him the article was that it was an excellent story about great men.

"Thanks for getting the ball rolling on all of this," Mr. Wintenburg's words to me, after all of it was said and done. "It's helped me heal from the experience. I never thought I would be able to tell our story."

The final denouement on my whole experience at Fort Campbell, shaped by trying to make sure people heard Soldiers' stories. An experience that saw me go to war with my unit to even continue my military career; that saw me go from a kid who didn't even know how to write to become the source of news in Iraq for one of the most powerful militaries in the world.

All because an offhand remark one day said in jest that no one believed could happen, especially me. But I get ahead of myself. The story begins in 2016, a year of bizarre happenings.

What's one more to add to pile?

Chapter One- The Joke - April 2016

This all started because U.S. Army Maj. Ireka Sanders had a problem with no clear solution.

Sanders was the public affairs officer for her organization, the 2nd Brigade Combat Team "Strike" of the 101st Airborne Division, which was 4,000 people strong. She was running out of time; the brigade was about to send a contingent to Iraq to assist in the fight against the Islamic State of Iraq and the Levant as part of Operation Inherent Resolve and she had a few months before they departed. She needed help.

Fast.

Sanders was the prototypical United States Army Public Affairs Officer --- she had studied broadcast journalism in college, was good with people, and above all else-

She was a person who thought outside the box.

The New Orleans native had to be, especially as a female public affairs officer in an infantry brigade combat team (IBCT). Even more so since her previous branches had been the Signal and Chemical Corps, where officers could get screwed up fast career-wise if they didn't have the drive.

The U.S. Army had invested heavily in its public relations branch after Vietnam with thousands of public relations specialists filling spots across the force at multiple levels, all with one job: sell the Army to the public. PAOs were underestimated, especially in IBCTs, since commanders didn't know how to use them. Most people thought they just took pictures, or just updated the Facebook page, or wrote news articles that no one really paid attention to. For a solid amount of PAOs, these expectations met the reality. It was a job where you had to sell your usefulness to whoever was in charge since you competed with other officers with much more easily identifiable mission essential jobs, like the intelligence officer, signal officer, or the operations officer who wrote all the plans and ensured that the 4,000-person organization executed tasks.

If you couldn't compete, you'd easily fall to the wayside, be forgotten, and then find yourself going home since you didn't get promoted. Maj. Sanders wasn't going to allow herself to be one of those PAOs who got sent, as the saying went, "to the house".

"We fight where we're told and win where we fight," was the motto of the "Strike" brigade, which greeted her upon her arrival to Fort Campbell,

Kentucky, home of the 101st, in 2014. A phrase that to most of us sounded like it would be more in place for the head of an evil corporation to say instead of a United States Army unit.

2nd Brigade, "Strike", the Black Hearts, home of the storied 502d Infantry Regiment, with a history that stretched back to World War II. Normandy, the A Shau Valley, Desert Storm, Mosul. A unit with a lot of alumni in high places and a unit that could be recognized by civilians in the outside world, (at the division level at least.) A unit that would probably find itself on the call if the Army needed someone to rotate in whatever operation came up.

All these reasons, and others, was why Ireka Sanders chose to come to the unit.

With all the history came baggage, however; the 101st was a light infantry division, no longer an airborne one, only keeping the designator due to unit history. Now they specialized in air assault operations- massive movements by helicopters to target locations. Fort Campbell was the home of the storied Air Assault School, where personnel learned about the types of aircraft, how to connect equipment to aircraft, and how to rappel.

At least, that's what the course guide said.

Either way, all leaders in the division were strongly encouraged to attend Air Assault School. The problem was, unlike the 82nd Airborne division who still jumped out of planes, you don't have to be airborne qualified to get into a helicopter, ride to the objective, and jump out. That didn't stop the division, brigade, and battalion command teams from trying, however.

Like the rest of the division, the 2nd Brigade badge was worn on their helmets --- two black hearts, one on each side. It was a practice that was used in World War II, disappeared for about 60 years, and then came back for the Global War on Terror. The symbol was distinctive and, unfortunately, seemed indicative of a culture at some points. Three members of the 1st Battalion of the 502nd committed war crimes in 2005, murdering the Iraqi al-Janabi family of Yusufiyah: a father, mother, and six- and 14-year-old daughters. The book about the incident, aptly titled "Black Hearts," was required reading for most military officers, and for years afterwards the first response to if you told someone you were going to the unit was, "Didn't those guys commit war crimes?"

The deployments didn't stop however, with the brigade deploying about once every 18 months. Iraq, Iraq, Afghanistan, Afghanistan, and now Iraq once more. If you could survive the practically nonstop training schedule, the type A personalities, the cut-throat politics, and perhaps a deployment on top of that, your career was set. All you needed was drive, and a propensity to deal with a lot of crap thrown your way.

Fortunately, Ireka Sanders had that in spades and quickly figured out the unit culture. She went to Air Assault school, did the ruck marches, attended all the meetings, and made sure she got face time with the commander. For anyone working in corporate America, these things seem like common knowledge. You'd be shocked however to know how many PAOs in the Army didn't do it, however. She looked at Strike as a brand, which meant that she needed branding. Black Hearts stickers, Black Hearts water bottles, Black Hearts posters, Black Hearts newsletters that looked more like glossy magazines. If you came to visit her in her office, you left with something with a Black Heart on it, even if she had to put it together herself.

She was also savvier than most people at her rank when it came to utilizing social media, which was shockingly not as common as one would think. There were way too many social media pages for units that Soldiers and their families didn't care to follow because they thought it was useless. To be honest, even I didn't start paying attention to ours until Maj. Sanders started putting out posts with #BeStrike, a hashtag she created.

Part of the schemes Sanders ran also had to do with making sure the key audiences were involved. Like any good brand manager, she made sure to stay in touch with the Strike alumni through community outreach, organizing Strike Soldiers marching in parades as far as Chicago, meeting and greeting the Vietnam veterans, and anyone else who sometimes literally came walking through the door. After a year, everything was firing on all cylinders.

And now she had a big hole to fill in her team for the deployment.

Staff Sergeant Sierra Melendez was one of Sanders' photojournalists and though they clashed a fair bit the two were a great team. Staff Sgt. Melendez had just transferred over from being a military police officer and was willing to get into the weeds if need be to get photos or the stories required. She was also a good photographer.

In Melendez's first year, she was selected as the best new journalist in the entire United States Army. Her articles were getting run at high levels and her images were being posted by the U.S. Army social media accounts, above everyone else's. Even better, Melendez had just got to Fort Campbell, so she would be around in 2016 when the unit was slated to deploy to Iraq. Going into an operation with the attention Operation Inherent Resolve was getting, and having perhaps the best journalist in the Army? Doing it as part of the storied 101st Airborne Division too?

Things couldn't get any better.

One small issue -

Staff Sgt. Melendez was thinking about getting out of the Army, and just like that, Maj. Sanders' plan evaporated. She was now looking at the prospect of no help for what was shaping up to be the deployment opportunity of the lifetime. No other units wanted to give up their PAO personnel, and she sure wasn't going to get a new one from the pipeline.

So, when this random L.T. sent her an email out of the blue, asking her if she needed help, she pounced.

What was the worst that could happen?

In hindsight, it's funny how being considered unimportant led me into the whole absurd situation.

"Ma'am," I began the email to Maj. Sanders, typing quietly on the keyboard in front of me, heart pounding quickly in my chest. Going around my unit's leadership was a significant risk; it could go sideways fast. I paused, then thought about the situation for a moment, weighing my options: my career was over if I stayed in my unit, and probably even if this crazy idea worked and I went to Iraq, it'd still be over.

Why not go for it? Why not try to join my friends who would soon be risking their necks 7,000 miles away? How could I even claim to be a Soldier, an Officer, if I didn't try everything to get on this mission?

"If you were serious about needing help on the deployment," I continued. "I'll help you out."

I looked at the email one more time, then hit send.

There was no way this was going to work.

It was April of 2016 in Fort Polk, Louisiana, home to the Joint Readiness Training Center. The installation was created to train Soldiers going to Vietnam back in the day- heavily wooded, swampy, humid, hot. Made sense that Louisiana was chosen to be the spot for training for a jungle war. The Army continuing to use it to prepare Soldiers for Iraq didn't. My unit was at the tail end of the exercise there, a 30-day event where units preparing to deploy battled a simulated enemy.

Before I joined the Army, I thought the National Training Center in the deserts of California was where people training to go to Iraq went to.

Yeah, right.

Turned out that's where mechanized units that specialized in tanks, armored personnel carriers, and other highly mobile equipment went to. I wasn't in a mechanized infantry unit; 1st Battalion, 26th Infantry Regiment,

"Blue Spaders."- a light infantry unit through and through. Lots of walking, dismounted patrolling, and carrying what you needed to survive on your back for long periods of time. As an officer in a light infantry unit, you were expected to have graduated from the United States Army Ranger school located in Fort Benning, Georgia, to even have a shot of getting a chance to lead.

Most officers did.

And there was me.

1st Lt. Daniel Johnson, information-no-unit public affairs? No,-assistant signal officer? Wait, I got it, what they had just told me.

"Family Readiness Liaison," responsible for handling communications with families as we stayed back at Fort Campbell and everyone else went "forward" to Iraq.

Oh yeah, 1st Lt. Daniel Johnson --- infantry officer.

No Ranger Tab.

It was an actual thing for lieutenants to get "tabbed check" by their commanders when arriving at certain units. A quick glance at your left shoulder to see if you had the qualification. If not?

"What happened at Ranger School?"

I was dead in the water without even completing the first lap. I had fractured my hip at Fort Benning, GA trying to attempt to pass Ranger School; I didn't make it out of the first week. The joke about the infantry officer course at the time was that it was basically a pre ranger course- you weren't worth anything in the eyes of the Infantry Officer Basic Course cadre if you didn't have your Ranger Tab.

 And some units out in the force didn't want you either. A prime example: the 173rd Airborne Brigade, out of Vicenza, Italy, where people got their orders canceled in Infantry School if they were Ranger School incomplete.

Commanders in the 101st had the same general attitude too. I had been warned not to come to Fort Campbell without a tab, but I was injured, so I knew my Ranger School dreams were over. I arrived in October 2014, right as the rest of the brigade was getting back from the deployment.

"Tabless infantry officer? Throw him to 1-26."

There were only 100 personnel in the Battalion, a far cry from the 800+ when fully manned. It was a new unit, more historically associated with the 1st Infantry Division of Big Red One fame, but now brought to Fort Campbell for reasons I still haven't figured out.

Either way I had no hope of doing the job I needed to do to get promoted --- being an infantry platoon leader. As a lieutenant in almost any job subsection of the Army (separated into branches, like the Medical Branch, Aviation Branch, etc.), being a platoon leader was paramount. It was ostensibly where you learned how to lead. (Not allowing people leadership opportunities that can teach them leadership skills because you think they should get more leadership skills is not too surprising considering some other Army logic). At 22 years old, you had responsibility for sometimes up to 40+ people, leading them in training, home base operations, and, if need be, deployment to a combat zone. Only after being a platoon leader could you look to do other jobs, because if you never were one you were at risk to be non-promoted.

Separation from the service would follow soon after.

A year-plus in the unit, first as the unit's communications officer (I was part of a program where I would switch from the Infantry the Signal Corps if I got promoted), assistant communications officer, and then. battalion social media guy and photographer. That job especially was usually given to an officer who the battalion commander felt had no purpose. It was a joke, and I was so low on the totem pole to the point that people felt sorry for me.

For over a year I had floundered, finding myself working for a Captain that I didn't like, given no guidance, and no chance to prove myself. Late nights, never-ending tasks, and the constant reminder, as new lieutenants arrived and immediately got platoon leaders slots, that I was at the bottom of the pile. I was shit on, always.

What a way to "serve" my country.

I'm still surprised that I wasn't more beat down. I figured that even though I was probably screwed, I might as well do my job until the jig was up. Whatever task my bosses gave me, I did. I may have been a "loser," but I was damn sure going to be a productive one. Anything less would be a failure on my part as a Soldier, officer, or hell, human being. Growing up I had watched war movies with my father, who himself had served in the military. Professionalism, loyalty, dedication, continuing to try even when the situation was crap, not for any external reasons but because it was the right thing to do.

Those lessons stuck with me.

I went to work each day to do whatever B.S. came next, oddly enough, to everyone's surprise, happy. I was the most active photo guy in the brigade aside from the Brigade PAO. I wasn't sound mind you, but they never had to worry about me not making social media posts or sending pictures. It also allowed me to get to know Soldiers throughout the battalion, who I guess were shocked that I wasn't a horrible officer; just one that was getting screwed.

Maj. Sanders knew of me. In fact, it was her own words that led me to email her in the first place.

The scene, just before my unit had left for JRTC: a brigade headquarters company formation, the staff and the company commander at the time standing outside the HQ building. Me returning from the on base Burger King to get back to another day at the battalion, getting ready to be the vaguely defined "information officer" for my unit doing god knows what.

Maj. Sanders and Staff Sgt. Melendez were standing in the back, listening to what was going on in front. Lucky, I thought to myself. In a few months they'd be away from Fort Campbell supporting THE mission in the Army at the time.

"What's up!" I waved at them since Staff Sgt. Melendez would be coming down to support us during the JRTC rotation.

They greeted me back.

"Ah, our favorite Unit Public Affairs representative," Maj. Sanders nodded at me. Under my watch, 1-26's Facebook page had been...good? Or at least updated. I responded to everything she asked quickly.

"Hah," my reply. "If I'm so good, take me to Iraq!"

"You know Johnson," she said, laughing. "You do good work at 1-26. Keep it up, and I may just do that."

An offhand remark.

One that most reasonable people would probably forget by the end of the day.

But I was the only person foolish enough to take her words seriously.

Even when I emailed her as I sat in the building at Fort Polk, referencing what she said, I didn't think she would remember or care. My own unit didn't even care about me- illustrated during the rotation when I became a simulated casualty, was moved to the holding point on the base and was left to languish there for five days.

I eventually gathered up a group of Soldiers, and we marched out, breaking the rules by acting like we were on patrol. My buddies were shocked when I came marching up to the camp and explained what happened.

The event was fresh in my mind when I hit send on the email that would change my life.

The reply came back from her the same day, to my surprise.

"If you're serious," her words. " Can you come by my office when you get back from JRTC?"

What the hell? There was no way she was entertaining the thought. That was impossible.

I had no idea what I was going to say, even as I walked up the stairs to the brigade's public affairs office. It was in a shared open space with the brigade's supply element, adorned with cabinets that held all the camera equipment, a giant Strike insignia black heart to serve as a background for videos, and Maj. Sanders' large office, her desk hidden out of view until you entered.

As I prepared to knock on the door, I glanced over at the side office where Staff Sgt. Melendez and the other enlisted personnel worked. They looked busy, but there was an odd silence in the air.

They would be listening in.

Here I was going behind my unit's back with no expertise, no worthwhile experience, about to ask an officer in charge of the public relations for over 4,000 personnel to take me to a warzone with her. This was the pitch of a lifetime, and I couldn't even think of an opening sentence.

I was screwed, and Staff Sgt. Melendez and the others knew it. I can't blame them for wanting to hear what happened to the dumbass lieutenant.

"Come in." Maj. Sanders responded as I knocked. I entered her office, filled with stickers, Strike swag, and paperwork. The length between the door and where Maj. Sanders sat at her large wooden desk, watching me with calculating eyes, seemed like a football field.

She's just humoring me. She just wanted to hear what I had to say, no doubt. I started to nervously sweat as she motioned for me to take a seat.

"So, *L.T.*," Maj. Sanders began, waiting for me to sit down. I could have sworn she was smirking- this was foolish; she was going to eat me alive. "Why should I take you to Iraq. You know the numbers are tight."

It was less a question than a statement, the cold hard truth. Only a quarter of the brigade would be going, the "top tier" of personnel and officers. You had to be pretty good to be on that list and it was competitive, with people doing *everything* they could to get on the mission. Even people with great qualifications were getting left back, being told that, "The brigade wanted to spread the wealth around both forward and rear."

And here I was, with nothing but a gut feeling.

"I really want to tell the Soldiers' stories," I replied --- the statement entering my mind immediately. Like a torrent, the thoughts continued to pour out. "What they're doing out there, what they've done, people deserve to know. I used to watch them on T.V. when I was growing up, and I always wondered what made them do what they do."

I stopped, realizing how stupid I probably sounded to anyone with experience. This was reality- not a place where a kid got to do things because he wanted to see his childhood heroes in action.

I waited for the sure to be negative response. The unit had a mission, Maj. Sanders would no doubt say. I couldn't help with it, she would no doubt finish, before shooing me out of her office. She looked at me closer, as if she was looking through me. Her face had softened a bit.

It turned out the answer I gave was perfect.

"Do you know what we'll be doing in Iraq?" she asked, probing.

"We'll be fighting to defeat the Islamic State," my reply. I nodded. "Pretty special to think that out of the whole population of the United States, and the whole U.S. Army, they called on us. I don't want to miss that."

"What other positions have you held in the brigade?" she continued, seemingly happy with the answer I had given, almost nodding to herself. The most embarrassing question. I had done nothing of importance. I was a nobody.

"I was an assistant to the signal officer, ma'am.," I replied, haltingly. Technically, by Army standard, there was no such thing as an assistant signal officer. It was a throwaway job. This was it; She would see that I was a loser and kick me to the curb.

"And nothing else?" she asked, eyes narrowing.

"And nothing else," I replied, eyes downcast. "That's part of the reason I contacted you about going. I'm probably done, career-wise. They'll probably laugh me out of the Army at the next board." Suddenly I felt that surge of anger. Pride?

Youthful idealism.

I continued, pulling myself up, figuring that these would be the last words said on the matter. "My career may be done, but I want to do my part at least before I head home."

Maj. Sanders looked at me with an odd half-smile. "Even if that's the end of your career, at least you'll have a bunch of experiences, right?"

"It's what I joined the Army to do ma'am. Everything else, promotions, titles, positions, doesn't matter."

She continued to look at me as if calculating her options, weighing me. Everything came down to this.

"Well," she said after a few long moments. "I can't make any promises, but maybe I could get you to Kuwait."

A silence in the air, almost as if neither of us had expected for the conversation to reach this point.

She was agreeing to this.

"This job is important L.T.," she continued, speaking partly to me, and partly to herself. "We've got a lot of work to do in Iraq. No one's getting stuffed released, and it seems like the PAOs there aren't pushing." She shook her head. "I want to change that."

She glanced at me.

"I'm going to need motivated people to help me do that."

A nod towards the calendar.

"It's an election year. Mosul is big. There's going to be a lot of push to get there before the next person gets into office. What you have to understand was that Strike was hand-selected for this mission."

Really?

"Really." She continued as if reading my thoughts. "Look at the background of the people here and look at what we're getting tasked to do. They're putting faith in us to get the Iraqis to Mosul. There's going to be some heavy lifting in the next few months; the division headquarters is already there so we should have a lot more freedom to work." She nodded at the paperwork around her.

"We need multi-talented people L.T. We're going to have to do a whole lot with very little. How much do you know about writing in AP style?"

"Uhhhh,"

"Then go buy a book on it and start learning. I'm going to expect you to do a lot, by yourself. Can you do it?"

I couldn't believe the words I was hearing. The realization began to hit me -

I was in over my head.

"I'll try ma'am," my answer to her, my voice shaking with lack of confidence.

"Going to have to do more than try *L.T.*," Maj. Sanders' reply, all business. I came to recognize that tone as one that indicated she was already planning something.

"Especially if I'm able to convince the brigade leadership to bring you along."

We had a lengthy conversation at her plan for the operation before she dismissed me for the day to start getting ready. As I walked out, I glanced into the enlisted personnel's office ---

They looked just as surprised as I felt.

On the best of days, it seemed like my battalion commander and I, even when speaking *to* each other, were speaking *at* each other. Every conversation we had ever seemed…off. Like we both made each other uncomfortable for some strange reason that neither of us knew.

Based on his expression as I sat across from him at his desk this day, it didn't look like that feeling was about to end anytime soon.

Spader 6 was a West Pointer, a Ranger School graduate, a man with multiple combat deployments, and a Soldier who had presumably seen it all during his decades in service. The fact that what was going on perplexed him so much that I could see it on his face was…surprising.

"How'd this come about?" his question, sounding as taken aback as I had ever heard him. Spader 6 was a hard charger who had relished the task of taking over 1-26 and getting from 100 personnel and no equipment to deployment-ready in 15 months. He was the one that made me the photo guy and was talking about making me the family readiness person. And now, on a deployment with limited personnel, with commanders and their staff going through their rosters multiple times to pick the right set of skills and their best people, with political battles raging across the cantonment area, the brigade PAO wanted to take *me*?

"Maj. Sanders said she needed someone," my reply, shaking my head as if I was powerless in this turn of events. I was a mere lieutenant, and the brigade headquarters would get what it wanted — I omitted the minor detail of me emailing Maj. Sanders was in the first place behind Spader 6's back, of course.

"She wants to take you to do PAO stuff, and *that's it*?"

"Yes sir," my reply. "She has no personnel, and she wanted to pull from the best Unit Public Affairs program she had."

I nodded, as if this was exactly what she had said to me. I'm not the smartest person, but I knew that making him feel like this was a strategic move with the brigade carefully choosing its most skilled people sounded better than me emailing her at JRTC because I was going to be left in the rear.

There was a silence as he processed the information, weighing the options. It was surreal to watch a Lieutenant Colonel let their poker face down in front of a junior officer, since it never really happened. He was *legitimately* caught off guard by all of this.

"I...don't have any problem with it, I guess." His answer after thinking, his face changing as the benefits of this deal became readily apparent.

"It'll be good to have someone from 1-26 up there."

The unit's first deployment with the 101st, and someone who was at least friendly to his unit working in the brigade public affairs section? This was an in, and the only way to get promoted in the U.S. Army was to take those ins whenever they showed up.

"The only condition that I would have is that you're doing Public Affairs work, and not anything else crazy."

It was my turn to show confusion. *Why did he care?*

"That's exactly what Maj. Sanders was thinking, sir." My reply, as if this was all common knowledge and not me making this all up as I went along. I could tell that he wanted to ensure that I would be in the right spot when the time came for this to pay off. It's not like he needed me anyway, so anything I'd do up there would be a bonus. This was turning into a brilliant boon for everyone, and the best part about it was: Maj. Sanders and Spader 6 each believed the other person had thought this up. Of course, *it had to be*, lieutenants in the Army didn't try to make these moves.

It wasn't long until the deal was done, and I reported up to the PAO office for my "first" day.

"So," Maj. Sanders spoke as I walked in. "Welcome aboard!" she thought for a second. "Wait, are you going to be detached to us or actually be in the unit?"

"I'd rather be in the unit ma'am?" my reply, with a hopeful tone. "I don't think Spader 6 much cares."

"I'll get you assigned to us, no problem." Her reply, as she turned to make some calls, shooing me out of the office.

"So, sir," Staff Sgt. Melendez poked her head out of the other room, as Maj. Sanders did whatever it was Majors did to make these backroom deals. "How much do you know about how to be a PAO?"

"I have absolutely no idea," my reply, with a shrug. "I'll just go out there and take pictures and write some stuff I guess." I nodded my head as I spoke, physically matching my thinking. Yeah, sounded like a good plan. It'd all buff out.

Melendez and the other Soldiers in the office tried to stifle the laughs that were about to come out, and I couldn't blame them.

"Do you know how to do cut lines?"

"Cut lines? What's that?"

"The photo captions..."

"Just write out what's going on right?"

".... Ok, we're going to have to teach you a lot of stuff before you go."

As I started my crash course in how to be a journalist, Maj. Sanders was getting the personnel issues fixed by doing exactly what she needed to do: going behind some people's backs. It was the first of many such incidents in this scheme.

The brigade personnel officer was another Major, who in fact was also an Appalachian State graduate. She didn't quite agree with the plan to get me assigned to the brigade headquarters company since the deployment roster was almost already set, she said. There was no way that the Brigade X.O. and the commander would agree with this. Her and Maj. Sanders were the same rank, so nothing that each other said or did would get either to budge. But the lieutenant who worked under the brigade personnel officer, however-

Maj. Sanders outranked her. And with an email saying that this was a critical move needed because of the deployment and that she had the backing of the Brigade Commander, the deal was made.

The personnel officer wasn't happy, but Major Sanders' reply when I asked about the situation?

"I'll handle it."

And that was that.

Except of course, it wasn't, judging by the brigade executive officer's face when I walked into the meeting Maj. Sanders had set up to introduce me. I had never spoken to the man before and he struck me as one of the Soldiers you see on the posters: Perfect uniform, haircut, badges, obviously in shape, standing at over 6 feet tall. A Soldier's Soldier, in it for the long haul.

Yet just like with Spader 6, there was immediately something off the second we laid eyes on each other.

"This is your new Lieutenant?" he asked gruffly as he looked over my uniform. Air Assault, ok. No Ranger tab? Must have been a non-infantry officer.

I saluted, and we shook hands, an odd feeling hanging in the air- it was like I was making him uncomfortable as much as he was making me. The man looked closer at me, obviously not impressed.

"You're a chemical officer? Signal?" I had to be. How else would I get this job?

"Infantry officer, sir." My reply.

"What happened at Ranger school?"

"I fractured my hip." I shrugged.

A pause, as we looked at each other.

"Did you ever do platoon leader time?"

"No, sir."

The X.O looked to Major Sanders.

"Lt. Johnson will get to Ranger school after we get back from the deployment," she said, nodding as if this was a discussion we had before, trying to smooth over a situation that was obviously going bad, fast. "But I need him now. He volunteered, and I think he'll be a great asset to the team."

The Brigade X.O. wasn't buying that at all. He looked closer at me, his expression saying, "What the hell is this?"

"You and I need to talk Ireka," he said, shaking his head. I quickly left the room, heading back to the Public Affairs office. At least Maj. Sanders had tried, and I couldn't blame her. The numbers were tight. I was a nobody, no skills, no special training — just a kid who had bit off more than I could chew.

Maj. Sanders returned a little while later, calling for me to meet her in her office.

"Well, the discussion with the X.O. was fruitful. You're going, but only as far as Kuwait."

I nodded my head.

"I understand ma'am."

"I'll try to get you into Iraq at least once for the combat patch." She continued, an odd tone entering her voice - what I would come to recognize as a sign she was plotting something. By the end of this whole thing, I would learn that once she decided on something, it was going to happen one way or the other --- other people's opinions be damned.

"Alright, that car over there, take the photo!" I pulled out the camera and clicked the button. I pulled it down afterward for the Sgt. 1st Class who was the NCO in charge of the PAO section to look.

It was blurry and off center, taken as I had tried to get everything in focus for a manual photo shot.

I didn't even know cameras had anything other than automatic mode before that morning.

"Solid shot, sir, you'll be fine out there." The NCO said, patting me on the back. And that was it; my training was complete. Thirty minutes in a parking lot trying to catch a photo of moving cars.

"You'll learn the rest through practice," his words as we walked back up the stairs to the PAO office so we could start looking at the equipment I would take to Kuwait.

"Can I get a Canon camera?" My question, the spread before us on the table. The EO5S D, new by Army standards, used by any public affairs person and combat cameraman who was up to snuff. Capable of H.D. video and photos, it was the kit you wanted to have if you were going overseas.

"Nope, we need those here," the reply from Staff Sgt. Melendez. "What are we going to take pictures with?"

"The extra cameras?" my reply.

"You won't need the Canon in Kuwait anyway. But we do have Nikons you can use."

She pointed out my tools of…choice. Three Nikon D90s, which didn't look like they had been used for years. For the years they *had* been used, it looked like the experience was rough.

"Here you go, sir," Staff Sgt. Melendez, handing me the equipment. "We don't have too many lenses for them…just 55-200mm. That's about all you should need. It's pretty much all-purpose."

"What lens do you use?"

"Oh, I usually use a 50mm lens, for better shots. But we don't have any of those for the Nikons."

I would later learn the 55-200mm lens should not be used as the primary lens, but instead "a complement to other ones in a photographer's kit". I didn't have the aforementioned "other" lenses. I took inventory of the dusty, ragged pieces of plastic. Three lenses, nothing else. 8 G.B. memory cards, barely enough to take pictures in Raw format, which at the time I didn't even know existed. Two batteries and a charger finished out the "kit"--- not much room for loss of anything or damage over a span of nine months.

"Here's your video camera," Melendez continued the layout, pulling out the massive piece of equipment, a big black block that looked to be about 10 years old. I ended up being wrong on my estimation- it was over 15 years. Developed by Sony back in the day, it didn't even use USB C cards or have the option to. Its storage device was the large USB A that looked more like video tapes than digital technology. To get your footage onto the computer, you had to connect the USB A cord and watch as it took forever to pull 10 minutes of video.

Oh yeah, I would be getting only one USB-A Cord.

"Don't forget the tripod," Maj. Sanders' voice from her office, which now looked akin to a storage room as she gathered the things she would take with her to Iraq. Staff Sgt. Melendez smirked and went into her office, soon carrying out a large bulky bag that looked like it could fit a sniper rifle. With a thud, she placed it on the ground next to the table.

"I have to carry that around?" The thing was big, bulky, and heavy, and on top of that, it would take too long to set up and break down if there was a lot of action going on. There's no way I would -

"I don't want shaky shots L.T.," Sanders's voice carried out again as if she could read my mind.

If there's one phrase I learned while working at 1-26, it was that ounces equals pounds, and that pounds equals pain. Especially if I was the one who was going to be carrying all this around.

"Anything else you think you'll need?" Melendez asked as we looked over the spread. I didn't know what I needed, even less so what I wanted. Glancing into the locker that still held equipment, something caught my eye.

"I want some GoPros," I said as I noticed the grey Hero 3s sitting there, looking as if they had never been touched.

"What are you going to need that for?" Melendez's reply.

"It's always good to have backups to this thing," I patted the Sony Camera. "And people may like GoPro footage, gives you the Soldiers' perspective." There were entire websites dedicated to military footage; there had to be some play from a Point of View clip, right? There was also the fact that I didn't need to be an academy award-winning director to get a first-person shot. I may have been bad, *but I knew it.*

"Alright, how many do you want?"

"All of them."

All told, I would have a laptop, a Macintosh computer for editing photos and videos (not the new, fast one of course), the camera equipment, and whatever extra memory storage devices or extras I could think of bringing. I somehow got it all to fit in a tough box I had bought that had wheels on it.

Everything but the damn tripod.

On top of that I had two duffle bags, my Operation Enduring Freedom Style Medium Rucksack, (different from the large rucksacks because they looked and operated more akin to bookbags), my assault pack (a smaller version of the rucksack, used for a purpose the name explains all for), and then finally, my body armor. I was a walking public affairs section --- one from the early 2000s probably by the state of the "top of the line" equipment I was given, but one, nonetheless.

Since I was going to be based in Kuwait the whole time, the hardest part would just be getting to whatever quarters I would have and where the equipment would stay for the rest of the deployment.

Right?

"I didn't think you would ever end up going to Iraq." The words of my father, to me, as I visited him in Fayetteville, North Carolina on pre-deployment leave. "Afghanistan, maybe…"

I had been in the Army for a few years at that point, so me deploying wasn't a shock.

It was me deploying to Iraq part.

It was almost 25 years to the day my father deployed from Italy to northern Iraq as part of Operation Provide Comfort as an infantryman. He missed my birth by a few days, and now, at almost the same age he was, I was heading to Iraq myself.

For the sequel to the sequel of his war.

Provide Comfort was the bookend of the Gulf War after the Kurds had revolted against Saddam Hussein in the northern part of the country. They expected America to help; they didn't get it. Outmanned and outgunned, the humanitarian crisis became so great that eventually a coalition was formed to re-invade the country and create a safe zone for the Kurds. It was a humanitarian operation that was part war of maneuver, part peacekeeping, and part providing aid. My father's unit, the 3rd Battalion, 325th Airborne Infantry Regiment of the 82nd Airborne Division, from Vicenza, Italy was part of the operation. 3 Soldiers from the Battalion were wounded, and one, Pfc. Lars Chew, was killed by a landmine. When the unit came home, I don't think any of the Soldiers expected their little babies would end up going to the same part of the world decades later, yet here we were.

When I was in ROTC in college, the Iraq war was drawing down; President Obama had campaigned on that. To his credit, he ensured that the drawdown started by President Bush was completed. He was right, of course, all the way up to about late 2015 when ISIL came on the scene.

It was an odd feeling, seeing my family for the last time before going into the unknown. I had been independent since going to college, true, was stationed all the way in Tennessee, and had traveled all around the world.

But this felt different. Everyone acted differently. Even when I said I would most likely be in Kuwait, that didn't make things any better. We all knew how fast plans changed in the military.

Near the end of my leave, I visited my sister and her husband, who was stationed in Alaska. My brother-in-law was an Iraq and Afghanistan war veteran, both deployments being with the 82nd Airborne Division as a 60mm mortarman.

He gave me some advice. Don't just carry around a pistol if I could avoid it, carry my M4 always since that would be more useful if shit hit the fan. Be prepared for anything to happen, because everything went out the window in a combat zone, but most of all:

"When you come back, you may feel a little different." His last words to me before I went back to Tennessee, as we sat outside on his balcony. "You won't notice it at first. You'll probably be in such a rush to go on vacation once you get back you won't have to think about it."

"But give it a few months. You'll notice things are different. Trust me."

I didn't understand at the time. I understand it all too well now.

Chapter Two- INHERENT RESOLVE- - May 2016

The Brigade X.O. was shocked, his expression one of a man who had seen a ghost the second I walked into the tent. I couldn't blame him; I was just as amazed as he was to be in Iraq only two weeks into the deployment. Maj. Sanders had said she had cleared the move, but as the X.O. and I stared at each other for the next few moments, we both knew that wasn't the case.

There was a "force cap" in place established by the Iraqi government that allowed only a certain amount of U.S. personnel in the country at a time. Each person that came in had to get cleared by the brigade leadership, who went through name by name analyzing the reason those personnel were coming into Iraq. Obviously, that hadn't happened for me.

"When you see your boss," his voice was even, seemingly unable to muster anger at me through bewilderment, and since I couldn't pull strings to get into country. "Tell her to come talk to me."

He obviously wanted me gone as soon as possible.

I scurried out of the command tent and towards the tent where Maj. Sanders was currently located. The interior of it was half constructed, the desks that everyone would be sitting at to conduct operations either not there or in pieces. Along with the other ramshackle group of tents nearby, this was our new staging area: "Life Support Area Strike." The "Life support" part was very bare bones, since the whole idea of expanding into northern Iraq was new. In the deployments from the past decade U.S. forces would usually fall in on some sort of "hard" structures as we called them, like buildings and already wired networks. Not here however; the Brigade would have to practically build its way towards Mosul on a scale the Army hadn't done for at least five to six years.

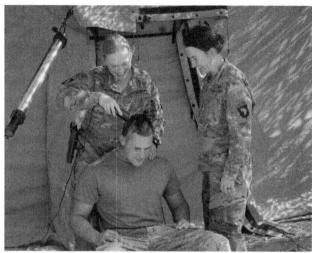

1st Lt. Amanda Veen, left, and 1st Lt. Katlin Forward, right, platoon leaders deployed with Company D, 39th Brigade Engineer Battalion, Task Force Strike, cut the hair of Spc. Mark Herron with Company C, 39th BEB, September, 2016 at LSA Strike. U.S. Army photo by Daniel Johnson

"Johnson, what are you doing here?" the Brigade's personnel officer asked as soon I entered the tent. "I wasn't tracking you were coming in."

I shuffled past her to where my boss sat. How the hell did she get me on a flight if the people who make the rosters didn't know I was on it? Maj. Sanders turned to look at me from her table, which was just a giant tough box that was set up on its side. She gave me a smirk, obviously pleased at how things were unfolding.

"Ah, *L.T.*," Sanders said, standing up. "How was your trip?"

"It was, er, something, ma'am."

A few days before, Maj. Sanders had told me that I would be coming into Iraq for a couple of weeks to help cover the change of responsibility that was about to happen between 2nd Brigade and the 10th Mountain Division. I had packed for two weeks too --- leaving all my extra uniform tops and other gear in my tent in Kuwait since I would no doubt be back soon.

That morning, I joined the other Soldiers who were going to catch the same flight into Iraq, most of whom were artillerymen. Our excitement was contagious; most of the other Soldiers, had, like me, been stuck outside of the country for the past few weeks, bored out of our minds. Gym, eat, nap, repeat. But now we'd be joining the main body in the country.

Most of us were in our early 20s or even late teens, another generation of kids going off into the great unknown; with the high amount of personnel turnover in the Army, a substantial amount of us had never been on an actual deployment. Looking into the night sky as we sat there waiting on our transportation to our flight location, I reflected on what was happening. After spending years watching American Soldiers in Iraq and Afghanistan, *I was finally going to be one of them.*

Leaving our base camp, we rode across the desert in busses with the windows covered by blinds so that outside observers couldn't see the American troops within. The drive was peaceful, filled with scenes of desert life like camels or small villages dotting the horizon. When we arrived at our next location, we were told that our flight would be in three days. Disappointing, but hey, at least we were going in. Two hours after we were told it was going to be three days, we got more info.

It was going to be three hours.

A runner went to grab everyone at the camp coffee shop, and we began to hastily gather our things to throw into the truck that would take it down to our departure area. In the confusion one Soldier would outright miss the flight in, having to get on another mission later.

The Army has a variety of transport aircraft, the C-130 (the transport variant of the widely known AC-130 from every modern shooter ever fame), which was a little tight on the inside, the C-17, which was larger, and the C5, which was large enough to fly in vehicles such as tanks. The C-130 would be our chariot that day.

Forming in a single file line, we entered the aircraft with our kit and helmets on and whatever carry-on bags held in our hands. The interior of the plane consisted of long benches which served as our seats-there were four rows, with the two on the right-hand side facing each other and the two on the opposite doing the same. In-between Soldiers on the benches, there was about an inch of space, and in-between seats, there was about two feet. It was a tight and uncomfortable squeeze, even before you add in the fact that we were fully kitted up.

At this point it was about 115 degrees, but we were in good spirits. Settling into our seats, we buckled up and got ready for the flight ahead; once everyone was in, all we'd have to do was wait for a few minutes.

Which turned into 15 minutes. Which turned into 45 minutes. Which turned into two hours. Due to a mechanical issue, the plane couldn't lift off. Usually that wouldn't be a problem, except the plane was off the entire time, meaning that the climate control was off too. Packed in like Sardines and wearing equipment that added another 15 degrees to our body heat, we started to bake like we were about the be the main course on Thanksgiving. Even better, there was no water on the plane either.

"God, will they at least let us out of here?" a Soldier asked, the sweat dripping down his face. The air was quickly growing thicker, and the smell of body odor was getting worse by the minute. Whether it was the first time in the Middle East or their third, everyone on that aircraft was sucking, including me. I had never been so hot in my life and started to regret signing up for all of this, calculating the odds that I would become a heat casualty before I even entered Iraq. It felt like we were there forever, cut off from the outside world.

Finally, the engine started, sending a sigh of relief through the cabin. It was short-lived, however, because the door opened and an airman poked his head inside, all the while looking quite comfortable.

"We got another plane for you guys," he said, sounding as if we were sitting in a nice, air-conditioned, waiting room at the airport.

"They could have told us that earlier," the same Soldier who had spoken up before said under his breath as we all unbuckled.

The next plane lay only a few hundred yards away, but after our massive loss of water we all kind of stumbled towards it. Every one of us was glad to be out of the oven and glad to see that at least this plane had power, and A.C. Once again, we executed the boarding process, much more subdued than earlier. This time, a few minutes was only a few minutes and we were off.

Beyond the constant buzzing of the aircraft filling the compartment, we flew in silence, each of us lost in our thoughts, or asleep. Iraq was a place of myths, video footage, war stories. It seemed *unreal*, and soon we would be there.

The plane lurched as we began our final approach towards the airport, beginning what the military calls a combat landing. Rapid, filled with turns, flares being released to confuse any heat-seeking missiles. Shocking if you're asleep, as most of us were. Guys woke with a start, and curses filled the air as the maneuvers began. Suddenly we touched down, a rough bump shuddering through the aircraft and tossing us around.

I began to understand why paratroopers joked that they would rather jump out of an aircraft than land in one as we bounced around, arms and equipment going everywhere.

The first thing I remember stepping out into the Erbil summer was thinking just how cool it was. We had traveled almost the entire length of the country and northern Iraq was about 30 degrees cooler than our starting point, giving the area a comfortable spring feel. In the distance outside of the airport, we could see the city and the mountains that lay beyond; in another life under different circumstances, I would call it one of the better views I've experienced when disembarking from an aircraft.

Erbil, Iraq, was separated by just 60 miles from the ISIL stronghold of Mosul. Even though the front was less than an hour's drive, you wouldn't know a war was on if you were in the city. With its cool weather and well-designed city blocks, the town was and remained a tourist destination even as the conflict raged. The city had bars, malls, and an airport that continued to have great business. On the radio one could hear a happy American-sounding DJ playing the latest pop culture hits, with commercials talking about the wide-ranging vacation opportunities in beautiful northern Iraq, which, judging by the aircraft flying in, still had backpackers and travelers continuing to take up the offer.

We were backpackers too, of a different kind.

Consisting of about 12 tents, the LSA wasn't much to look at in its current state. There were only about 40 personnel at the LSA since the artillerymen split off towards another camp on the compound, leaving a sad looking place that I would later learn was on a flood plain. Jumping out of the vehicle that had carried me to the location, I had wandered around lost looking for direction before another Soldier helpfully led me towards the command tent.

Where the X.O. had seen me.

"Thanks for getting me into country ma'am," I continued my reply, glad I wasn't baking in an airplane anymore. Looking back, I nodded back towards the personnel officer. "How'd you do it?"

"That's not important," Maj. Sanders said, her grin growing.

"I think the Brigade X.O. wants to talk to you about it."

"Don't worry; I'll handle that. I've got work for you to do." She shrugged, as if whatever he had to say would be a minor detail, looking around the empty workspace. "Now that you're here, we need to start pushing up products. Nothing's been coming out of here for months." She shook her head. "I don't know what the PAO before us was doing, but I need you to go out there and start getting stuff so we can send it up."

"Where do I need to go, ma'am?" My question. I was eager. I didn't know what I would be doing, but I was ready to do it.

"First," she picked up some tools. "We need to build our workspace."

My face blanched.

".... Really?"

"Really. You wanted to be here, didn't you?" The question was a statement. She had me trapped, and she knew it.

"Yes?" I replied sheepishly.

"Then you have to earn your keep. And then tomorrow, you need to start getting some footage."

By the time ISIL had crashed into northern Iraq in January 2014, the ground was ripe for a Sunni uprising against the Shia Maliki government. Overreaching after the U.S. departed in 2011, the Iraqi government started cracking down on minority groups in the country. Seeing the government backed by Shia militia groups, or PMFs (paramilitary forces) as we called them, who were in turn backed by Iran, Sunnis were especially unhappy with the new political atmosphere. When the small number of ISIL fighters came from Syria talking about overthrowing the Shia government, a substantial number of Sunnis joined in. In June of 2014, everything went haywire as ISIL began seizing towns along the Syria and Jordan border; on June 10th they captured Mosul, the largest city in northern Iraq.

The fall of Mosul was an utter embarrassment, as about 1200 fighters from ISL caused 30,000 Iraqi troops to flee, most of them leaving their equipment behind. Abrams Tanks, Up-Armored vehicles, weapons, the works. Billions of dollars down the drain, and an estimated 4,000 Iraqi security force prisoners were also executed in the aftermath of the battle.

The advance continued as ISIL seized the Sinjar area of Northern Iraq which was home of the Yazidis, a minority group in the country. 2,000 Yazidi men were massacred, thousands of Yazidi women were taken into slavery, and 50,000 more fled into the Sinjar mountains to hold out, hoping for international aid. The Kurds stepped in, and with the assistance of American firepower, weapons, and Soldiers that started flowing in, halted the ISIL advance.

The front stabilized about 40 miles from Erbil, causing the war to settle into a stalemate as the Iraqi Security Forces and the Kurdish built up the required troop strength, supplies, and firepower to counterattack.

About 25 miles east of the Tigris River lies the small town of Makhmur, which ISIL had seized during their offensive in 2014. The ISF had pushed ISIL back and set up a joint command post there called Camp Swift, where American, Kurdish, and Iraqi officials could coordinate their plans in the counteroffensive against the terrorist group. One critical need was for coalition fire support; air support was already being flexed into the area, but there were gaps in coverage due to weather or refuel time, plus the limited number of aircraft committed to Iraq. Another, riskier, way was also to invest indirect fire assets such as artillery. The U.S. Army unit at the time, the 1st

Brigade of the 10th Mountain Division, did not have artillery support in country with them. Fortunately, there was a Marine Expeditionary Unit nearby, the 26th MEU, which had a battery available.

MEUs are forward-deployed Marine units who can respond to crises. Within a few weeks of being notified, they were on the ground, setting up just west of Makhmur at a location they named Fire Base Bell. As soon as Bell was established it came under immediate attack in the form of constant rockets and ISIL conducting ground probes of the perimeter.

On March 19th, 2016, Staff Sgt. Louis Cardin of the 26th MEU was killed in an indirect fire attack, and several other Marines were wounded. Up until this point Firebase Bell was a closely held secret but now questions were being asked, and of course, people wanted access. The Pentagon went into defense mode, talking about how this was only a continuation of current policy while skirting around the whole "boots on the ground" issue.

A week after Cardin was killed, the Combined Joint Task Force (CJTF)-Operation Inherent Resolve, which was run by a 3-Star general and oversaw Operations in Iraq and Syria, sent a Marine combat cameraman to the base to get imagery so they could get a better look at what was going on. There was no issue and the young Marine, Cpl. Andre Dakis, completed his mission easily. Returning to his base, he started working on captioning his photos when he got an email from a random lieutenant colonel in Baghdad.

The Marines firing at ISIL from Fire Base Bell in March of 2016. USMC Photo by Cpl. Andre Dakis

"Do you mind sending me those photos too?" was the gist of the email and Cpl. Dakis, following what he thought were lawful orders, complied.

Dakis was misled.

By the end of the week, his photos had ended up in the hands of news organizations across the world, an inside look at conventional American forces on the ground in Iraq doing exactly what the politicians said they weren't doing.

The military released small snippets of news on the Firebase over the next few months, slickly changing its name of it to the Kara Soar Counter Fire Complex, as if all operations there were in response to enemy forces firing on the base or Iraqi Soldiers. Somewhere along the line, it changed again to the Kara Soar Base, for reasons I still don't know.

In May of 2016, Company C of the 1st Battalion, 320th Field Artillery Regiment, replaced the Marines at Fire Base Bell/Kara Soar, and imagery could once again start getting collected. On the very first day that 1-320th occupied the location, I dropped off a combat cameraman to go with them. I wanted to go, but Maj. Sanders went with the "tried hands."

Combat camera personnel usually operate with Special Forces elements, documenting their operations and assisting with site exploitation. Neither are meant to be publicly released, so they don't really focus on the "public release" part. Now, the combat camera element was being totally misused in a public affairs capacity in Iraq because of some strange chain of command in Kuwait.

Maj. Sanders and the 101st Airborne Division Public Affairs in the Baghdad office wanted more footage, and even further, news organizations wanted access to the base. Due to a languid and reactive public affairs guidance put out by CJTF-OIR, news organizations getting access was a no go.

However, news organizations getting first access to footage from the base was just fine.

_____

I had been in the country for about two and a half weeks, doing necessary public affairs work. Video-taping shout outs (messages to families back home) that we posted on Facebook, some photos, and a couple of low impact articles. Things like the building of LSA Strike, signal operations, and some ceremonies held by Soldiers down further south. It wasn't fantastic work, but with the help of Maj. Sanders and the PAO personnel at the division headquarters, it was competent enough.

The articles were posted on the Defense Visual Information Distribution Service, or DVIDs, which was an online repository for DoD media. The best civilian equivalent to it would be the Associated Press or Reuters --- a place where you upload your products and local and national news organizations, along with other government entities, could download them and use as they saw fit. The most significant difference, of course- it was all free.

People could subscribe to units or news feeds if there was something exciting going on. Being that we were from the Clarksville, Tennessee area, 2nd Brigade's main followers at the time were the papers there. They posted just about everything we wrote, accomplishing our mission of informing the local community back home. No one wanted just the gimmes, however.

"Get ready for a KSB rotation," Maj. Sanders informed me over the phone. "I need you to get up here from Taji as soon as possible."

I couldn't help but smile. I had been sent down to Taji, just north of Baghdad, to get footage of anti-drone weaponry and advise and assist missions down there. I was still a rookie cameraman however and I failed miserably at my task, to the point that none of it was usable — even Maj. Sanders seemed disappointed in my efforts. I knew nothing about photography and nothing about videography; all I had was my writing, and even that wasn't amazing. Now, here was my chance for redemption.

"What happened to the combat cameramen?" I asked.

"They're not doing what we need them to do," Maj. Sanders replied oddly. "They answer to a totally separate chain of command. The division wants to get some footage of the base we can use. They have a plan to give it to the BBC."

I furrowed my eyebrows as if she could see me through the phone. We were going to do what now?

"They don't want to let the BBC go out there?" I replied. "Isn't it kind of odd to be relying on me?"

"No one has any access," Maj. Sanders replied. She paused for a second. "It's making it almost impossible to do my job up here. The plan is for them to come up to Camp Swift and do an interview there. You'll get the footage from the Firebase and give it to them later."

"Isn't that kind of odd to have someone from the military go out there to get the footage for the purpose of giving it to the media?"

"Yes. But this is where we're at L.T."

Camp Swift had been open to the media for about two months. There the media could interview the Brigade Commander and get some photos of the joint America/Iraqi operation center. Every-time they asked to go to KSB however, the answer was the same: no.

What CJTF tried to do to help bridge the gap was hold interviews at the commanding general level, like Lt. Gen. Sean MacFarland who oversaw

CJTF, or, Maj. Gen. Gary Volesky, the commander of our division. Every media inquiry was met with a, "We can't do that, but you can talk to the general". Even better, even if the media wanted to interview personnel at Camp Swift, they still had to meet with Volesky or McFarland first. It was getting old; the story people wanted was at the firebase.

"And we need to start getting products out there," Maj. Sanders continued. "We need to start building our audience, telling people what's going on."

There was an implied statement in what she was saying. Anything you get is ours to use, immediately. There was also the fact that while I wasn't a great journalist at the time, I had one characteristic she needed for this: I was dependable.

"I want to get video of the living conditions," she began going down the list. "Footage of the guns firing, and an article, since you like to write."

"I'm a better writer than a photographer," my response.

"I know," she sighed. A major news organization needed footage, and the only person she had in all of Iraq was me, a guy who had no idea what he was doing. I would be the first actual photojournalist to get to the firebase, and I had full access. The scheme sounded absurd but when you don't have a lot of options, you use what you have.

"I'll catch a flight up there as soon as possible," I replied. "See you in a day."

The issue with the "new" war in Iraq we were in was that mixed messages were coming from the military about the nature of what American forces were doing. The military, instead of simply admitting that there were troops on the ground, some of whom were engaged in combat operations, was behind the power curve the entire time. And now it was about to get more schizophrenic.

Maj. Sanders hung up, and I began to make my plans. I had no idea what to expect when I got to KSB; this whole mission to get footage for use by the news sounded like something I'd never heard of. The Army would get B-roll, (supplemental or alternative footage intercut with the main shot) true. But that B-roll usually wasn't literally the *only* footage there was.

This whole scheme sounded harebrained to me, but I figured I'd give it my best shot.

Chapter Three- THE GUN LINE - June 2016

The Kara Soar Base felt like a different world even though it was only a few hours from Erbil and its sky rises, neat streets, and brand name car dealerships. It had been a wheat field when the Marines occupied the base. but based on the dust cloud that greeted me when I jumped out of my vehicle, those days were long gone. Moon dust, the Soldiers called it, and it was everywhere, in your food, in your weapons, in your laptop, on your clothes.

In the distance, battles could be seen raging near the Tigris River through the thick dust smoke, and missiles could be heard launching nearby as clouds on the horizon confirmed a successful strike. Through the heat of the day and into the night, this small patch of land was where the United States military had decided to deploy a substantial amount of firepower to assist the push towards Mosul.

I picked up my bags and walked towards my place of stay, the radar defense station led by CW2 Rafael Miranda, which was used for tracking incoming mortars and rockets. Miranda and his crew, which consisted of Sgt. Kevin Villarreal and two other Soldiers, were there to watch the variety of screens in their shelter and alert the base if the trajectory of one of those rounds ended up on top of their heads. A slow beep would sound to let the user know if a round was fired, tapering off if it was safe. If the shot were coming straight in however, the screen would turn red and a louder more threatening beep would sound. That sound would continue until the incoming dot and your position met. On average, from red beep of death to round landing was about 5 seconds. Miranda and his men would have just enough time to flip the switch and then head to the bunker that was just behind them. If the switch didn't work however, they would physically have to speak the words over the loudspeaker to warn the base. It was a thankless job, but a critically important one.

Miranda and Maj. Sanders were friends back at Fort Campbell, and her advice to me before I left Erbil was to find him first.

"Sir!" Chief Miranda approached, shaking my hand. "What are you doing out here?"

I dropped my bags in the dust and pointed all around me.

"Maj. Sanders sent me out here to get some footage," I replied, trying to recall everything she had told me during my brief stay in Erbil.

B-roll. Used to support interviews, or A-Roll. The footage of cop cars driving while someone speaks about crime, or college students walking across campus when there's a report about education. A good B-roll package consists of a few minutes of clips on a subject, further cut into 5-7 second sections of footage that news organizations or other groups could use.

I had learned about the term that morning.

The plan was to get all the footage she could and then send it up to the division headquarters in Baghdad to get it approved. Once that was done, we would post what we could or store footage for later use if visitors came by.

"How have things been?" I asked, looking around the area. We had all flown in from Kuwait together and occupied the same tent in Erbil before they pushed out to KSB. They looked much worse for the wear since the last time I saw them.

"It's been pretty rough, sir." Villarreal said as he walked out of the sleep bunker, sweat pouring off his face. "We didn't even have this when we first got here."

He pointed to their area: a truck, two stone bunkers, and a camo net. "Isn't it nice? We've got it pretty good now."

He nodded at their home away from home. "Wish the rest of our air defense cell at Camp Swift could see this."

Good to see his sarcasm hadn't been burned out.

I turned to investigate their bunker, where one of their Soldiers was currently resting in-between shifts.

He was in a pool of sweat.

There was no climate control of any kind, besides the radar shelter itself, which *had* to be kept cool lest the computer equipment overheated. Outside of that, though? You had to be utterly exhausted to be able to sleep in these conditions. Judging by the looks on their faces, they had crossed that threshold weeks ago.

I walked to the edge of the shelter and looked out.

"If someone's got to use the bathroom?" I asked.

"Over there, sir." Villarreal pointed to a hole in the perimeter barrier a few hundred yards away. "Porta potties are there, along with the showers. We usually go about twice a week due to the water shortages. When we first got here, it had E-Coli in it."

"Full kit to head over there too?"

"Yep."

Let's just say it's not exactly easy to try to strip off gear while dying from the heat and straining not to poop yourself.

"And what about those poles?" My reply, pointing towards tubes that seemed to dot areas randomly across the base. "I've never seen those before."

"Oh yeah. Those are the piss tubes if you can't make it to the porta-potties."

No internet, no connectivity to the outside world, pissing in tubes, barely any respite from the heat unless you worked in the operations center or fire direction center, laundry only done once a week, and one hot meal a day.

These guys might well have been on a different planet from the rest of the brigade.

"How long are you staying?" Villarreal's question.

"Until I get the footage, at least," my response, shrugging.

"Really?" his reply. "That's interesting; most people stay only long enough to visit a few spots on the base before heading out."

With a good luck to Miranda's crew, I dropped some of my gear and began my walk towards the artillery pieces, a few hundred meters away.

I had arrived early that morning, but the temperature was fast approaching 110+ degrees, pure dry heat. Now and then, a Soldier would emerge to walk to some location, trudging through the dust. Their usually green Multicam was often discolored by all the dust, now looking like a form of the old Desert Camouflage Soldiers in 2003 wore.

Bunkers dotted the area indicating sleeping quarters or unit HQs. Some vehicles rumbled around, up-armored Maximum Protection vehicles as we called them, giant trucks explicitly designed to reduce casualties from IEDs.

I walked into a gun pit as all this was going on, tripod in hand.

"Hey, guys!" I said as I approached, the Soldiers looking up at me with questioning expressions. They sat around their gun with their body armor on, their skin and uniforms caked in dust, with plainly visible salt stains splotched all over the fabric. Nearby sat their helmets at the ready to don, while along the side of lay sandbags and a weapons rack for their M4s. Snacks and other mementos lined the area, an attempt to give their small piece of Earth a homey feeling.

"Sir?" Staff Sgt. Carlos Mont, the gun's crew chief, questioned as he approached.

Mont, 28, was already on his third deployment, and he *looked* much older than his section, both in appearance and behavior. The weight of responsibility was evident in his features and in his movement.

Even though all the Soldiers looked tired, dirty, and ragged, their ages stood out. It's an odd thing --- in the rest of life, being in your late 20s or early 30s is considered young. In the military, however? You're considered an "old man." Makes sense in a profession where you can start at 18 and retire by 38, I guess, and where the company commanders responsible for up to 200+ personnel were sometimes *26 years old.*

As crew chief Mont was the most experienced Soldier in the section on the M777 weapon system, responsible for the safety of his crew as they operated the weapon. It was a complicated job, where a mistake could cause serious injury or fatalities to the team or friendly forces.

"I'm from the brigade public affairs section," I offered to break the ice. "I was sent out here to get footage from the BBC and world news organizations."

Staff Sgt. Mont looked at me in disbelief, no doubt thrown off by a random lieutenant materializing out of the dust. I felt my brave front begin to drop; what if he laughed? Around him though, the men perked up. Who was the guy talking about the BBC?

"I want to get you guys out there," I continued, making my pitch. "Millions will see you in action?"

Mont looked thoughtful.

It seemed like forever, the air growing eerily silent in my mind.

He grinned.

"Alright, sir, you can hang," Mont replied. "We're the best section around here anyway. The last guy who came up, the combat cameraman, he stayed with us and got some good shots."

"You're going to get us on T.V. sir?" one of Mont's crew, Pfc. Alexander Sabol, asked as he approached. He looked like a surfer dude who had somehow ended up in Iraq. I looked closer, how the hell was he maintaining a hair "flow" out here?

"That's the plan!" I said, confidence growing, the question I wanted to ask hanging at the tip of my tongue. Just two weeks before, I had taken a video so bad the reviewer at CJTF hadn't even finished watching it. But I couldn't fail here. I couldn't allow myself to fail the guys who were making it happen.

Sabol nodded and went to go grab his go-pro to put on his helmet, as if he had been waiting for this moment.

"The BBC is a pretty big deal," another Soldier, Pfc. Tristan Trammel, said as he sat on the wall. He looked young, and it turned out that he was 19, but something was discerning in his eyes. He seemed like one of those types who had ended up here for a specific reason.

The rest of Mont's section was relatively fresh-faced; only one of them had a previous deployment. I could tell they looked to the older Soldier for leadership and guidance.

As I studied the gun and its crew, a call came over the radio.

"Fire mission!"

The crew leaped into action, quickly donning their helmets as they sprinted toward the gun line. Mont barked orders to the Soldiers as they moved in a synchronized war dance; each member on a team had a role, from loading the round, to making the calculations, to pulling the lanyard that fired the weapon.

Once the Soldiers finished loading the M777 howitzer, Mont raised his hand in the air and swiftly brought it down, yelling, "FIRE!"

The ground shuddered as the explosion sounded, the reverberation appearing to shake the body armor of the Soldiers on the team. The overpressure from the gun knocked the breath out of anyone standing nearby. Dust and smoke filled the air, and if you watched closely enough, you could see ghostly outlines of us created out of the particles in the air.

Immediately after the round was fired the mission continued with other artillery pieces joining the battle, the reverberations of the pieces rumbling across the perimeter. The M777 was a 155 MM howitzer, the biggest in use by U.S. Army forces, with a range of over 20 miles. Each of its high explosive shells had a *kill* radius of 50 meters.

To put it bluntly, one shell dropped on the 50-yard line of a football field would damage everything from end-zone to end-zone, both team's sidelines, and even the objects in the stands.

There was a cheeriness apparent on the crew's features. Here they were 7,000 miles away from home living in austere conditions with limited communication with the outside world, and it appeared that this repetitive act of firing their weapon is what made them happy. We're an all-volunteer force, and as morbid as it sounds morbid, they had chosen the artillery branch for one reason, based on the Army's manuals: *to* destroy, neutralize, or suppress the enemy by cannon, rocket, and missile fires.

The High Mobility Artillery Rocket Systems (HIMARs) joined in the fray, two trucks pulling out of their covered positions to a spot just outside the base. Their missiles launched with a boom as a yellow line streaked off into the sky towards Mosul, each rocket carrying dozens of small bomblets that dispersed and exploded immediately upon hitting their target.

The rounds had a higher-than-average dud rate however, and the victims of the rounds weren't always the intended target, whether that day, or the months after.

Two missiles.

Four.

Eight.

They were aiming for some *big* targets.

It wasn't until afterward that I thought about the civilians in Mosul who were caught in between ISIL, Shia militias, and now missiles raining down from the sky by the dozens. A few years later I would do a news briefing about civilian casualties that occurred during coalition operations in Operation Inherent Resolve.

Some of my fellow officers *blamed* the civilians for being there.

HIMARs systems weren't exactly common to see in the U.S., due to the way they operated. There's not a lot of places with the airspace open enough to send massive, to be honest, *cruise missiles,* into the air safely. A strange feeling, hearing and feeling rounds from the weapons systems cutting through the dust into the air towards their spots thousands of feet above us.

And then there were the Paladins.

Boom. A round fired from them, the vehicle becoming a giant metal monster roaring to life, belching fire. A shudder as the wave hit you. Unlike the M777, the Paladin was an enclosed armor vehicle with a 155 MM gun on it. The crew wasn't visible, and the telltale signs of personnel moving couldn't be heard to warn you they were going to shoot. No grabbing of equipment, no yelling. Just a sudden thud, the shaking of the ground, and the dispersion of dust. It was as if some giant still monster was awakening from slumber each time, spitting out destructive fire at its unwitting victim. It's the type of image that would inspire a giant machine of death in a sci-fi movie.

On the public relations level, the Paladins were additions to KSB that had rarely been spoken about. Why? Because they could rapidly move to new positions and shoot if they could drive there. And they were being used in just that fashion, taking up positions at KSB in between sallying forth.

Coalition jets appeared overhead, in between the HIMARs launches, conducting strikes on targets that were sometimes close enough that you could hear the booms and see the smoke clouds from the missile impact. They added to the plumes in the distance, more firepower as the fight raged.

We had a ringside seat to something that looked like it was from a sci-fi movie; something that no movie, video game, or photo experience would ever be able to match.

Destruction on an *industrialized* scale.

I began to realize how infinitely small I was in all of this as I began to understand that what I was seeing wasn't even a fraction of what the military could bring to bear.

But then again, lack of firepower wasn't the reason we found ourselves in this predicament of being in Iraq in 2016.

GoPro footage from PFC Sabol of Staff Sergeant Carlos Mont with Battery C, 1st Battalion, 320th Field Artillery Regiment, Task Force Strike, inspecting a round during a fires mission in Kara Soar, Iraq, June 10, 2016. U.S. Army photo by Alexander Sabol.

ISIL fighters knew that KSB was the lynchpin of the counter-attack efforts against them, and there were frequent reports of ISIL fighters breaking off towards the base. In some cases, the artillerymen were firing to stop enemy fighters from coming *directly* towards them in the distance, either by denying terrain or causing casualties with HE shells. Combat, advising, whatever people want to call it, the intent of the artillerymen was simple: kill the enemy before they kill you. Or "neutralize" or "destroy" the enemy before they reached you, because kill was too "harsh" of a word for an organization that engaged in the most brutal of human endeavors.

At some point, I broke off from Mont and his crew towards the other guns on the line, approaching one right as the team was getting ready to fire.

"Well, well," came the voice of the NCO who was watching his crew in action. "I was wondering when you would leave Mont's section and come over here." I studied the Soldier more closely. Staff Sgt? Joseph?

"They're pretty good," I replied, pulling up my camera to catch more action. Another fire mission had come down, and Joseph's Soldiers were loading a round.

"We're better," Joseph replied, with the self-assured confidence of a man who had done this many times before. The spirit of competition was alive and well.

To see who could blow up people the fastest.

What a world.

The Soldiers in front of Joseph began to go through their crew drill, their section sergeant pushing them with commands. They looked...different from Mont's crew. The way they moved, the way they loaded, the way they spoke. Different methods to do the same procedure. Personal touches that demonstrated that they all weren't a bunch of automatons.

"Fire!" the chief yelled. Boom, one round off. The crew moved to reload another one, and Joseph grinned. His guys were looking pretty good for the cameras.

The next round was loaded. The crew chief brought his arm up again. "Fire!"

Click.

"Damn," came a voice from Joseph. "It's a malfunction; you know what to do."

The crew went through the troubleshooting procedure in seconds, making minor adjustments. They nodded at their chief once more.

"Fire!"

Click. Nothing.

I looked down at Joseph, who looked up at me.

"That thing isn't about to blow up, is it?" I asked. I started to sweat even more than I was already sweating due to the heat. A whole gun crew, and cameraman, wiped out by a malfunctioning piece of artillery. It had happened to M777s before, especially when continuously fired in less than perfect conditions.

The red haze filling the air sure seemed to indicate less than perfect conditions.

"We'll be good, sir," Joseph replied, shaking his head. "Our gun's going to be down for a while, though."

"This happens a lot?"

"Yeah. These guns are the ones from Campbell. We got six new ones in the theater that they're not letting us use."

"Why?"

"Word is they need it for something else."

We both shared a look at each other as if saying, "What could be more important than this?"

The next year, one of the artillery pieces *did* explode, killing Sgt. Roshain E. Brooks, 30, and Spc. Allen L. Stigler Jr., 22, from the 82nd Airborne Division, our replacements. Five other soldiers from their cannon crew were injured in the incident when a 155mm artillery round blew up inside the tube of the M777 howitzer that they were firing.

I thought I knew for a fact that their battery took over the same guns that 1-320th was using, a fact I would be mistaken on as was I informed later that C Battery took their guns home with them (I thank the personnel from C Battery for correcting my error). I had the feeling that getting new guns from Kuwait would have prevented that malfunction; but people higher than us who thought they knew better determined the guns were better served sitting there in a warehouse.

I nodded my head, assured by the veteran. If the expert said we were safe, we were safe. "I'll be back."

Joseph nodded before turning to walk to get a closer look. "I'll hold you to it."

There was a lull in the action as I returned to Mont and his crew, who were returning to their positions just a few feet away from the gun.

This was their life. Fire. Wait. Fire, wait.

Then they would get off shift and get some rest, which just a few weeks before had consisted of sleeping in the dirt right next to the artillery piece. The bunkers that now held their sleeping equipment were better due to the fact they provided some shade --- but the temperatures inside them still rose over 105+ degrees. Inside was almost as bad as out.

"Got the shots you need?" Mont asked, grinning. Taking off his helmet he moved to sit on an ammo box, the radio that transmitted their fire missions set up nearby. Throughout the day we had spoken, and I had gotten to know him a little better.

In my excitement to get down to the guns, I had forgotten my Nikon camera.

"Sure did," I replied, then glanced around at their living area. "Truth be told, no one really knows how you guys are living out here."

Sgt. Nicholas Davis, Mont's second in command, laughed.

"I don't think they would want to know, sir," he replied, shrugging his shoulders. "Doesn't help that we're totally out of contact here."

I pointed down at the video camera I had been lugging around all day. "I can show them, hopefully. If I get this video up to division, who knows."

"Alright," said Davis. "Feel free to check out whatever you want L.T."

Pfc. Sabol led me into the section's bunker complex, pointing out their sleeping area. It was placed just outside of the bunkers, with a sandbag barrier covering them from the outside world. Their area of repose consisted of cots, packed together, some with small army pup tents on top of them.

Nearby lay the Soldiers' gear, rucksacks, assault packs, toiletries. If you tried to catch a nap during the day, good luck. Soldiers had to do it in full kit, body armor and all, minus their helmets.

Inside the actual bunker itself were the section's packages, at least the ones that made it through to them. Trammel came walking in and he and Sabol began to dig through boxes.

"We've got a few good things, sir," Trammel said, pulling out a…baseball glove? I didn't expect to see that in a box. I had never been on the other side of a care package, but it had the desired effect, based on the Soldiers' faces.

Sabol walked over, patting his GoPro. "Got some good footage today, you want it?"

"Sure, I think people would like a first-person video." I nodded confidently, as if I did not actually have no idea what people would like.

"A lot of these guys haven't deployed before," Mont said, gesturing back towards his crew as we sat on ammo boxes that were serving as stools. "Naturally, they were asking me, 'Chief, how are things going to be out there?' I told them, 'Honestly, I've never been to Iraq, so I can't tell you about where we're going and what to expect.'"

"I've been in the Army for nine years, deployed twice to Afghanistan before this. One of them we were out at an outpost kind of like this, living in the same type of conditions. With those deployments, though, the mission was a little more concrete. Here in Iraq since the war died down five or six years ago…. the mission is a little bit unclear."

It was a surprisingly honest assessment, one that surprised even me.

I was starting to see the disconnection between the people in charge and the Soldiers on the ground quick.

"Our mission is vague. We're not supposed to be here, but we're here. So, what are we doing? 'Providing counter-fire and supporting the ISF with indirect fire.' That's all we've been told. That's all I can tell the Soldiers. The bad guys are right now trying to, or have tried to kill us, and we've killed a lot of the enemy already."

The word kill. A dirty word that no one wanted to use in official DoD parlance. It was "enabling through fires", "deny terrain", "reduce". Words that could blur what was being done, whether it was by the Air Force, Special Forces Soldiers with the Iraqis, or artillerymen.

Mont continued. "All that I could do before we left was prepare them the best that I could. I enjoy this, being able to teach and mentor the guys to hopefully be good Soldiers and good human beings. Still, I can't wait to be able to see my family again when we get home."

"It's kind of hard to explain all of this to people, unless they were here." He paused, nodding at me. "How'd you get this job? Kind of strange to see a lieutenant running around with a camera."

"Oh," my reply. "I'm a uh, infantry officer. They never gave me a platoon and were going to leave me at home, so I volunteered to do this."

"Really?" he seemed surprised. "You volunteered to do the job that's usually done by an enlisted Soldier?"

"Yeah."

"Haven't met a lot of officers who would choose to do that," he continued, shaking his head. "Infantrymen aren't doing too much on this deployment anyway. Smart move to work with the superior MOS." He laughed, amused at the turn of events.

The conversation trailed off. I fumbled over my words, trying to say what I was feeling at the moment. I could not.

I moved on to interview Mont's crew, who also had a lot of information about their mission and themselves; it was a crash course for me in how an artillery section worked, what they did, and how they did it.

"Tell me a little about yourself, Trammel," I asked the young man as he sat on the wall of the firing pit, something telling me he had something interesting to say.

The usual story; he had been in the unit since it was created the year before. Before coming to Iraq, he had done the typical training, ranges, and menial tasks expected of Soldiers of his rank.

"Why'd you join the Army?" I asked, the question coming into my head. It was a blind ask, but I had the strangest feeling about what the response would be.

Trammel looked off towards the Tigris river, then back to the gun. "I was watching videos on the internet last year."

Ah. Another kid, just like most of us, drawn in by a slick recruiting video that made the military look awesome all the time. I could laugh at it then, but-

51

It had worked on me.

"I saw the videos of the atrocities ISIL was committing," he continued, not in the direction I was anticipating. "It pissed me off, what they were doing. I had been thinking of joining the Air Force, but I wanted to be closer to the action."

ISIL's Information Operations campaign was surprisingly robust for a terrorist organization. Social media posts, video footage that was shot and edited professionally, targeted audiences. It had caught the West off guard. Some of their footage even had an ISIL fighter from the U.K. narrating like it was some NATGEO documentary. It was like a bizarro world version of western military recruitment videos, targeting young men and women. The crazy part was how well it had worked, drawing on foreigners by the *thousands* to fight for ISIL.

And, as in the case of Tristan Trammel, driving people to fight *against* them.

Negative propaganda? Was that even a term? I'd find out later that it was called a boomerang effect, and no one is really sure how or why it happens.

"I asked the Army recruiter about what had the best chance of getting me there, and he told me about the combat arms jobs."

Still, Trammel's odds of getting to Iraq with the *one* M777 battery deployed there in May of 2016 were slim. He didn't get a choice in his duty station, type of artillery piece he was operating, or what unit he was assigned; all he had done was sign up as an artilleryman, going where the needs of the army dictated. At the time, Charlie Battery of the 1-320th *didn't even exist.*

Yet he had enlisted, got sent Fort Campbell, then to 1-320th, then to the new M777 battery of the unit, and then due to a mission that wasn't even anticipated when he went to the recruiter's office to raise his right hand, now found himself launching artillery rounds at ISIL. I can't count the number of times I met people in the military who wanted to do the same thing, yet never, over a 5 or 6-year career, got the opportunity.

Trammel had however, just over a year in, "reverse radicalized" by the internet after the footage he saw elicited such a strong emotional response in him. Most people his age worried about college, summer vacation, or their status on social media, not about firing high explosive shells in a fight against the world's foremost terrorist organization. At 19 years old, he had found himself a part of history. I remembered something my ROTC instructor, Master Sgt. Chalk Wetmore, had said when he spoke about returning home Afghanistan and talking to people he had known since childhood.

He had told them he was in the history books.

"I'm not kidding sir," Trammel replied to my quizzical expression, shaking his head. "To assuage my mother, I decided to join the artillery, since it was a little further from the front lines." He smirked knowingly, realizing how that had turned out, then shrugged.

My mother thought I was sitting in the rear with the gear, in a nice totally safe office, sending out Soldiers to grab the footage. I hadn't told her I would be grabbing the footage *myself.*

"It sucks out here, but I'm glad to be doing my job."

Trammel's mother was a big follower of our unit on Facebook, I would find out, always commenting with pride whenever she saw a picture or video of her son. He was just a kid-

We all were, really. Drawn together by chance or purpose, intentional act or spur of the moment decision. Or, in my case, an offhand joke. Our conversations continued as the sky darkened, signifying dusk.

I figured that things would eventually calm down around the base. I was wrong.

The other-worldly effect of the weapons being used was even more distinct. KSB operated under blackout conditions for security reasons; when the HIMARS went off, it was like someone throwing an amber flashlight over the base.

Hissing, multiple times after an explosion --- the telltale sound or the rocket systems in action, or the night suddenly going white as an artillery piece sounded off. The sight of flares fired by the artillerymen floating down in the distance, giving artificial moonlight. Sometimes to support firefights. Other times to guide refugees as they escaped from ISIL.

And then the drones came out.

Hovering around the base, observing our location. Too small to be ours and flying way too close to the ground. You could see them if you looked through your night vision goggles, small shapes hovering on the horizon. The United States Military proudly claims that it controls the air. Bombers, fighters, UAVs- by controlling that dimension, we control the battlefield. But now we were being challenged.

By a terrorist group buying toys offline.

The military thought that the drones were enough of a credible threat that KSB had just been fielded anti-drone weapons called drone defenders a few weeks before. They looked like sci-fi props- futuristic weapons that fired invisible beams at UAVs to bring them down. You could tell when you had a "hit" because the drone would stop in place, and then begin following the barrel of the drone defender like it was attached to an absurdly powerful magnet. We were among the first units fielded them; my horrible video footage weeks before was of the fielding exercise.

There was a fear in June of 2016 that the UAVs would eventually be armed with grenades or used as ramming objects, which did eventually happen. Everything on KSB was stationary, so why wouldn't they?

If the UAVs got too close to the base, the security forces on the perimeter would engage: first, with the drone defender, and if that didn't work, plan B: machine guns and rifles, lighting up the night with gunfire. They were participants in a struggle battling killer robots during a "war" with no name, for which they were not "boots on ground" in. The Army doctrine for counter drone operations would not be published until 2017, so we found ourselves in literally uncharted territory, working with the Army's Asymmetric Warfare Group to create it as we went. To emphasize the point --- the drone defenders weren't made by the Army, they had to be brought from commercial companies as a *stop gap* solution.

And here I thought reality being stranger than fiction was just a pithy saying.

Trammel's words stuck with me as Soldiers began to appear, trudging through the dust towards the feeding line. Artillerymen, engineers, cavalry scouts, radar technicians --- over 200 personnel all told. Their legs looked heavy, the soil beneath them doing nothing to help their footing. There was no central area to eat food at this point, so once one received their dinner serving, they either trudged back to whatever position they were in or sat down somewhere in the sand.

Dust storms and dust devils were a common occurrence, an unnatural *natural* event considering that this part of Iraq was mostly grassland. Anytime wind blew, the moon dust would carry into a Soldier's dinner, adding a distinct *earthy* flavor. The mix of dirt and fruit juice or water was *especially* memorable.

"I heard you were down with Mont's crew," a voice called to me from outside the serving line. I looked over and squinted my eyes. A Sgt. 1st Class regarded me, multiple radios on his body armor, his face weathered by experience. I looked closer at his name tag: Young.

"I was," I replied. "They were pretty good."

Sgt. 1st Class Young smiled with pride. "Of course. We are the best platoon out here after all." He nodded towards the perimeter.

"They sent you down to just get footage of the guns? When the combat camera guys came by, that's all they were looking for."

"They did," I replied. "I'm from the Brigade PAO section. My boss also wants to get a little more."

"A little more?" Young replied, a tone of distinctly piqued interest in his voice.

"No one knows how you guys are living out here," I replied. "We want to send footage up, hopefully, get it released. Show what you guys are doing to help fight ISIL." I shrugged my shoulders. "Even if the news doesn't run it, at least people at Campbell can see it."

"*Really.*" his reply. "Odd for a PAO to ask for the full story. Come with me."

With a wave of his hand, Young started walking off, leaving me to grab my camera to follow him hastily.

"I'm the 'mayor' for the base," he continued as we walked off behind the chow line. "Basically, I try to make sure the base has services, generators were repaired, people have places to live."

He was also the gunnery sergeant for 2nd Platoon, which Mont's section was a part of.

"We've been working to make this place better," Young said as we walked through the dusk. "The Marines were living pretty rough since they knew they'd only be here a while. We're getting more overhead cover, and hopefully next week we'll have our DFAC up and running."

"It'll hopefully help us with the rat problem too." Young continued.

"I keep on hearing about these rats," my reply. "What's going on with them?"

Young stopped and pointed at something on the ground. A sizeable dirty creature, with multiple puncture wounds.

Stabbed to death.

Young explained. "When we set up here and started disturbing the ground, they started showing up."

He gestured to the mess near the rat- seemingly torn open MRE bags, crumbs spilling out of them and forming a trail towards the creature.

"They even started eating through our MRE and care package bags." Young shook his head. "These things are bold; they'll crawl over us at night."

We passed a sign that had a rat kill count, the words "MISIS neutralized" in big, bold letters, emphasizing the point. Beyond it lay an opening in the Earth.

A trench, one looked like something out of an old World War I movie. Dug a few feet into the ground, it was wide enough for one man to move through at a time, the paths crisscrossing just like in the stock footage.

"Almost home," Young called back to me, jumping into the battlement. I followed, landing with a dull thud. The pathway narrowed as we continued, moving past small openings that had sleeping gear set up in them.

"This is where I live." Young stopped, pointing at a dugout, carved hastily into the "wall" of the trench. It was sparsely decorated, with some photos of his family and his bags tucked into the back wall. Underground positions in the dirt were some of the oldest and most effective ways to protect personnel against explosives. Most earthen works are, hence the proliferation of HESCO barriers filled with sand around forward located military outposts. Usually, along with sandbags on top of and around bunkers, that was enough to serve as indirect fire protection.

There weren't enough bunkers of other materials to go around when the Marines arrived. So, like Soldiers in the early 1900s, they literally dug *into* the Earth.

"To think," Young said. "This is better than when we found them." He sat down on his cot to show the relative size of the position, bending over so that his head wouldn't hit the roof — the view he had to look forward to at the end of his shift each day.

For the next three months.

"They don't talk about this at all," I said, at a loss of words. To be honest, I felt someone had to see it to believe it.

"And they won't sir. They never do," Young replied, stepping out. "It's not that we're complaining that it's rough out here. We get it. It's a firebase. It's meant to be temporary. But," he pointed back towards his hole.

"It's important that people understand what we go through, what it takes to make things happen. Everything isn't as clean as they make it out to be. And who knows, a video might make them improve conditions." Young laughed bitterly.

Sgt. 1st Class Young's Sleep area. Photo By Daniel Johnson

Yeah, right. I could almost hear him thinking. I learned that Young was a photographer himself; this was deployment number *four.* Unlike some of his previous rotations, this rodeo saw the artillerymen being used as.... artillerymen. In the Surge days, the Army was short on bodies, so anyone and everyone were drafted to augment infantry units, including artillery ones. It was so common that some had fired their M4/M16 in combat more than their assigned big guns, finding themselves embroiled in the urban combat that was the trademark of Operation Iraqi Freedom. Still, even with those experiences of living in Combat Outposts and dealing with an insurgency, Young considered KSB one of the roughest living arrangements *he had ever experienced.*

"Do you mind giving us the footage you take while you're here?" his question, near the end of the conversation.

"Of course, it's of you guys. I'm just capturing the stuff," my reply. "Isn't that what usually happens?"

"Not always, in my experience."

That made no sense, to me at least.

Young showed me out of the trench, and I began the walk back to the radar station, using the outlines of the terrain as my compass in the blackout condition. Glancing up at the sky, I had to admit that it was kind of beautiful. No light pollution, giving the stars a clarity like I had seen back in Boone.

My sleeping spot would be the in-between a hole and bunker- the open under the camouflage netting of the radar truck. There wasn't enough room for me in CW2 Miranda's shelter, but we all figured that if something did happen it was only a split-second scramble into the stone enclosure.

"Not going to head back to Camp Swift tonight?" Sgt. Villarreal's question as I settled in. I glanced in his direction and he seemed amused.

"Why would I? The story's here, right?"

"It is."

I glanced down at one of the MREs near the entrance to the radar vehicle, gesturing to it.

"Why does it seem you only have six types of MREs? Aren't there 24?"

He laughed. "Yeah, for some reason we received nothing but menus 1-6. The one hot meal a day helps though. We sometimes get to send our laundry back to Erbil too, but it has a habit of getting lost. At least the water doesn't have germs that wreck your stomach anymore." He made a movement that silently said, "Things could be worse."

"Why aren't the guys at Swift making sure that's taken care of?"

"That's the question, sir. It's almost like they don't care." A resigned shrug of his shoulders. "We'll still do our job though. If all we get at the end of this is the satisfaction of knowing that we helped keep these guys safe, so be it. I'd rather have that than anything else; I'd rather be here than Camp Swift." He nodded his head towards the blackness of the night. "Hopefully we can help make sure everyone gets home safely."

"And not riding your bike?" I offered.

"Ok, I would rather be doing that then this, but that would be a pain to carry all the way out here and we barely have enough space as it is!"

"Fair point." I admitted. "Thank you for letting me crash with you guys. I really appreciate it – I know you guys are busy enough as it is without me being an extra burden."

"You're not a burden."

He paused for a moment, his tone suddenly turning much more serious.

"It's strange, you can come all the way out here and choose to stay with us, but our own bosses ten minutes away can't do that. *Funny* how that works."

"Isn't this what officers or other people with rank are supposed to do? You guys are out here, so I should be out here too."

He laughed at my response, shaking his head with a smile. "Good to see someone gets it. *Odd* that it's the assistant PAO of all people though. You're a good guy L.T." He stopped for a moment, looking at my sleeping area --- a cot with my bags under it. "You can stay with us anytime."

With that, he turned to head back to the bunker, leaving me with more questions than answers. I couldn't be the only person *choosing* to stay out here, right? Because if the Soldiers' own leaders were abandoning them, or giving the *appearance* that they were abandoning them, that suggested that they didn't care.

And if they didn't care, *who* did?

Chapter Four -Good Morning Iraq

I walked into the bunker where Sgt. Arturo Hernandez stood watch, carefully picking out my steps. Grenades, machine gun rounds, rocket launchers. Flytraps, mouse traps, sector sketches. Hernandez and his fellow Soldier looking towards the horizon, for anything out of the ordinary, or just anything at all.

"Sir," the veteran Soldier regarded me as I walked in with my camera. He tilted his head; when people came to visit KSB they usually didn't stop by the battle positions ringing the base which served as the duty stations for their unit: 1st Squadron, 75th Cavalry Regiment. Their mission: keep the base secure. Thankless on most days, or the target of ire on others when they opened fire on the ISIL drones.

But mostly, as with all wars in human history, boring.

A Soldier from 1-75 CAV standing guard in one of the bunkers around KSB, June, 2016. U.S. Army photo by Daniel Johnson.

Even though they had one of the most important jobs out there by protecting the guns so they could fire, it was a challenge for the Cavalry Soldiers to see that in the day-to-day grind. Who could blame them? You waited for something to happen for long periods, then when something *did* happen, it seemed like it was over in an instant. And who could forget what they had to look forward to in their off time: one hot meal per day, laundry service that steadily lost their clothes, and a hole in the ground to sleep in under the Earth.

"I'm from the Brigade PAO," I announced to the two Soldiers, pulling up my camera as if it would add believability. "I want to get some photos and footage of you guys for everyone back home, get it in the news if I can."

Hernandez smiled. "That's great," his reply. "It's been pretty quiet out here, though when we first got here, we could practically see the Iraqis fighting. Are you going to do a story on us? My wife was upset during our last deployment; she never heard about 1-75 Cav while we were in Afghanistan."

"Sure," I replied. A story was forming in my head about the firebase: one on the artillery pieces and the variety of units like the security forces who made their operation possible.

We spoke for a while longer about the base and…life. Just talking about home, Iraq, anything. Hernandez eventually informed me that his shift was about up. I was glad for the info he shared with me about operations at KSB, and, even better, he pointed me in the direction of who to talk to next.

Except that he was acting odd.

Well past his shift ending, Hernandez stood in the bunker, as if waiting for something, occasionally glancing down at the radio. I was a little confused. Was he supposed to get some sort of message before he left?

"This is my favorite part of the day," Hernandez announced after a while. I looked out of the bunker into the Iraqi morning. He was right, it was kind of serene out here if you really thought about it-

"Gooooood Morning Vietnam! I mean -Iraaaaq! Break!"

A voice sounded from the radio, seemingly out of nowhere. Hernandez and the other Soldiers, including the ones who had arrived to replace him, leaned in. A jingle played after the voice's words, immediately recognizable as mimicking a famous line used in the 1987 military comedy-drama film, "Good Morning Vietnam." The movie, inspired by the life of Adrian Cronauer – played by Robin Williams – a former U.S. Air Force sergeant and radio personality, depicted Cronauer's experiences as an innovative disc jockey during the war.

I glanced outside again, half expecting Hueys to be flying overhead blaring Creedence Clearwater Revival, the open grasslands replaced by dense Southeast Asian Foliage. No. We were still in what looked like Iraq. And glancing around the bunker, our uniforms had not transformed into olive drab with the trademark round steel helmet. But the Soldiers were still gathered around the radio like we were in 1968.

1st Lt. Jared Thomas, the announcer and er, *host,* of this guerilla-style program, worked in the intelligence element of the Cav. It was a random idea of his to come up with the program, one his leadership obliged to due to the thinking, "The guys are bored out of their minds so why not."

And it was a hit. With an excitement and mannerisms that were eerily reminiscent of the Robin Williams character, Thomas would wake up and inform his fellow Soldiers on what was going on in the world that day.

Sports news, political news, world news, every topic was covered in detail, albeit in a funny manner. Thomas ensured that each portion of his audience heard something they were interested in. For most, this was the only outside news they would get for days, and the broadcast was one of their only tangible connections to the outside world.

The internet on the base was slow, and it could only be used a few times a week. The entire installation had to share a minimal amount of connections. When Soldiers *did* get connected, most of the short time available was spent just trying to contact the family. With this Good Morning Vietnam --- *Good Morning Iraq,* you could receive updates every day. Like you were back home.

Almost.

1st. Lt. Thomas was funny, his goofy imitations of some of the subjects in the topics he selected adding that extra bit of pizazz and drawing chuckles. His impression of Donald Trump was especially spot on. This kept up for about 30 minutes as he hit topic to topic with impressive speaking ability, not even pausing to gather his thoughts. Even when he reached the end of his allotted block, he was obviously prepared to go on for much longer.

"This is Lt. Thomas wishing you all a good day. Stay hydrated, and don't die!"

And that was that.

"Lt. Thomas?" I asked, still transfixed by what had occurred. "Who's that?"

"He's an intel guy who works in the Tactical Operations Center (TOC). He does this every day," Hernandez replied as he prepared to leave and then paused at the doorway of the bunker.

"When we first got here, we were sleeping on the ground behind our bunkers, it was pretty rough. Thomas started doing the show about then, it helps a ton with the morale around here."

As I continued around the perimeter, other Soldiers confirmed his words. They loved it. Most morale "raisers" were looked at with amusement at best, sheer hatred at worst. But "Good Morning Iraq" was actually...serving its purpose. The fact that Soldiers were willing to push back going to sleep to listen in was the most tell-tale sign.

They also didn't mind speaking about what they were doing. I always thought that most Soldiers would be bothered whenever I came by, but a shocking number of them wanted to tell their story, or just talk about life. It turned out that beyond the local leadership that was on base it was rare for anyone else in their chain of commands to ever stop by and just have a conversation, or even stay the night. Must have been too busy with the advising and assisting stuff, I guess. Leave it to *unimportant* people like me to do that.

The younger ones were also more than willing to send video messages back home to their friends and family, which I taped using my cell phone and put on the brigade Facebook page every Saturday. This wasn't the war they had expected, but at least they were finding purpose in trying to make their situation better.

As I moved towards the center of the base, I encountered one of the medics. He seemed different from the other ones, most immediately in his appearance, or at least his helmet. It was a CRYE helmet, one usually worn by Special Operations Soldiers. I nodded at him in passing.

"How's it going sir!" his response in a cheery voice.

A cheery voice with an *English* accent.

I cocked my head at him as he walked off, thrown off by what I had heard.

"Got a question, guys," I said as I approached some Soldiers who were enjoying the off time in one of the most tried and true methods- playing cards." I could have sworn I heard a medic with an English accent when I was walking."

"Oh yeah, that's Sgt. Gary," one of the Soldiers replied, focusing on his hand. 4 players. Two teams. Spades. I swear I had never seen the game before I joined the Army. "You would probably want to speak to him; his story's pretty crazy."

His teammate placed down one of his cards, and the speaking Soldier shook his head.

Looked like a wrong move.

"Crazy even for here, sir," the Soldier continued, nonplussed. "He was in a rock band in the U.K. or something before he joined."

Hmmm, that was intriguing. How many former U.K. rockers were hanging around in the U.S. Army?

"He was also an actor in a few episodes of Band of Brothers."

"What?"

"Yeah, he pointed himself out in a few scenes."

Going from playing as a Soldier in the 101st in a T.V. series to being one in a conflict? I shook my head; my "source" went back to his cards. Guessing by the voices when I walked off, his card strategy worked, and his team won the hand.

We gathered behind the TOC for the nightly meeting, headed by Maj. Kurt Knoedler, the 1-320th X.O. and de-facto leader of the base since he was the highest-ranking officer there. The commanders from each of the units would gather to discuss the day's events and tasks for the next under the night sky, and unlike the meetings usually conducted back in the states there were no PowerPoints, computers, or even chairs.

Knoedler acknowledged me when I walked into the area with my tripod in hand, glancing down at the gathered personnel who were sitting on either the dirt or their helmets. He was in his early 30s and had been in the Army for about a decade. This wasn't his first rodeo, and he seemed at ease with the whole situation. Based on my meetings with him at KSB, in Erbil, or even back at home, he had the same calm demeanor whether he oversaw *the* firebase in Iraq or was grabbing some coffee at Starbucks.

"Getting all the B-roll you need, Johnson?" he asked. I was thrown for a second; most people wouldn't know about B-roll. Heck, I didn't know until Maj. Sanders had told me a few days before. Maj. Knoedler would be the only person during my entire time in Iraq to use that term, and I still wonder if he studied film or something in college. It wouldn't be the weirdest jump into the military, that's for sure. I would later discover that one of the First Sergeants in the brigade had studied journalism in college, a fact which made him very amused when I told him I had no training at all.

It was an odd feeling, having a field grade officer (outside of Maj. Sanders, of course) who genuinely…liked me: no weird looks, curious questions, or furrowed brows. As soon as Maj. Sanders had informed him that she was sending a cameraman to the base, he had put out the word that I was to have free reign. The rest of my encounters with 1-320th would have the same atmosphere; they seemed to like having me around.

There was a weird dynamic between the artillerymen and the rest of the brigade- due to some force realignments, they were no longer "part" of the brigade but attached. The fact that Charlie Battery was added to the deployment mere months before made the relationship even more strained; the battery was, to be honest, a strategic asset that was going to be moved and used by commanders in echelons well above the Brigade Commander at

Camp Swift. Which meant that there were some…sore feelings about the whole thing.

Especially when it comes to getting credit.

Once the last Soldiers arrived, trudging up to the hill, Maj. Knoedler started the gathering by going over events he had thought happened during the day. The assorted personnel represented all the disparate elements on base and their missions: Security forces, route clearance guys sallying forth with the Paladins, HIMARs, engineers. All were looking exhausted.

His part done, Knoedler opened the ground to the next person up, a Captain who I didn't recognize.

"Sir," the Captain began, his calm briefing voice in contrast to his run-down appearance. "Today we conducted-"

BOOM.

The Captain paused, and everyone looked at each other.

"Was that an artillery piece firing?" someone asked.

"No, that sounded different."

I looked around the gathered group. The air started to feel tense. It's subtle, but when people sense danger or are readying for a fight, you can see it. You can *feel it* — a slight shifting of the shoulders, leaning forward, expression change. The adrenaline starts to flow, and it happens subconsciously.

"Hey, look!" someone called from the top of the dirt mound. "There's smoke coming from right outside the base."

Some of us clambered up the hill, straining for a look like we were a bunch of tourists looking for a geyser- not Soldiers in a war. I climbed up with them, grabbing a spot to observe. He wasn't lying; a giant white smoke plume was flowing into the evening sky.

"Hey Chief!" I called down to CW2 Miranda, who hadn't moved to join us. "Take a look at this!"

Miranda shook his head. "I'm good sir, trust me."

I glanced down, smiling, then stopped.

I swore I could almost see him sinking into his body armor.

"Let's break this meeting, everyone," Maj. Knoedler said as he put on his ACH. "Someone fired at us --- and they don't usually just send one."

Everyone started moving quickly, breaking off to their positions in the base. I grabbed my tripod, putting it into my bag, and then started my trudge back to CW2 Miranda's post. With my tripod bag and other kit, the sprint to a bunker would be awkward-

INCOMING. INCOMING. INCOMING.

God damn it.

Without even thinking my feet picked up their pace and I began moving towards a bunker at the edge of the L.Z. At about the same time I started running, there was a loud explosion from behind the base, shaking the Earth noticeably. The weird thing about bombs in real life versus in movies is just how...hollow they sound. Not a loud high bang, but a low boom, that began and ended suddenly, like bass drums playing in a large empty cave. Crashing into the dark stone interior of a bunker with a huff, I was soon joined by about four other Soldiers who had moved even faster than I did.

ISIL fighters had made a run with a vehicle borne Improvised Explosive Device (IED) towards the firebase, no doubt acting in conjunction with the rockets that had been called in. They knew that the IDF would send us into cover, giving them the opening they needed to reach the perimeter and blow a hole in our defenses.

On the perimeter, the 1-75 Soldiers in the guard bunkers spotted two ISIL fighters in the distance, the observers for the rocket attack. Their job done, the two black figures emerged and began to make a run for a waiting motorbike.

The Kurds on the outskirts of the base scrambled, attempting to stop the VBIED. They did, with only about 200 meters to spare before it would have reached the base walls, and by the trembling of the Earth, a good portion of the rest of the base.

The Soldiers on the perimeter were ready to eliminate the two ISIL spotters. They asked the TOC for permission to engage. Hostile intent was clear- unless people just liked to lie in the prone with binoculars and watch an American firebase just before rocket attacks.

Yeah right.

The artillerymen on the gun line begin to spin their M777s to conduct a counter-fire mission. The radar system that CW2 Miranda and his crew were running could give anyone who needed it a grid, distance, and direction to any large caliber weapon that targeted the base. That's all you needed for a fire mission, and the crews were trained to execute counter-battery fire quickly; they had to. Chances were that as soon as the rocket left the ISIL position, they were already on the move.

Meanwhile, in the bunker I was occupying, it was quickly turning into a sauna and then an oven. About 8 of us were crammed into a 7 foot by 3-foot space, each of us adding our body heat to each other. We couldn't leave until the "all clear" signal came on, and the seconds passed slowly, each drop of sweat seeming to drip off of our faces dramatically. It seemed like forever, the questions eating away at our brains.

Would there be more?

I'll never bring this tripod again.

It's so hot.

How would it feel if a rocket landed in that little space and killed us?

Can these bunkers take a direct hit from a missile?

Would I see the flame? Would I feel the shrapnel?

I'd rather be outside risking it then inside this damn oven.

The fear of the unknown, that cold hard reality, deep in your stomach, that you could not escape from. The wait is one of the worst parts of the whole experience, I would learn. The maddening feeling of waiting for danger that may or may not happen, your brain constantly creating scenarios of danger or safety. It's like standing in line for a roller coaster you're afraid of.

It's just that the line can stretch for hours, days, or weeks, and as soon as that moment hits, that adrenaline rush once you realize you're still alive or the firing is over? You're right back to it.

There's no other feeling like it.

"Johnson? Is that you?" came a familiar voice, bringing me out of thoughts. I hadn't heard it since I had left Kuwait a few weeks before.

"Finch?" I asked, peering down the corridor. The last time I had seen Finch, 1st Lt. Anthony Finch, was at the TOC in Kuwait. He was the battle captain there, the military equivalent of a shift lead. I didn't even know he had gotten into Iraq.

"Strange place to run into each other again." His words.

I laughed, and somehow the mood seemed to have lifted. As morbid as it sounds, something is relieving about knowing someone who's going through the same things you are. We caught up a bit about our adventures, and how we both had ended up at KSB at the same time. We even took a selfie together.

The counter-fire requests, both from the artillerymen and cavalry Soldiers, went up the chain. First through the TOC on base, then to Camp Swift, then even further. At this time in the campaign, extremely tight control was being kept on any use of American firepower, even on enemies who had fired or called in fire on coalition troops. The stringent rules of engagement seemed to dissipate depending on the "value" of the threat, however.

Both requests were denied, though by the time the word had been received it was too late anyway. The ISIL spotters got on their motorcycle and sped off as the Soldiers on guard watched, their weapons following the vehicle until it was out of sight. The enemy rocket system that had fired at us also drove off, unmolested by a counter-battery fire.

It was odd, that at a base ostensibly set up counter-fire missions, that an actual counter-fire couldn't be executed. The Soldiers in the towers and on the gun line weren't happy to have missed their chance to engage the enemy because of a decision made by some high-ranking guy hundreds of miles away. I guess the radio show wasn't the only comparison to draw between then and Vietnam.

Returning to my cot, I dropped my tripod bag in the dirt. I hated carrying that thing and after the experience of running to cover with it, I decided it was done. Sure, my videos would be more "shaky," but the bosses would take what they could get. That and they weren't the ones running around Iraq to try to get the footage.

Maj. Sanders rankled her nose at me the second I walked into the tent back at Erbil, even though I had followed her command to report to her immediately after I arrived, sweat stains and all.

"You smell like you've been rolling around in the dirt," her words to me before I could even open my mouth. I gave her a shrug.

"You could put it that way." My dry response.

"You get the footage?"

I patted my camera. "Of course." I began to approach her desk.

She put a hand up to stop me as if warding off my smell.

"Take a shower first," her words, holding her nose. I guess the stench was enough to make even her be willing to wait on the footage everyone was wanting. I smiled inwardly, I kind of wanted some time to get settled in myself. I returned a bit later, after one of the best showers I felt I had ever taken, with the one uniform set that I had worn that past few days safely tucked away in a laundry bag to be dropped off at a different time to the cleaning tent on base.

"Let's see what you got, L.T.," Maj. Sanders as we sat at the desk, the video footage slowly being transferred over to the Mac Computer due to the ancient USB Cable. That wasn't the only technical issue, since MAC computers weren't set up to connect to the "tactical" internet our satellite vehicles provided and since there wasn't precisely google fiber available in Kurdistan.... We had to buy our internet. 35$ for a blazing 15 gigs per month, provided by WIFI "PUCs", sold to us by a friendly convenience store in Erbil. I wonder how much of a profit they made.

"I got everything you asked for ma'am," I reported with a smirk. "Quality of life, fire missions, even the chaplain's service."

I looked at her expression to see if I would get anything readable. She seemed happy enough by what she was seeing appear on the MAC Computer. Would I finally get a "Good job kid,"?...

"Good, good," she said as she nodded her head.

And that was it. I was waiting for more, but it wasn't coming. Her tone implied that she knew I would come through. That, or she knew she didn't have any other choice in the matter, so getting anything was a victory.

"Did you get any good photos?" her next question, not letting me enjoy the brief feeling of victory I was having.

I looked up at her, the confidence draining from my face.

In my rush to get to the gun line at KSB, I had left my Nikon up with Chief Miranda on the radar and when I picked it up again, I was focused on walking the perimeter. All those days, and I had gotten zero photos of the artillerymen in action.

"So, you only got video." Maj. Sanders continued, reading my expression. She had a "God Help Me" look on her face that shifted to disappointment for a moment, and then finally ended as a strange look that seemed to say: I wasn't totally incompetent. I had gotten what she asked for, so there was that.

"Never leave any of your cameras LT." she began to lecture. "Three products for everything you go out to do: photos, videos, and news articles if you can get a good interview. Remember that. If you do that, you'll be way ahead of everyone else."

Three products per going out?

"That's crazy," I blurted out. "Who does that? I'll be going back and forth between a camera and a video camera."

"That's what it takes, L.T.," Maj. Sanders finished, expression unchanged. "That's what we used to do in my old unit." She paused, looking thoughtful. "I thought you said you were willing to do what it takes? If not, you can head back to Kuwait..."

I sighed. She had me, and she knew it.

"I'll try ma'am."

She nodded as if she knew what the outcome of this conversation was going to be the entire time.

"Good, let's start cutting this footage."

We poured over the footage for hours. This wasn't even supposed to be for a complete video package, yet there we were looking over every clip, moment by moment.

"Five to seven second cuts L.T.," Maj. Sanders' voice as we played around with the adobe premiere program that we had on our MacBooks. "News organizations look for five to seven second cuts to use for B-roll."

Great, wish I knew that before I went out there.

"No, that's too close. That's too far. There, that clip there, that's what we want. We want this B-roll to tell a story too."

Themes. Messages. She was talking about things I had only seen in theory. I was learning that she wasn't just worried about the media: she wanted something she could use when generals, members of congress, or anyone else asked questions.

We were building a picture.

The fire mission footage was rough. I didn't quite know what to look for, so it was all over the place. Still, the HIMARs footage, some artillerymen loading their guns, and Mont's crew firing made the first cut. Maj. Sanders didn't want it to be too long, only about 2 minutes tops. But even with everything I shot, we barely had that.

"Anything else?" she asked, rubbing her head at what we had to work with.

"I-"

Then it hit me, as I remembered the information Pfc. Sabol had given to me, along with data, before I had come back to Erbil.

"The guys gave me their GoPro footage to use, ma'am." I opened one of the files, shot by the Soldier during the same time as my other video footage. Loud, sweaty, his helmet visible in the frame as he moved and loaded rounds. It was chaotic, rough, a totally different perspective from the clean clips usually released. Maj. Sanders thought about it for a few moments, looking closer at the images playing out on the screen, then signaled for me to stop.

"There, that clip there, that's *it.*" Her words as I replayed the clip, footage of Pfc. Sabol not only ramming rounds but also spinning one to get the fuse on during a fire mission. "I think you're onto something with this GoPro stuff L.T. Do you have more?"

"Gigs of it, ma'am."

"Perfect."

I edited the footage in, and the clip in its entirety was under two minutes. All it had taken was four hours of work.

We moved on to the editing quality of life footage. The first thing that immediately caught Maj. Sanders' eyes was the clip of Sgt. 1st Class Young sitting in his bunker.

"That's perfect!" she exclaimed. "That's exactly what I'm looking for. We're going to start with that for a full 7 seconds," I glanced back at her in surprise. "That perfectly shows what life at KSB is like. How'd you get it?"

"He just asked me to follow him, honestly."

She had a laugh at that, and by the end of the night, we had put together about six minutes of assorted footage for review by the Division Public Affairs Office. We uploaded and sent it up to the Division PAO's non-commissioned officer in charge, Sgt. 1st Class Nathan Hoskins.

Hoskins was a public affairs photojournalist and an extremely efficient one at that, having won multiple Keith L. Ware Awards. The awards were given only to selected public affairs professionals in the Army after their entries or personnel records were compared with other competitors. He had about a decade of experience in the job, at multiple levels, one of the reasons he was selected to go forward to Iraq with the challenging job of reviewing the submissions from every public affairs asset in the Combined Joint Forces Land Component Command- Operation Inherent Resolve, (CJFLCC-OIR) for short.

Hoskins and his boss, Lt. Col. Chevelle Thomas, were also the 101st Airborne Division's PAOs. Without delving too deep, CJFLCC-OIR and the 101st Airborne Division were not one and the same, even though it consisted of the same personnel. Due to the pure chance of 2BCT Strike being chosen to go to Iraq while the 101st HQ element was still there, the lines kind of blurred, which worked out in everyone's favor.

When Maj. Sanders had informed Sgt. 1st Class Hoskins of her plan to deploy me to Iraq, he thought it was extremely odd, especially since the best new journalist in the entire U.S. Army was available. He didn't quite know what to make of me based on my first few stories sent up, but the fact that he took the time to look over everything I submitted showed a dedication to the job that some of his peers didn't have.

Hoskins and Thomas wanted to publicize the Division above all else since their boss was the 101st Airborne Division commander, and the scheme to send someone to KSB to get footage for the media?

That was *their* idea.

It didn't take Hoskins long to get back to us.

"This is exactly what we needed," he started, the excitement audibly apparent over the speakerphone. "Some of it looks a little...red, though."

71

Maj. Sanders looked at me. I shrugged.

"Yeah, the white balance was off," her reply.

I didn't even know what white balance was until that day. And I felt the red coloring really brought out the heat aspect of what was going on, but...

"Have to take care of that next time," Hoskins continued. "But, the GoPro footage, where'd you get that from?"

"I got it from the guys," my reply. "They gave me a ton of footage of what was going on."

"We need *more of that,*" he continued. "That's pretty stellar --- the whole thing is. These clips will go a long way once they're released."

Hoskins paused for a moment, his tone changing when he continued speaking.

"The quality-of-life footage though, with the guy staring at the wall. That's pretty morbid. With all the silence and him staring at the wall I felt like the screen was going to go black and we were going to hear a gunshot."

"Go on," Sanders prodded, already planning for the conversation to take this turn.

"Everything is well shot, but if we release this, the phones will be ringing off the hook. We have talk to Lt. Col. Thomas on this one."

Maj. Sanders grabbed the phone. "I'll handle this," she said, switching it from speaker to the device. For the next 10 to 15 minutes she spoke to Sgt. 1st Class Hoskins, agreeing that while the quality-of-life footage looked rough, *that was the reality.* He agreed, but of course he wasn't the one calling the shots-soon enough, Maj. Sanders and Lt. Col. Thomas were speaking to each other. Some disagreement talk about how other elements of the division were out of touch, what the role of a PAO was, and above all else: the difference between the two's marching orders. Both were adamant about their points of view, and it was the first sign that while we were all working together, we all weren't *really* working together.

"Alright," Maj. Sanders said after she put down the phone after the conversation ended, rubbing her head. "Division doesn't want to release the other footage, but that's ok, we can use it for ourselves." The unspoken words: *which was precisely the plan all along.*

"You did a good job out there, L.T. Got anything for stories?"

I rapidly listed off the angles I had discovered.

"Good," she replied. "I can see you've been working. We have the footage, so I'm sending you back out there tomorrow."

Soldiers from 1-502 during a break at KSB in-between missions, June, 2016. U.S. Army photo by Daniel Johnson.

Maj. Sanders seemed to consider articles a bonus rather than a purpose, but figured that since I was nearby anyway, she might as well see what I came up with. She even expressed some amusement that I had the habit of writing stories about anything and everything I encountered. There was no grand plan or expectation from her beyond writing what I thought would work, which at the time was...vague. The joke about U.S. military press releases is that they're considered cold, impersonal, sanitized and manufactured in the public relations factories of the Pentagon.

For the next eight months, that public relations factory would be some 25-year-old kid who was basically told to write whatever I felt, however I felt. So, I just decided to write about what I saw and portray the information from the Soldiers' perspective, if I could. Good images elicit an emotional response, and good writing can also create those results. There's a space for straight news, but a straight story wouldn't be able to try to convey what was going on at KSB properly. The goal of public affairs is to inform people, right?

No one is going to be informed if they're not paying attention in the first place. The final product I created was not what they taught the U.S. Army's public affairs school, however, as I soon found out.

"I like it," Maj. Sanders' words after I sent her my first drafts. "But what are you trying to say?"

"What do you mean?" My reply. "I'm just writing about what's going on. I'm not really trying to say anything."

She sighed.

"But what about the messaging?"

"Messaging? Messaging about what?"

My opinion on U.S. Army public affairs is that the job to *inform* stakeholders/the population is paramount above all else. An *informed* populace can make better decisions about how *their* armed forces should be used. If Soldiers were sleeping in holes while burning up in 130-degree weather, their families and everyone else should know; especially since, even through all the conditions, they were delivering the tactical effects required by their chain of command.

To me, *that* was the story. I watched the invasion of Iraq on T.V. as a middle schooler in 2003 and had heard and read the rosy reports about coalition progress. And yet here we were in 2016, fighting an enemy who quite literally formed *because* of our invasion of the country. Strategic messaging wasn't going to cut it if no one believed a word you were saying. If the American people, with the information we provided, decided the mission wasn't worth it, then that's how things should work.

"I don't know how to message ma'am," my reply, half right. I didn't *want* to either.

"You're going to have to learn."

"I'll try, but I'm just a lieutenant. My world is at the level I can see."

"But the world is much bigger than that L.T, and the audience is too. People in the U.S. aren't the only ones looking at this."

"I'll add some blurbs to make everyone happy," she finished, her lecture complete. I was shocked; she didn't remove anything I had written, a perfect "compromise."

Sgt. 1st Class Hoskins was the next step on the ladder, and he was surprisingly accepting. If I had been a student at the Defense Information School, I probably would have gotten laughed out of the course, yet here we were with Hoskins sending back his suggested edits.

"How far do you want these to go?" His question after his review.

"Honestly, I would be glad to get them in the local post newspaper and Clarksville so the families could see them," I replied. "Who *else* would run them?"

"We can do that," his reply. "Getting it in the Clarksville area papers is no problem.

He sent the article up to the next level so that they could do their final review. Since the goal was only to reach the local outlets, it shouldn't be too much of a struggle, he told me.

"Hey, what is this?" read the email from Sgt. 1st Class Hoskins one day. I looked at the attached screenshot, Maj. Sanders joining me when I told her about the message. The scheme to hand the BBC the footage from KSB had failed. "We're getting our footage," their words. "We won't rely on an Army cameraman."

Remember that quote for later, trust me.

Either way, with that scheme ruined, we now had B-roll sitting around unused, and I had uploaded it to DVIDS. The best way to think of DVIDs is like a cloud service for all DoD Media. Military journalists upload their articles, photos, and videos there for use by government employees, media companies, or the public.

That's why me uploading the file a week before without it technically being approved was a problem. Sgt. 1st Class Hoskins let Maj. Sanders and I know that we had jumped the gun, so we took it down in 30 minutes, which was more than enough time in the digital age.

"Task Force Strike Artillerymen conduct fire missions." the title of the YouTube video read. I was confused --- the combat cameramen had taken footage weeks before-

"Video by 1st Lt. Daniel Johnson."

Maj. Sanders and I glanced at each other, shaking our heads almost in unison. Neither of us had seen this coming.

The YouTube channel with the clip was on Funker530, which was a Facebook page, website, and YouTube channel set up during the height of OEF/OIF that posted combat footage, usually submitted by Soldiers. Military friendly, and with considerable audience size.

Which made the whole thing confusing. I wasn't a person worth following on DVIDs at the time, so how had they gotten the clip so *fast?*

"It wasn't me," I replied to Sgt. 1st Class Hoskins. "I just sent it up and to no one else."

"Wasn't me either." Maj. Sanders replied, hiding a smile. It was *such a tragedy* that the footage was being viewed by thousands, perhaps hundreds of thousands of people! *How unfortunate.*

Sgt. 1st Class Hoskins wasn't happy that the cat was out of the bag, but it was too late: the footage was going viral. The main hook?

The GoPro footage.

The Army Reserve, GoArmy.com, random war footage groups, Twitter, Instagram. Horrible white balance and all, it was going more places than a year's worth of previous footage from the brigade. To say that all of us were surprised was an understatement, with Maj. Sanders occasionally recounting to me communications she had received from others in the brigade about how they were getting messages from their family members back home with links to the footage.

It was some beyond the looking glass type stuff.

"The Gun Line," was the name of the companion article that I wrote to go along with the footage, based on my interview with the artillerymen. A generic title to be sure, but that's what the article was about, and no one *else* had any ideas. The final set of edits from CJTF-OIR had some choice comments:

"Next time you do this, you need more actual *quotes*." The note began. "And some more photos." Obviously, they weren't fans of the video stills I had pulled of the action since I had forgotten my Nikon.

"But since this is only going local, learn for next time." The review finished.

The Clarksville and Fort Campbell papers shared the article, as expected.

The United States Central Command, the highest headquarters in the Middle East and responsible for everything from Afghanistan through Iraq, shared it as featured news of all the operations in the area.

Then the headquarters of the United States Army shared it as the featured news of the entire *branch*, putting the article (after some slight rewrites and a title change to "Life on the Gun Line"), on the front page of Army.Mil.

For once, I could say Maj. Sanders had been caught off guard, based on her reaction. Most journalists in the Army considered their crowning achievement to be making the front page of Army.Mil, and usually crafted their articles and made the connections to do so. The article hadn't trended because of my writing, that's for sure: the article was going places because people wanted to hear stories from the ground level. That is what *drew people in*.

I knew from the start that I wouldn't ever be able to get the unfiltered truth out; the reaction to the video of the living conditions at KSB proved that. But that didn't mean I couldn't get as much out there as possible. The heat, the sleeping conditions, the dust. Little descriptors that set the scene but also tried to illuminate what the Soldiers were going through. Sometimes it got edited out; sometimes it didn't. But considering that I could interpret a note saying, "Find a way to reword this," as I wished…

I also shared the article on the U.S. Army Reddit page. I figured two things: Soldiers want to hear about what's going on with other Soldiers, and, if the article didn't pass *their* test, then I had utterly failed in my mission. I was pleasantly surprised that the article got good reviews from them, (with some good-natured ribbing of course) and some shares.

"Don't get too cocky," Maj. Sanders words after the article was released. "It takes a lot to get back up there."

The article on Lt. Thomas' "Good Morning Iraq" radio broadcast came out next, after working its way through the system. It was supposed to be about all of what 1-75 CAV was doing on the base, but CJTF-OIR's reviewers grew excited when the saw the radio show portion and suggested a cut in half. Why? The public affairs branch *started* from radio broadcasts during conflicts used to keep American Soldiers informed about what was going home.

"Sure," my reply at the time. "Works for me." I was a little miffed, considering that I felt that the full story wasn't getting out there. Maj. Sanders simply shrugged her shoulders; it was an excellent article for the people back home, at least. There would be other opportunities, she said.

When the Department of Defense's official twitter page, highly watched because it was the social media account of one of *the most powerful militaries on Earth*, posted a link to the Good Morning Iraq article, the floodgates opened. The subscribers on our DVIDs page almost doubled, our social media accounts saw increased activity, and even better, media organizations started emailing *us*.

Since we had arrived, Maj. Sanders had been trying to get in contact with the Armed Forces Network, Stripes, the Army Times, anyone, to see if she could get some brigade focused coverage. Those that did respond were usually directed to the division headquarters first since you know, what did a small brigade combat team have to offer?

Then the Army Times contacted us directly. They wanted to do a follow-up article on Lt. Thomas and his radio broadcast. *Nothing else.* The crazy part of it? The Army Times sent an email asking to talk to *me so I could coordinate it.*

Maj. Sanders jumped on it when I told her what was up, making sure to let them know that she was the PAO in Iraq, not me, of course. When she notified the division, they were understandably confused --- outside media *never* usually went and contacted a writer of an article about something that was written to do follow-ups. It was often the other way around.

There was also some chagrin from the Division HQ; the Army Times wanted to interview some random lieutenant at a far-flung firebase. What was going on?

There are three different "levels" talked about in Army doctrine when speaking about delivered effects. The tactical level, where individual battles and engagements are fought. The operational level, which is concerned with employing military forces in a theater of war, for example Iraq with Operation Inherent Resolve. And then finally the strategic level, which focuses on defining and supporting national policy and relates directly to the outcome of a war or the conflict. Strategic communication is part of that, all the concerted efforts like marketing, advertising, community relations, and news releases. For my articles to jump up to the Pentagon level meant that someone up there saw fit to use them to support their *strategic* goals. Reports don't just get chosen to be featured by "Big Army"; they're chosen to support whatever communications objective that's in place at the time.

Whatever that was, however, I sure didn't know it. I was just glad the guys were getting their names out there.

"You know," stated Maj. Sanders on a call one day as the situation developed and the footage and news started to blow up, or at least got more widespread than we all thought it would. "What you're throwing up there isn't quite right, but," she paused, and I thought I could hear a chuckle. "It's working."

"Isn't that all that matters?" my reply.

"No," her words. "I feel like you could just post a guy walking and still get a ton of shares right now."

"Isn't that the whole point?"

"You're thinking like an infantryman, L.T.," she chided.

".... But that's what I am, technically."

"No, you're working in *public affairs* now. You've got to start thinking about the big picture, because whether you believe it or not -"

"We're in it."

Interlude I- App State - 2010

Maj. Sanders wasn't the first person to take a chance on me, as the figure that was standing near the stairway to block my path that day at Appalachian State would show.

"Hey stud!" he called out, shifting from his position of leaning on the rail looking out over the entranceway to one where he stood directly in front of my line of advance.

No escape.

Master Sgt. Chalk Wetmore hadn't been selected to serve on a Special Forces A-Team for no reason. He didn't just come to Appalachian State to help shape future officers for no reason, either. I guess he wanted to help knuckleheads' like me find their path.

Or not.

"We need to talk," he began, looking straight at me.

Looking straight *through* me.

"You haven't been able to pass a P.T. test all year." Not a question, a statement, not even a hint of emotion in his voice.

"Shin splints, Sergeant Major." My reply.

My excuse.

I had fallen into the Appalachian State ROTC program after one of my roommates suggested that I try it out. My GPA in school at the time was subpar, the result of me not really caring about showing up to class and never taking the time to study the textbooks. I hadn't gone to college thinking I would be interested in the military, and I hadn't started the program with any real goal in mind, so on a whim I said why not.

I was a slacker.

Or at least I thought I was.

The ROTC program held physical training three times a week, with me waking up at 5:30 A.M. to walk through the freezing Boone air. Beyond the pushups, sit-ups, and other usual military exercises, there was also the 2.0 mile run around downtown Boone which was practically right next to App State due to how small the "city" was. Each time I'd run until my shins gave out, an effect of spending my teenage years playing too many video games. Even still, I was even taking the ROTC classes twice a week and doing the ROTC "labs" every Thursday, where we dressed in our ACUs and did "tactical" exercises at State Farm Field. The name was aptly descriptive; it was quite literally a large open field right next to the one large off campus parking lot for all of App's students.

The odd part was, I was doing it all for *free.*

You either get an ROTC scholarship, which pays for four years of school, or get "contracted" separately, where unlike scholarship cadets you don't get your school paid for while getting the other benefits like a stipend. I was not part of either program and soon I would be a junior in college, which was critical for ROTC cadets due to the way the evaluation system worked. The big question was coming up.

What was I going to choose?

Master Sgt. Wetmore knew the answer, even though I didn't know it for myself at the time.

"You need to pass at least one P.T. test this year if you want to get contracted next year," he continued, laying out the stakes.

"You have one more chance."

"Sgt. Major-"

"I talk, you listen, roger?"

"Roger," for a moment I wanted to run, turn, and never come back.

But I couldn't.

"If you can't meet the standard, we don't need you. You have to *set* the standard if you want to be an officer."

A pause.

The unspoken question.

Do you *want* this?

"The next P.T. test is in a month." He walked past me towards the door, brushing me to the side. Suddenly, he paused at the entrance, speaking while not looking back. "You think about it for a while. Nothing is stopping you from leaving if you want. You're not contracted, you don't have to do this. All you have to do is simply stop showing up."

With that, he walked off, his words hanging in the air.

He was daring me. Daring me to be better than I was - to *believe* I could be better than I was.

Tap tap tap.

Snow falling all around me.

My feet hitting the pavement of King St., the "downtown' of Boone, North Carolina, weighed down by the Brooks running shoes.

Damn, these things are heavy.

The last turn up the next street, a sprint to the finish.

Still a few seconds off.

My shins burning as I began the toe-tapping exercise I found online to strengthen the muscles.

I wasn't going to make it.

Morning P.T.

Wetmore watching me like a hawk as I ran around the track.

"You have to pick it up, Johnson," his words, carrying through the sound of huffing and puffing. "You have to start pushing!"

My legs were burning as the laps stretched on. 18 laps on the small track in the student recreation center on campus to complete the required two miles. I wanted to stop, to just go back home to my dorm and forget about all this Army stuff. I wasn't even getting paid.

My legs kept on moving forward though.

"To complete the required two miles, you must run *eleven* laps."

The Holmes Convocation Center, home of the App State Basketball team of "Worst Free throw of all time" fame, and the only good indoor track near campus for inclement weather. The briefing continued, the details of the physical fitness test being laid out. Pushups, sit-ups, two-mile run. The last test of the semester.

And my last chance.

The test began, butterflies in my stomach, to the point I was shaking. Push Ups- no problem. Sit Ups- No problem.

They never were.

Finally, the run. My heart racing as we stood on the starting line.

This was it.

The sounding whistle, us moving, the fast guys speeding off.

One lap.

Two laps.

Breathing getting ragged.

Lap eight.

Shins are burning.

Lap eleven. Time ticking down.

The realization- Master Sgt. Wetmore only gave me another chance because he had faith in me.

Me, of all people.

I didn't deserve it.

But I couldn't let his belief in me be a waste.

I crossed the finish line with seconds to spare, huffing and puffing, eventually collapsing on the side, laughing.

I had did it.

Wetmore walked over, his face stern as always.

But not surprised.

"Good work." For the briefest of moments, a flicker of pride, before returning to the instructor visage.

"You'll have to get faster, though; you can't just *meet* the standard."

With that, he turned around, his words hanging in the air, daring me to do better. Daring *me* to *believe* I could do better.

By next year I wouldn't be just a few seconds from failing the run, but a few seconds from maxing it.

Chapter Five-Camp Taji- July 2016

"They're deciding who's going to get what awards," one of my fellow lieutenants spoke as I investigated the small office space at Camp Swift where the Brigade X.O., the sergeant major, and other high up guys looked grimly through papers sitting on the table.

"How are they deciding that now, we've only been here two months?" My reply.

"What do you think?" A sigh of understanding- the awards were going to be given out based on rank, not contribution.

"Yeah, but what if a guy charges a machine gun nest or something a couple of months from now?"

"Army Commendation Medal with a Valor Device, of course."

I glanced at him with a silent laugh, but we both knew he was right. The big joke about the Army awards is that people in higher ranks got the "better" awards like the Bronze Star, even if all they did was answer emails. If you didn't have face time with a high-level official, and you were lower ranking, you get an Army Achievement Medal or maybe, if they *liked* you, an ARCOM.

Yes, you could run directly into an active minefield to pull out a comrade wounded by an IED, and still receive a "lower" award than some guy who sat at Starbucks all day; it had happened before.

I guess it was like the Combat Action Badge and the odd criteria for it. By doctrine, it reads: "(The CAB) may be awarded to any Soldier performing assigned duties in an area where hostile fire pay or imminent danger pay is authorized, who is personally present and actively engaging or being engaged by the enemy…"

Sounds like the guys at KSB, right? The leaders of the 1st Armored and 1st Infantry Division Soldiers who operated the Paladin Artillery vehicles thought so, and so they got theirs. 1-320th *didn't*, doing the exact same thing. Seems like one set of standards was different than the others, at least on the face of it.

Now, if the standards were fair, our brigade's stringent interaction of what combat was would be followed everywhere right? Except that when Camp Swift had a mortar round land hundreds of meters away, the personnel there got Combat Action Badges. I wonder if it was because there were some higher-ranking officers that worked with the Brigade Commander that lobbied for it? Maybe I was being too distrustful, but then again-

I was directly witnessing "end of tour" awards being decided on *at the beginning of the tour*. And by the end of the whole show, based on the awards given, you'd think the brigade headquarters was leading the way the whole time, what with the number of bronze stars, combat action badges, and even the Combat Infantrymen badges that were rolling around at the end.

I wasn't the only one who noticed it, based on the comments I would receive from the Soldiers during and after the deployment.

Running the brigade's Facebook page, while mostly enjoyable, could be a real pain. The enjoyable part came from seeing family members of Soldiers respond to posts that featured their loved ones, be it a photo, news article, or shout-out.

What had started in Kuwait to put up content because we had just gotten on ground and didn't have anything else to post yet had turned into "Shoutout Saturdays", a day where nothing but videos of Soldiers saying hello to the friends and family back home were featured on the webpage. It was a hit, to the point that people were anticipating the next edition and even asking for us to find certain Soldiers to get a video message. *Especially* from the guys at the farther locations where internet and phone connectivity were spotted and limited.

The whole thing about the shoutouts was that sometimes it took a little coaxing- ok, begging- to get people to participate. Not always though --- CW2 Miranda's crew at KSB were one of the first ones to volunteer, Sgt. Villarreal being at the front of the line. Soon after other personnel on the base joined in figuring they'd might as well get on the internet too.

The random photos we posted were also popular. Whatever got approved of Soldiers in their daily lives would go up on the Facebook page. Standing guard? Uploaded. Working out? Uploaded. Talking to Iraqis? Uploaded. Boring, exciting, in-between, it did not matter. If there was content that showcased the Soldiers, it was put up for the most important audience of all- the families of the personnel. Unfortunately, they were not the only audience.

There was nothing better than a message, usually from an older retired Soldier, who would usually presage it about how "they just wanted to make sure the Soldiers' looked professional". Before complaining about the lack of standards, or how back in 85... Sometimes, it bordered on the absurd, like complaints about Soldiers sometimes not wearing eye protection even though the reason they were doing so was because their eye protection had broken and there were *no replacements*. Maj. Sanders took it in stride, however.

As time went on, I grew more savvy on the little pet peeves of each audience we were engaging. I had to, considering my boss was leaving most of the social media posting to my judgement. She was happy because the followers kept on increasing, the likes kept on going up, and the hashtags #OIR and #BeStrike were catching on at levels above our own in the Army.

However, we were back to the original problem.

"People at home don't know what we're doing out here," Maj. Sanders said as we spoke near her desk in Erbil, rubbing her head from across the table. "The *Brigade Commander* feels that the families don't understand the mission. Since the division is-"she paused for a moment, looking at me, then shook her head. "-Not allowing a lot of media into the country, we'll just have to publicize what we're doing ourselves."

She still could not explain it, and none of us understood it, but if she had someone who had a direct line straight to the big public affairs people up in the Pentagon, why not use him? That meant she controlled the message *directly*. Based on her expression as we spoke, however, she was not quite sure what I would give her. Her problem of not having content had been solved, but now she had another one-

There was no theme to them. Public Affairs officers *hate* having no theme to their output.

"We are publicizing what we're doing," my reply. I started counting off on my fingers. "Shout outs, posting photos, the news articles…"

"Yes, but what are you trying to say?"

"That the Soldiers are out here?"

"For *what* purpose."

I shrugged. The Soldiers were still out there risking their necks in sometimes horrid conditions, and the more people who were informed what American foreign policy looked like in action, the better in my mind. The articles were vague because our purpose was vague, and if the American people felt that their military shouldn't be used in pursuit of vague objectives, so be it. If the planners of "the most powerful military on Earth" couldn't tell me what was going on, how was it I was going to tell *them*.

This war didn't even have a freaking name.

"What are we doing out here, ma'am?" I replied. "I don't get this advise and assist thing. I've heard the term, but what does it mean? I'm in Iraq, and I *still don't know* what's going on."

U.S. forces had been committed to "stop ISIL". But what did stopping ISIL even look like? The Tigris river? Taking Mosul? Even further? How about the Iranians and their plans for the country, or the question of Kurdish independence? What about the death squads that were rolling around taking retribution on civilians as the ISF advanced? Or, how were 5,000 personnel supposed to build the capacity of the ISF when 100,000 plus years before hadn't been able to do it?

All that I had seen was vague proclamations that we were doing good, almost straight copy and pasted from the Iraq War a few years before. From my observations at Camp Swift and Erbil, a lot of the advising seemed to be ...people talking to each other. Cool and all, but even I could read between the lines and see the ISF hadn't really started making large gains until American firepower had been provided in the form of artillery, Apaches, and Air Force bombing runs. That was *tangible*. That made a *difference* on the ground along with supplies and other assets like ISR. During the Vietnam War, the South Vietnamese government didn't collapse until the U.S. stopped providing firepower. That's probably what the Iraqis cared about the most, and who could blame them?

"Each story and photo are a piece of the bigger puzzle," her reply. "This is a planned operation; you can't keep on going out there and hoping something sticks."

But it has stuck. My thoughts, and I guess my expression too.

"You start getting a little success and your head starts getting big."

"My head isn't big!"

"Uh huh. Your expressions say a lot L.T. I get the feeling you don't really *respect* anything," I tilted my head at that statement.

"It's like no one knows what you're going to do." She laughed. "But you work hard, I'll give you that."

"We're doing a lot of things, L.T.," she continued, leaving me wondering what she meant. "Working with the Kurds, enabling the ISF with fires, advising their logistics operations, the Baghdad Operations Command, training special units. The fundamental tenets are building partner capacity (training the Iraqis), advising the ISF (the TOC operations,) and assisting them with enablers (the artillery unit or UAVs.) The Brigade Commander wants all of this highlighted, so I want you to go hit all of those spots."

It only took him *two months* to figure out that he wanted all this highlighted, I guess.

"If they're not going to let me get any media access, I'm going to use *you*," she continued, pointing at me to emphasize the words. "I need you to go out there and interview the key players in all of those operations. Things are building up, and there's about to be some major movements soon. If we can start getting articles out, maybe we can start getting media in. You're the only one of us free to move around. And...." She paused as if calculating her next words. "The only one I can trust right now, *God Help Me.*"

"I need you to stay mobile LT.," she continued, looking around. "You can only stay in the country 90 days on TDY before you have to go back to Kuwait, so I need out as much as possible. Who knows if I'll get you back," There was an inflection change? I'd known her long enough to know what it was.

"I'm trusting you, L.T. Remember, *I'm* your only boss. You only answer to *me.* Don't let anyone waste your time or try to use you. It's up to you to do the right thing and get what we need. *Don't bring any attention to yourself.* Get to Taji as soon as possible and start there."

There was a seriousness in her tone that I'd rarely heard before; she was trusting a lieutenant she had known for two months to his own devices to find the right people, get the proper footage, and then, hopefully, turn it into something useful. Even further, it seemed like she was *hiding* me from something. Or, *someone.*

I found the whole concept absurd: the entire public affairs apparatus of the United States Army, with all its strategic thinkers, DINFOS trained journalists, and buckets of cash was relying on *me,* some random guy, to report on one of the most important efforts in the military during 2016.

At the peak of the Iraq War, Camp Taji held over 20,000 coalition Soldiers on an installation that was about 25 square miles. It was the logistics hub for all operations in the Baghdad region, and had a large and essential airfield where the coalition could fly in all manner of supplies.

We were a long way from the peak of the Iraq War.

I flew into Camp Taji on a Chinook, the American workhorse helicopter that had been in use since the Vietnam War. As we started our ascent, the crew chief at the back of the helicopter opened the ramp revealing the lights of Baghdad slowly moving below us. Signs of life in a city that was over a thousand years old, had been a center of learning and empires. I felt...small.

It was surreal, being one of those people that I had watched on T.V. as a kid: A Soldier part of an armed confrontation with the most well-known terrorist group on Earth at the time. The crew chief and I continued to stare out of the back of the Chinook, transfixed by the sight, as thoughts raced through my head about everything that was happening.

I was no longer a spectator to history.

I was a part of it.

Me, the joke of my battalion, an infantry officer with no platoon, no ranger tab, and no future. The assistant S-6, the photo guy, the *loser*. Yet here I was, trying to publicize a war that no one wanted to talk about as one of those few thousand Soldiers in the entire U.S. Army in Iraq at the time.

What in the world had I gotten myself into? It didn't feel real.

It still doesn't.

When we landed, there were barely 2,000 personnel on a small patch of land that stretched perhaps five sq miles, called the "American Side" Of Camp Taji. The airfield still existed but couldn't support the large aircraft it had in its heyday; the coalition was trying to improve the facilities, sending out construction crews at night for security and heat reasons. Outside of the coalition compound, on the "Iraqi side", the rest of the base was now overgrown, occupied by the Iraqis who used it as a training and logistics hub themselves.

It also served as the site for most of the advising efforts in the area.

"Come in," the voice of Lt. Col. Christopher Brown, the commander of the 526th Brigade Sustainment Battalion, in response to my knock on the door. I opened it and approached his desk as he grinned.

"Lt. Johnson, good to see you," he said, shaking my hand.

Brown had a bear grip and the build of a football player, and with his southern drawl he looked and acted like the type of guy you would see in a stereotypical war movie. He had started off as an enlisted infantryman before commissioning and switching over to logistics as an officer; now, after a lengthy career, he was the commander of 526th Brigade Support Battalion (BSB). The BSB was 2nd BCT's logistics element, with all the cooks, transportation, a medical company, and other support assets. Due to the nature of the deployment, Brown's elements were all over the world. Some were in Kuwait, Taji, or in Erbil, with still more at Fort Campbell preparing to come over once certain conditions had been met in Iraq. As the "mayor" of an installation with a few thousand personnel from multiple nationalities, he had all the access I could ever need.

Brown didn't have much of a battalion to command; due to a weird split of the forces it was mostly up to him and his acting sergeant major, Master Sgt. Jarrod Gozy, to do all of the "mayor" duties. A handful of people to oversee the whole base was a stretch; Gozy was a veteran Soldier and he was everywhere, keeping track of housing, personnel, the SECFOR, the training, and all the other little things that were needed to keep the base operating.

There was practically no one else, and I couldn't quite understand why they were so understaffed compared to other spots in the brigade, like the brigade headquarters.

"Sir," I replied, returning his handshake. "Maj. Sanders sent me down here to help out and cover what you're doing." I took a seat on one of the chairs, glancing around the office. It was nice, spacious, comfortable. Heck, it was probably better than the offices back at Campbell.

"The Brigade Commander wants people back home to learn about our mission," I continued my pitch, exactly as Maj. Sanders had told me. "I understand that you're doing logistics advise and assist, and there's Ranger training? Also, Maj. Sanders let me know to help out with anything else you need."

Brown's face lit up in the same expression I had seen on many a field grade officer when an opportunity presented itself that would lead to a positive outcome for their career.

He was having someone from the brigade cover what he was doing down at Taji?

And he could also use his skills for other projects?

Even better.

"Reka is always looking out for me," Brown said fondly and eagerly, the wheels no doubt turning as plots and schemes revealed themselves.

"That's no problem; I can get you out there. You can with roll me with when I go out for my circulation, speak to the Iraqis." He was nodding his head as he spoke, obviously pleased at this turn of events.

Everybody loves good P.R.

"I'll talk to the units and let them know you're coming," He paused for a moment. "You're going to need some space, aren't you? I'll put you in the office down the hall so you can be *nearby*."

Inwardly I groaned. I hated being *nearby* to high-ranking people.

Outwardly, I nodded my head vigorously, one of the most critical skills needed when dealing with people who outrank you.

"Talk to Lt. Brooker down there."

Brown smiled as I stood there in shock for a moment. A battalion commander that didn't just blow me off? Things were looking up. Saluting, I stepped out of the office and into the hallway of the building, nicknamed the "Taj Mahal." The "Tahj" had been an office building used during the halcyon days of Camp Taji, as the story went. Well equipped, with its air-conditioned hallways and operational bathrooms stocked with toilet paper, it was a far cry from Maj. Knoedler and his tent bunker…hill at KSB. Walking around lost for a moment, I stepped into an office that belonged to someone I thought was Lt. Brooker. Computers lined the desks, and a female lieutenant stood behind one of them, working on something that looked like serious business.

"Sorry, to interrupt," I started as she glanced up at me. "Is this Lt. Brooker's office?"

"No," she replied, looking at me closer. "She works down the hall. Hey, I remember you, aren't you the photographer guy who was here a few weeks ago?"

"Yes?" I replied. "I just came back from KSB up north; it was kind of rough."

"I heard it was bad," she replied. "What do you mean by 'rough'?"

I thought about the best description to give.

"Guys are walking around in full kit all day, can barely get clean clothes and are sleeping in holes underground, with the threat of drones and ground attacks," I replied. "It's kind of- "

"That sounds so cool!"

I paused, confused.

I thought about the response for a moment then looked at our surroundings. This was a very different part of Iraq, with a different mission, and a different way of life. There was an actual DFAC, fast internet, two gyms, substantive air-conditioned sleep areas, cots, and shower trailers. From our sleep area to the Taj Mahal was about 50 feet.

Still 7,000 miles away from home, however, doing what was asked of her. The *idea* of KSB might seem cool to others if they hadn't experienced it. On a macro-level, saying that war was "cool" is what got millions of young men and women throughout history to join the military.

Wasn't that part of my job, to *sell* the coolness or intensity of military service?

"Yeah," I replied, trying to process what I would call it if asked. "I guess it was *cool.* Have a good day?" I quickly waved and walked out of the office, reaching the next office in a few short steps.

"What brings you here?" a 2nd Lt. called as he saw me walk in. He had multiple computer screens at his desk, looking like someone at a command center in a computer strategy game. I looked down at the lieutenant's nametape. Howlett.

"I've been sent by the brigade to cover your operations," I replied with a friendly grin. "I work in the brigade public affairs office."

"Really?" Howlett replied, standing up and looking at my rank, then my face. "I didn't know Public Affairs had lieutenants, how'd you get that job?"

He was right. This was kind of irregular. I decided to be honest. "I volunteered."

Howlett looked at me incredulously. A 1st Lt. was assigned to take pictures in Iraq?

That made no sense.

"Don't you have an enlisted guy with you?"

"Nope."

"Alright…" Howlett finished, shaking his head before shrugging. He reached out his hand. "Connor Howlett, battalion S2."

I shook it and then paused.

"Battalion S2?" I replied. "Did the actual S2 have to go home?"

"No," Howlett replied. "I'm the *actual* S2."

I looked at Howlett again; he had been on active duty for less than a year. He was a 2nd Lieutenant, just out of school, doing the job of a person two ranks his senior. Intelligence officers were supposed to be assistant S2s, then Military Intelligence platoon leaders, before going to an advanced course and becoming an actual S2 as a Captain. All Howlett had received was the absolute basic instruction on military intelligence operations, and now he was the head honcho for all intelligence operations for 2,000 personnel on Camp Taji?

Then again, he had more training for his job than I sure did.

I was shocked there weren't Captains who were dying to fill his spot, considering deployments were hard to come by those days in the Army. We talked for a little bit more, and I learned Howlett had attended the United States Military Academy at West Point; while his buddies were just getting started at their units, he was now the intelligence chief for a brigade sized element.

As we spoke, another lieutenant walked in, brusquely pushing past us.

"Lt. Brooker!" I called.

The young woman had been in the Brigade for as long as I had, holding a platoon leader position before getting sent to the battalion headquarters. She hadn't exactly wanted to come to Fort Campbell; when she commissioned, she wanted to work as a parachute rigger but through the infinite foresight of the United States Army Human Resources command, she hadn't got it.

Army HRC had a habit of doing that to people.

"I heard you're working here now," she said as she walked towards the back of the room, placing her M4 on the table. She didn't exactly seem happy that I was there. "What do you do exactly again?"

"I'm the brigade journalist-"

"You work for the brigade?" she replied, shaking her head. "And they sent you down to Taji? You're not up there with the Brigade Commander?"

I frowned. I had only spoken to the guy once back at Fort Campbell when Maj. Sanders introduced me. He gave me the weirdest look like he couldn't believe I was there, then gave a generic, "I expect great production out of a lieutenant, blah blah blah."

"Maj. Sanders can take care of the Brigade Commander," my reply." I'm more of a Soldier's level type of guy."

Brooker wasn't buying it. "So, your boss is up north, and you're traveling around Iraq by yourself taking pictures and writing news articles?"

"…Yes?" my reply.

"That's crazy." Brooker finished.

"It's a crazy world." My reply, my grin growing wider. In the background, I could almost hear Howlett rolling his eyes.

Looking around, she pointed at a desk. "I don't know why they send all the 'attachments' to this office. You can share that desk with Lt. Waltz, I guess."

"Waltz?" I replied, searching for the name in my memory. "He wasn't here the last time. He a new platoon leader or something?"

"He is," Brooker replied. "With 1-502."

"Where's his company commander? Kind of odd for him to be working by himself in the BSB HQ, unless his commander is somewhere else in the country."

"He's still back in the United States," a voice answered behind us.

Turning around, I saw Lt. Waltz, first named Craig, walking in the office towards his desk, dropping his kit in front of it. The way he said it, the fact that his supervisor was 7,000 miles away was like water being wet: a simple fact of life.

"Good to meet you." He said dryly.

"What do you do here Brooker?" I asked, figuring that it was an innocent question.

"What I'm told." With that, Brooker sat at her desk with a huff as I looked to Howlett, who gave me an understanding look before jumping back on his monitor array. Shrugging, I turned to Waltz, who was cleaning up my side of the desk. "Guess it's time to settle in," I said to no one in particular — four lieutenants, with four different missions, and practically no guidance.

If this was the best Army in the world, how did the worst one operate?

I sprinted down the steps and into the waiting vehicle driven by Howlett.

"Ready to roll?" he asked, M4 at his side, his dark eye pro covering his facial expression and making him appear to look like someone off an Army recruiting poster.

"Sure thing," I replied, patting my camera and assault pack.

Lt. Col. Brown emerged from the headquarters building soon after, striding down the steps like a cowboy. With his patrol cap tilted, M9 pistol on his hip, and dark sunglasses, he kind of looked like one too.

Brown was going on a full tour of the base today to talk to the Iraqi garrison commander and thought it would be a good idea to support the brigade's mission, and *his*, by getting photos of himself at work. Higher headquarters was looking for pictures of American leaders talking to Iraqi leaders, and Brown was going to give it to them.

"Alright, let's go," Lt. Col. Brown's driver radioed to us, and off we went, our two-vehicle SUV convoy driving through the dusty camp streets.

"You do this a lot?" I asked Howlett as he maneuvered the vehicle.

"Every now and then." He replied.

We passed through the installation, driving past the bazaar which had, among other things, a hookah bar and a place where you could buy knock-off electronics. Further down the road past the market was the headquarters of the local security force element --- My old buddies from 1-26.

"We're stopping over here," the driver over the radio, as Brown spotted a high-ranking Iraqi who just happened to be visiting the camp. We pulled off the road as Brown jumped out and began talking and pointing with the Iraqi like we were in some educational video on how to make friends and influence people.

It looked suitable for photos though, and he knew it.

We finished up, and Brown looked at me with a head nod and a smirk. Jumping back into our vehicles, we began moving again towards our main objective: the Iraqi garrison commander on their side of the base.

"He's totally hamming it up," Howlett spoke up as he drove, shaking his head at the whole situation. "They didn't even really talk about anything."

"What? Of course," I replied, looking through my camera at the photos. "But you have to admit, that's what the Army says we're doing, 'working with the Iraqis.' If they want to see Lt. Cols having random conversations with the Iraqis, then who am I to argue."

"That's what they want? Really? To see Lt. Col. Brown talking to the garrison commander about security here?"

"They want to see Americans and Iraqis working together. Shows that it's their fight, and we're supporting them." I shrugged my shoulders. "I think it's wacky too, it's not like all that talking worked out for us the first time."

"You don't seem to have much faith in this, yet you're taking the photos."

"I'm just a lieutenant in the United States Army. Who am I to argue with general whoever in wherever?"

"An *infantry* lieutenant at that. You never explained that part."

"I was getting screwed. Maj. Sanders needed a journalist."

"*You're* the one who emailed her. She didn't just find you, based on what you've told me."

"Yeah, if my career is over, so be it. I didn't join the Army to get promoted."

"That's fair," A pause. "Then why *did* you join?"

"…I don't know. I just kind of fell into it I guess."

"Fell all the way into Iraq? Yeah, right. For a guy who doesn't seem to take anything seriously, you sure do *care* a lot."

"I have to care. I'm a *strategic* asset."

Howlett groaned. "Not this *again*."

"Hey, I don't get mad when you and Waltz watch all those Gregg Plitt videos every night."

"Did you see his gains though?"

It was my turn to groan.

"I'll continue talking about my high-fidelity photos then."

"Do you even know what the word fidelity means?"

"No. Me and you would make a good buddy cop movie, I feel." My reply, intentionally trying to annoy him.

"I feel like I'm already in one," he interrupted. "Needs better jokes though, yours are pretty bad."

Lt. Col. Brown, the commander of 526 BSB, conducting a "KLE" at Camp Taji in July of 2016. U.S. Army photo by Daniel Johnson.

He smiled as I gave a, "Ah, touché", and silence ensued between us, with him achieving the W on that one. Howlett shook his head as we hit the gate that separated the coalition compound from the Iraqi side; our signal to jump out of our vehicles and to chamber a round in the barrel of our weapons. A sad fact of life: even on an Iraqi logistics base, going to talk to the *garrison commander,* the threat of someone deciding to turn on us still existed. It had happened before, and it didn't help that there were reports of an Iranian backed Paramilitary Force operating on the installation.

The Iraqi side felt like a monument to the last war. The once-bustling base was now empty, with overgrowth, skeletal buildings, and junk *everywhere.* Some dogs watched us from the side of the road, a mother and two puppies. Mangy and thin, they were barely scraping by; I wondered if they were descendants of dogs brought in by coalition forces.

"You can tell what the good Iraqi Army units are by how well they keep their area." Howlett's words as we glanced out, passing some well-kept buildings flying the Iraqi flag. It was a far cry from some of the roughshod areas of the camp.

"Think they have an area beautification detail? Would love to see the order for that."

There was a chuckle from both of us. How many sergeant majors back in the states ranted about keeping their unit areas clean? "Stay off the SGM's grass," was the age-old joke, along with the ever-present cleaning details that usually found some unlucky privates mowing grass and hacking weeds in 100-degree weather.

We continued deeper into the camp where we began to hear a rumbling noise. A cloud of dust approached us, obviously a large convoy; we pulled off to the side and as several mine-resistant vehicles in a tight formation drove past, flying the Commonwealth Flag. Some of the personnel in the convoy waved to us, their green uniforms different from ours.

"Australians," Howlett informed me. "Their main mission out here is to train the Iraqis. They have the largest contingent here. Technically, *they're* in charge of this base, not us."

I nodded, noticing how serious they took security compared to our two little up-armored SUVs. Granted, the IED threat was practically non-existent, but you never know, right?

We soon pulled up to a well-kept building with a well-kept lawn, disembarking from our vehicles and walking inside, Lt. Col. Brown at the lead. It wasn't long before we were in the office of the Iraqi garrison commander, a middle-aged man who looked like a schoolteacher. He invited Brown to sit down, calling for tea to be served, and the conversation began.

It was dull.

Army training suggests that you never jump straight to business when conducting a KLE with Iraqis due to their culture, and Brown followed that guidance *to the lett*er. A very long letter, with conversation about the weather, family backgrounds, children, schooling, and other topics for what seemed like *forever*. It may have been about an hour before the actual business portion began.

Brown did not run all the coalition forces on Camp Taji, but he did have to make sure that they had everything they needed and that there were no significant issues from the Iraqi garrison. He was the face, the mayor, the *fixer*, handling any problems that arose so the other unit could focus on their missions.

Coalition forces were not just advising the ISF on the best practices for their logistics operations, but also giving them supplies at Camp Taji for use in future operations. We called it the ITEF program- the Iraq Train and Equip Fund (ITEF). The base was like the Amazon warehouse of the war on ISIL; equipment would be handed off, training conducted, and then that new capability or unit would be pushed north. The bridging equipment that was about to be used by the ISF to cross the Tigris came from Taji, and the Iraqi Soldiers who were going to conduct that critical mission had been trained there by an American engineering training team.

Brown nodded to Howlett, signaling him for the next part of this conversation and Howlett pulled out a map, handing it to the colonel.

"We want to make everyone's lives easier and give you this map so we can know where you're located, and the same for us," Brown said through the translator, smiling.

"We are guests on this installation," he continued, laying it on thick. "We don't want anyone to think we're hiding anything."

The ISF commander was pleased, a broad smile on his face. Freely giving up this information, showing deference to our Iraqi counterparts? He expressed his thanks.

But there was a kicker of course.

There always is.

"Yes," Brown replied as they looked over the map. "If you could also mark your units on the map," A subtle glance towards Howlett, who for his part, had a good poker face as he stood there trying to look grim. "It would greatly help all of us."

The Iraqi garrison commander happily accepted. He got to see that the coalition was on the up and up and Brown and Howlett got to see what Iraqi units were on the base. For example, *Iranian backed PMFs*. Both parties were satisfied by the meeting, and everyone was all smiles. Even I pasted on one, looking like a crony in some crime movie.

There was some commotion outside.

Suddenly, another high-ranking Iraqi officer burst into the area. Everyone looked at the newcomer as he studied the room, waiting for him to speak. Which he did, obviously agitated about something.

"He's saying that our guys wouldn't let him onto our side of the base and that since it's an Iraqi base, they can't do that," the interpreter told the colonel. Brown shook his head and weighed his options before responding, obviously not believing the newcomer's accusation.

"Here's probably here for another reason," Brown said under his breath, then put on an eyeless smile.

"Let's figure this out together!" he offered to the newcomer.

The newcomer greeted each of us as he pulled up his seat, then stopped and stared at me and my camera. He looked uncomfortable for some strange reason.

"Paparazzi," Col. Brown said, doing the hand signal for a camera and making a clicking noise. "He's making us look good to the people back home," I knew I had to play my part, pulling up my camera and grinning as if I didn't know I was in a foreign country armed to the teeth.

There was some talk, some overdramatic threats from the new guy about how since this was an Iraqi base, his guards could prevent the coalition from moving around, along with some other back and forth. After a while of this, he seemed appeased, and Lt. Col. Brown agreed that he would investigate the issues.

"Well, I have another meeting to go to," Brown said as the conversation wound down, nodding to us, who nodded back to him as if we all understood that he had an appointment that couldn't be missed. I think Howlett even glanced at his watch. "We'll swing back around with the map and updates on what we talked about." He nodded to the garrison commander.

Brown paused for a moment, looking at me.

"How about we all get a photo?" He offered to the gathered group. The garrison commander was more than happy to. The newcomer wasn't, judging by his awkward stance in the shot, but he joined in anyway.

"What do you think, Howlett?" Lt. Col. Brown asked as we returned to our vehicles.

"Something about the new guy, sir," Howlett replied, looking at his notes. "That seemed to be more of a power play of him trying to force himself into our meeting. It seems he doesn't want to be cut out of what's happening here."

"That's what I was thinking," Brown replied, deep in thought. "I've never heard of him before, and I know everyone out here. We need to investigate him. You get a good picture of him, Johnson?"

"I did, sir," I replied, looking through my camera. "Helped that you stopped to pose with him."

"Of course," Brown replied. "*Funny how that works*. Pass it to Howlett and me, and we'll start building a better picture of what's going on." He went to step into the vehicle and stopped, looking at Howlett. "See, PAO isn't useless after all."

"Roger sir." Howlett replied as I grinned.

"I told you I was a *strategic* asset!" My words of victory.

"Don't get too cocky." Howlett replied, grimacing as we both got into the Pajero.

Chapter Six- Ranger Training

Having a meeting where nothing was accomplished but trying to spy on the Iraqi units on base was indicative of the whole advise and assist mission. Brown was true to his word and kept on hooking me in with the units on base, but the more I went out, the thinner it all seemed. Logistics advising, medical advising, tactical advising, there was a lot of it going on. Still, no one could seem to tell me *what was being accomplished.* It was not due to a lack of effort; just like at KSB and other locations personnel were accomplishing any of the tactical missions given to them by higher headquarters. It's just that the purpose was missing. All the rosy proclamations being made seemed empty, especially when the same ones were made six years before and then promptly were revealed as false in 2014 when ISIL invaded. There was also the fact that in the last Iraq war, these same missions were being conducted by 10s of thousands of more troops.

On a deeper, existential level, there was also knowledge that ISIL wouldn't have existed if not for some…subpar strategic decisions during the "last" Iraq War in the first place. It's no secret that Al Qaeda in Iraq came to be *because* of the 2003 invasion, and then the subsequent policy of de-Baathification. Abu Musab-al-Zarqawi, the leader of the group, was one of the many foreign fighters who found a fertile ground for jihadism in Iraq due to the chaos there. The current head of ISIL, Abu Bakr- al Baghdadi, had formed the essential connections for the group while in American military prisons. Now we were cleaning up the mess. Our own mess? Or just a continuation of the last mess? Were we in a sequel or just in an extended epilogue?

Even the Security Forces on Camp Taji from Delta Company of 1-26, felt like they were flapping in the wind. The conversations I had with the senior Soldiers in the unit were telling.

"Well, at least someone cares about us." One officer said, shaking his head as we sat in the Joint Operations Center, where the D Company Soldiers watched the security feeds from around the base. "Spader 6 hasn't visited us once."

"Isn't he just down in Baghdad?"

"Yeah. Must be *too busy* to care about us though. Meanwhile we're barely getting information. Like when the CJTF Sergeant Major busted into our barracks here and got mad when no one knew who he was. *We didn't even know he was coming."*

He turned to me and tilted his head.

"You work for the brigade; you know what's going on?"

"No idea," my reply, shrugging. "I was told to 'Make sure people know what's going on,' without being told *what was going on."*

His face to my comment said it all.

The aimlessness seemed to infect everything; boredom was rampant, and the outlets for relieving it ranged from the mundane to odd. Once a week, Brown and his staff would hold a political fight club in the Tahj, participation voluntary of course. With the presidential election season in full swing, they discussed everything from gun control to the positive aspects of Jeb Bush, and how Donald Trump stood no chance. Everyone got their say in and then once they left the room the unspoken rule was no politics at all until the next round. Considering the strong opinions that the election was bringing out in people around the world, the fact that this arrangement never spilled out of control was peculiar.

Unlike the *actual* fight club on Camp Taji. Launched by some lieutenants, Soldiers would meet up in an empty building with no prying eyes and then commence relieving stress with "organized" fighting tournaments. The cover story was that it was just Army combative practice being held in the dead of night, but it didn't take long for Soldiers to start getting injured and start talking about how. Reprimands were swift.

For those who didn't want to get the crap beat out of them or argue about the difference between socialism and capitalism, there was always the Hookah place at the bazaar, or pickup basketball games at the gym. The basketball games and other sports were popular and even drew some Australians and British Soldiers to join.

I found myself on advising missions, KLES, security patrols, gun ranges, tenant unit meetings, and anything else that I could find. That included things like riding around the Iraqi side trying to figure out where the PMF were at, and then stealthily jumping out of the Pajero and pretending to take a photo of Lt. Brooker and Howlett while actually taking a photo of the PMF flag.

I can't make this stuff up.

After I came back from an outing, I would return to Lt. Brooker's office and upload the footage or edit it. Us four lieutenants in that small office in Taji became fast friends, and like people our age, began to waste time. Youtube memes, movies that we brought from home, cheesy jokes. It felt like what I imagined working in an office with other young professionals would be like in the states, minus the loaded M4s sitting near our desks, the body armor on the floor, or the feed that Howlett looked at each day that informed him about potential threats that were trying to enter the base to kill Americans.

All in all, normal.

None of it made any sense, but I did my due diligence and sent up everything I could to Maj. Sanders, who was pleased with my progress. I wasn't the only one trying to figure out what to do with myself, however. The longer I stayed in the "Lieutenant cave" with Waltz, Howlett, and Brooker, the more I realized that the lack of information and purpose was *almost total*. Howlett was stuck behind his desk all day, watching all the different screens as he got intelligence reports from the brigade, the division, the camp, and whoever else was in the area at the time. Less than a year in the Army, Captains and Majors were coming to *him* for information, considering him the most knowledgeable person on the base. He was drowning in work and it didn't help that through some bizarre manning he had only one intelligence Soldier with him to balance the workload. She was stuck in the Joint Operations Center all day. Meanwhile, the brigade S2 at Camp Swift kept on expecting stuff from him and he did a pretty good job keeping up, all things considered.

Waltz was technically a platoon leader for a maintenance section in the country, but his maintenance section practically ran itself. He found himself with the awful fate of being the guy trying to answer questions in the brigade maintenance meetings with no idea of what was going on. He was stoic about the situation; even when I kept on asking him on how he was going to be rated by a commander 7,000 miles away or when a warrant officer who was known to be ruthless put him on blast for stuff he had absolutely no control over.

Brooker meanwhile was working all day and even into the night, on something. *Everyone* was, even when there was nothing going on. It was like they didn't want to leave the office until 10 P.M, and I couldn't understand it. Finally, I had to know why.

"What exactly are you working on for so long?" I asked her as I sat in the office with her one evening, the dusk having turned into full night.

"I'm working on Operation Jonah and some other stuff for the commander," Brooker replied gruffly, and yet-

She sounded disappointed.

"What's Operation Jonah?" I asked, expecting a scoop on a story.

"Well," Brooker said, clicking through her slides as I moved around to get a look at her screen. "It's a plan to evacuate in case the Mosul Dam fails. If it goes this whole area will flood and we'll have to evacuate everyone and everything fast."

"That sounds like it takes a lot."

"It does," Brooker replied. "But the B.C. keeps on changing what he wants, and I feel like this is just a project to keep me busy." The frustration was evident in her voice. "I almost feel like coming out here was pointless; I'm not doing anything like you are."

"What, you mean highlighting the American fighting man and-or woman with the highest levels of image fidelity as they participate in the ultimate struggle?"

"And-or-woman?"

"I have to cover everyone equally."

"Where did they find you."

"In the college dorms of Appalachian State."

"And let me guess, you always planned on doing this."

"No," my reply, quickly. "I hate writing, it's why I stopped being an English major and switched to Criminal Justice. You know me, I have no plan."

She nodded her head, obviously agreeing with my assessment. "That's *definitely* true. You don't even have a plan to get furniture!"

"Hey, I have a couch and dresser! The world is home, I only have what I need to plan out the next adventure."

She chuckled at that, shaking her head.

"Can you get moved?" It had worked for me, at least.

"It's not easy," the response. "Everyone can't just barge into a Major's office."

"I didn't 'barge in,' I sent an email."

"Behind your commander's back."

"I-"

"Everyone isn't like you."

"I'm just a regular guy."

"A regular guy who doesn't seem to care about the consequences. It's not that easy for some of us."

Was that how I appeared to other people? Like anyone who started to go through the process of having to judge their actions and behaviors, I tried to change the subject.

"Well," I replied with a cheesy grin as I pulled up my camera, trying to cheer her up. "At least you're in the fight. I'm just a guy who takes photos!" I smiled inwardly. Once she looked at my situation, she wouldn't feel so bad.

"But you have a purpose." She replied, looking at me.

She caught me off guard. Did I have a purpose?

I looked at my job as being simple: telling people back home what American Soldiers were doing in Iraq. The more views we got, the better, but there was no end goal beyond that. Just tell the story, whatever it was, because service members deserved at least that much. If they were at KSB firing against ISIL, cool. If they were giving out weapons, awesome. At the end of the day, in my mind, no matter how you cut it, they were all away from home making the foreign policy speeches and movements on the giant maps in the Pentagon happen. As always, the people on the ground were the ones who brought ideas into reality.

We all just hoped that the people with the giant maps knew what that reality was.

My work was getting reach that I wasn't expecting. Each day when I came back to the office, I would see a new link, a new share, a comment. Something that showed that whatever we were doing was working.

But did I have a purpose?

"I'm just a failed infantryman," my reply, suddenly self-conscious. "What *did* you want to be doing?"

"I wanted to work with Soldiers," she looked around the office, at where she was now. "I loved being a platoon leader, I loved being able to help Soldiers out and hopefully make a difference. That's the whole reason I *joined.* I'm not doing any of that here. Updating slides for nine months isn't useful to the mission, or the Army."

"And what I'm doing is?'

"How many people can talk about their work being used by the Pentagon, or shared on websites, or constantly going out to do stuff and answering to no one."

"I answer to Maj. Sanders," my reply. "I'm following orders just like everyone else."

"But she's trusted you enough to send you down here by yourself, and she never gives you busy work. How many lieutenants can say that?"

I had no response.

"I hate wasting my life away here." She continued.

"But you're still doing it. Most people would have given up by now. Heck, they do it with 'actual' work. That's what makes you an *actual leader*."

Her expression shifted slightly, my positive words having only a slight effect, but I'd take it.

"I'm not leading anything here though."

"Being in charge doesn't make you a leader, I always say."

"And what does?"

"Caring."

"Then what are you? Do you consider yourself a leader?"

"No. I'm not anything until I earn it. The title is irrelevant; my actions are. There are a lot of people walking around here who call themselves leaders and aren't."

"I've never heard you say that," she laughed, obviously feeling a little better. "But you *do* talk a lot about how great you are."

"I mean, if no one else is going to, why not me?"

"Here we go again…." she rolled her eyes as I began my speech about my view on life.

Brooker was a hard worker, who wanted to help not in a "useful so I could look good" way, but because it was *the right thing to do.* Waltz and Howlett were the same way. A substantial majority of people in the military want to do their jobs and serve their nation, hence the happiness of the artillerymen at KSB when they got a fire mission or the pride of an infantryman being the individual that took and held ground.

But what was I? My usefulness to the Army up to this point had been negligible, and even working in public affairs was *not* going to be the tipping point that won the war. Yet, I found myself doing as I please, without the responsibility expected of someone at my rank, with the outcome of a critically important thing in this Army world: *credit.* Or the knowledge that your work wouldn't be forgotten.

I may not have cared about that, but other people did.

Brooker was a good officer, who even despite her frustrations, kept doing her best. She didn't care about rewards, awards, or accolades, just the knowledge that what she was doing was helping the mission.

Unfortunately, not everyone out there was like that.

The last time I had seen Capt. Pete Jacob, the commander of Company A, 1-502nd Infantry, was when we were both students at Appalachian State. Like me, he was a graduate of the ROTC program there and from what I remembered from him back at App State, he was just the type of guy you wanted to oversee a "Ranger training program."

ROTC programs have clubs within them for those cadets/students who want to...set themselves apart. There were clubs like the Scabbard and Blade, which did community service, and the Pershing Rifles, which specialized in drill and ceremony.

Then, at Appalachian at least, there was the commando club.

The commando club was where the more "hardcore" of us joined to increase their "tactical" (as tactical as ROTC cadets could get) knowledge. Like the other clubs, you got points towards your overall order of merit list score which decides your branch, or job, in the Army. If you wanted to go into the combat arms, and more specifically the infantry branch, you joined the Commando Club.

To get the "Commando Tab" (which looks like a Ranger Tab but just says commando instead), you had to earn it in an event called the commando's qualification course. It consisted of a physical fitness test, land navigation, tactical exercises, and other activities up in the hills around Boone in the middle of winter.

Challenging enough, before the whole encouragement by the current tabbed members of the commando club was added in. If you "survived" to the end, i.e., didn't quit, you earned your tab.

Not joining the commando club at App State, among other reasons, should have landed me far away from Fort Campbell and Iraq. One of my fellow cadets at the time was in the top 10 of cadets *in the nation,* and he participated in everything. He was a much better cadet and better officer than me, and I truly mean that. Perfect G.P.A., perfect PT scores, was the cadet battalion commander, did everything required. As one of the top 10 Cadets he not only got selected Active Duty, and then Infantry, but then should have gotten his duty station of choice: Fort Campbell, Kentucky.

In your junior year, you rank the 25 duty stations you would like to go to, and then based on your OML score, ROTC Cadet command assigned you to a duty station. I wanted to go to Fort Drum, New York, since it was up north, and put it in my top 5 duty stations. On the flip side, I ranked Fort Campbell, Kentucky at #25. I had barely made the active duty cut off and was a branch detailed infantry guy; Fort Campbell was highly desired for the high-speed types, there's no way I should have gotten it. People for some reason were down on Fort Drum, which made me figure that I would get it since I actually wanted to be stationed there.

My buddy, one of the best Cadets in the nation, got Fort Drum. It wasn't even in his top 5 since he wanted to stay down south; his unit was the one my brigade replaced in Iraq. I got Fort Campbell, which still to this day makes no sense. Now, I was the Pentagon's "best" hope to cover conventional forces in Operation Inherent Resolve.

What a world.

After Jacob commissioned, he went to Ranger School and passed, and then led a platoon in combat in Afghanistan with the 82nd Airborne Division. He then requested a place where he would get another crack at a deployment, and world events were working in his favor.

"Sir," Capt. Jacob said crisply, greeting Lt. Col. Brown as he walked up. "We're running the candidates through basic rifle marksmanship today if you want to take a look." He glanced over at me. "Guess you're trying to get some photos too?"

"It's what people want to see, sir," I replied. "A long way from Appalachian State, right? I'd wonder what the Sergeant Major would say if he saw us right now."

Jacob did a double-take and looked at me closer.

"Oh yeah, I remember you." Oddly enough, it never took long for people to recognize me from school. Then again, considering the school only had about 400 minorities on the entire campus of a school of 17,000, it made perfect sense. After traveling across the world, I can say that Boone, North Carolina, is one of the most least diverse places I've ever been, below even *Scandinavia.* Still was weird as hell though when professors who hadn't seen me in 6 years would just remember my face from across the crowd though.

"You took a photo with the brigade S1, didn't you? Saw it on the App State Facebook page. I'll have to tell the chaplain; he went to App too."

He turned to lead us towards the range. The training was part of the "build partner capacity" of our mission set, which sought to build a strong cadre of Iraqi Soldiers who would inevitably take over the battlefield once we departed.

The fact that Jacob and A CO were even doing this in 2016 was telling. It wasn't for lack of trying though, and the Iraqi Golden Division and Counter Terrorism Service were doing pretty well at that moment, having retaken Fallujah in early July. But they couldn't be everywhere at once, and they took horrific losses constantly being at the vanguard of every major operation.

Hence the idea behind the Ranger training, a shorter version that was akin to the U.S. Army's Ranger school. The U.S. Army's Ranger training program was established in 1951 at Fort Benning, Georgia, with the mission of building tactically proficient leaders who would spread their skills out into the force. It was a reaction to the Korean war and the thought process among senior leaders that performance there was the result of failures of the tactical level.

It wasn't like the generals during the Korean war were racist and thought the North Koreans would flee at first sight of American firepower, and then committed their forces piecemeal without the weaponry and personnel to fight off an invasion. *No*, it was the fault of the Soldiers on the ground sent to execute a horridly thought-out policy.

The program in Iraq had the same mission as the one back home, with an important difference: The United States Army didn't have a bunch of corrupt generals who had thousands of phantom Soldiers on the rolls like with what had happened with Mosul in 2014. We *also* didn't have to deal with the best fighters being sucked into paramilitary forces which were backed by a foreign state.

No Iraqi Soldier was forced to take the training, and the ones that did volunteer first had to go through a selection process that lasted 3 weeks before being allowed to learn advanced individual skills, like room clearing and heavy weaponry. Basic Rifle Marksmanship in initial entry training for the U.S. Army was about two weeks long, with simulators, dry firing, zeroing, and multiple range iterations.

A CO only had a few days.

We walked past the line of guardian angels, mostly younger Soldiers, who stood behind the firing line with body armor and rifles at the ready. If one of the people they had come 7,000 miles to "assist" made a move and turned his weapon on the American trainers, the guardian angels were instructed to eliminate the threat.

"Get a good sight picture," one of the trainers, Staff Sgt. William Meravy said through the interpreter, sighing as he looked down as the young Iraqi Soldier kneeling beside him.

"Remember what we practiced."

With his mechanical PELTOR ear protectors, dark eye pro, and combat shirt, Meravy looked in his element as a range instructor. This was his 3rd deployment, the last one being to Afghanistan where he had spent his days on patrol, looking for the Taliban. Still in his 20s, he had that same look I had seen in too many NCOs his age, the combination of stress, responsibility, and the lifestyle. It was already 100+ degrees in the morning in Taji, and he and the rest of the company had been up since before dawn to get everything ready.

Meravy continued to coach his student, as the other NCOs down the firing line did the same thing. All the familiar sights and sounds of military rifle range, except for these students, there was a war going on right outside the gates. Once the shooting iteration completed the Iraqis and their trainers marched down to their respective targets as the Iraqi and American leadership checked each one, the main grader being Sgt. 1st Class Joseph Perminas, the platoon sergeant, and 1st Lt. Gideon Bernthal, the platoon leader. Perminas and his group soon reached Meravy's Iraqi Soldier, and they gave each other a look.

Staff Sgt. William Meravy with A CO, 1-502 IN, training an Iraqi Soldier, July, 2016. U.S. Army Photo by Daniel Johnson

"Good," Perminas said, grabbing the target off the holder after he graded it.

"Good?!" The Iraqi replied, excited.

"Good." Perminas finished as they began to walk off.

Meravy looked at me, shaking his head.

"Why is a lieutenant taking photos?"

"I volunteered." My reply. "I'm here to make you famous."

"Famous, huh?" Some of his buddies chuckled. "People care about this?"

"I'll make them care?"

"Yeah, we'll see. What are you, a chemical officer or something?"

"No, I'm an infantry officer."

He furrowed his brow, then looked at my shoulder.

"Oh, so they screwed you because you didn't have a tab huh?"

"They did."

"But, you somehow got to Iraq."

"It's a crazy story."

Meravy laughed. "And I thought I had heard it all."

"So, the Brigade Commander wants a video of me talking about the Ranger training for the Facebook page." Jacob's question, incredulous.

"Yes sir," my reply. "At least that's what Maj. Sanders told me."

"You don't think that's odd?"

"I'm just following orders, sir, like everyone else." Jacob seemed amused by my response, understanding the situation we found ourselves in. Neither of us had any say in the matter at the end of the day.

You have about 30 seconds for a Facebook video before most of your viewers disappear. To be honest, there was a significant drop off at *10* seconds. Big Army public affairs loved doing long videos, which by social media standard was a couple of minutes. The problem was that if they didn't get to the point in the first few seconds, most of the message was lost unless someone was genuinely interested.

Maj. Sanders was pushing Facebook hard with the goal of getting 101,000 followers on our brigade's Facebook page by the 101st Airborne's birthday next month. It was a tell-tale mission creep; just thirty days before she was happy with getting *anything* released, and I think she *knew* that getting 101,000 followers in the timeframe we had was impossible.

It did brief well, however.

"What do you want me to say?" Jacob asked after we set up outside. "Or, what does the Brigade Commander want me to say?"

"I don't know, to be honest." My reply yelling over the power generator that was right outside the building, its buzzing noise drowning out everything in a 5-meter radius. I struggled with the tripod, trying to stabilize it and bring him into focus; Sanders had explicitly told me to use it.

"No shaky cam!" she had ordered as if she was going to materialize in Camp Taji and strangle me if I didn't.

"Just talk about the Ranger Training, I guess?"

"You don't have a script or something?"

"I don't plan these things out, they just kind of happen."

Jacob shook his head as he looked at me. He glanced back at the generator.

"You sure you don't want to do this inside?"

"Sorry, I didn't hear you."

"Do you want to move this inside?"

"No, I should be able to get buzzing noise out in the post process."

I had never touched the Adobe audio program in my life, but it would work.

I hoped.

I gave Jacob the thumbs up, and to his credit, he hit every key point about the Ranger Training program, even stopping a few times for better takes.

"This program is important because it lays the foundation for an elite Iraqi unit," he said, hitting all the buzz words. "Students start at day one as an individual and come away at the end of this course as part of a team."

I had heard that before- our ROTC instructor talking about the Commando Club at App State.

"The program itself starts with a 21-day selection process similar to special forces selection," he continued. "It's a 24 hour a day operation where our cadre go out and validate each student no matter what the rank..."

It didn't take us long to finish.

"That work?" Jacob asked as soon as I stopped recording.

"It did, sir," my reply as I started breaking down. "That'll work for the article too."

"You're doing an article, photos, and video? What'd you study at App?"

"Criminal Justice."

"Ha, just like everyone else in ROTC."

The criminal justice program didn't prepare me for how to reduce background noise, however.

"You're going to put this on the Facebook page L.T.?" Maj. Sanders was chiding me after being greeted by a buzz saw when she opened the video. "This is amateurish; we're a professional organization."

Wasn't I an amateur? My thoughts.

"Yes, ma'am," my words. "Do you still want to run it?"

There was a long pause. "I guess we have to." I could hear her audible sigh on the phone. It turned out she was right though: someone commented on Facebook that they couldn't hear the video because of the buzzing.

I spent the next few days with A CO as they continued training the Iraqi Ranger students, this time focused on room clearing and close quarters tactics. At a regular Army unit, this training is usually conducted over multiple phases, over a long period of time. There's rifle qualification, advanced rifle marksmanship, ready up drills, glass houses (just strips of tape on the ground simulating a room), dry room clearing, blank room clearing, and then finally, a live-fire shoot house.

A CO didn't have time.

"Well, look who it is," Meravy said as I stood outside on their building, a strange smirk on his face. "You didn't say that those pictures from the range would end up in the Army Times."

"They…did?" my reply.

"You didn't know?"

"No…."

We walked inside the building, and I watched in amazement as someone pulled up the article.

The XVIII Airborne Corps commanded by Lt. Gen. Stephen Townsend, was taking over CJTF-OIR and the fight against ISIL. Their lead image for the article: Staff. Sgt. Meravy, looking like a serious American trainer, watching the Iraqi Soldier firing in the kneeling position at the range a few weeks before.

"You should be happy," I laughed. "Your face will be all over the internet now."

"The first sergeant wasn't happy at first," Meravy replied, chuckling. "Something about me not wearing gloves and holding a water bottle." He shrugged, obviously pleased at the whole situation as we returned to the vehicles.

"Going to get me in the Army Times next?" a Soldier asked as I jumped into one of the Humvees outside that would take us to the range.

"I can't promise anything," I replied, grinning. "But I think I can get you that, and maybe even the front page of Army.Mil." A bold prediction coming from a guy who had just started two months ago, but why not, right?

The Iraqis were going through glass house drills when we arrived. A CO had trained the officers, all Iraqi lieutenants, on the tactics of room clearing and how it should be done in theory. If this whole advising thing were going to work, it would be up to them, *ostensibly*. Gathering the assembled Iraqis together in a group, one of the Iraqi lieutenants began to run the Soldiers through drills, doing it just like we did it back home.

Perminas, Bernthal, and the assembled Americans stood back, allowing them to run the show.

"This place has changed a lot since the last time I was here," Perminas said, looking around the training area. "I was here during Operation Iraqi Freedom- there were thousands of us on this base back then."

Perminas was now on his sixth deployment- he had joined the Army in 2002, and for a man considered "old" by Army standards, he didn't move or act like it.

"What was it like back then? I was in middle school." My attempt to break the ice.

Perminas glared at me comically, shaking his head. "Thanks for making me feel old."

There were some laughs in the background, but they dissipated as he continued speaking. "It was practically its own city. It's funny, ending up back here of all places. I met my wife here."

"Was she a civilian worker on base?"

"No, she was in the Army." A few more Soldiers had gathered nearby, subtly trying to listen to the story.

"My unit was here back then, and I noticed her because she worked with us. We spoke a few times, but I figured she wasn't interested. When we all got home, I was talking to one of our mutual friends about it, and they told me she thought I was interesting."

"We started dating, and then we got married," He paused, looking around. "I guess I can thank this place for that." he finished, with the face of a man who was *seeing,* not just remembering the past.

"My wife and I were both deployed to Afghanistan in 2010. We both ended up getting wounded. She got hit by small arms fire in Kunar province, and I was wounded by grenade shrapnel," He looked at me with an amused expression. "Needless to say, I'm glad she's not in the military anymore. Much safer that way."

We all chuckled at the ending, but it felt strange. It was an odd feeling being surrounded by ghosts of the "last" war, serving with people who were there. It felt like that all of this was unfinished business, a legacy that I was a stranger to. I had watched Soldiers like Perminas on T.V., and now I was standing next to him in Iraq, a decade-plus later?

What did that all mean? What was the *point?*

I wanted to ask him why he kept on doing it. He had given up more than enough years in service to his country, and also his body. What drove him? But then again, what place did *I* have to even ask that question? I didn't even know the answer for myself.

The Iraqi lieutenant running the training stopped and pointed at our assembled group.

"He wants us to show a few examples so they can see how the professionals do it." The interpreter informed us, looking to see who would volunteer.

"Sure, why not?" a Staff Sgt. Brandon Blanton replied, walking towards the stack of Iraqis. The students in the crowd perked up, watching him closely. The interpreter talked him through what the plan of action of, and nodding, he stood right behind the #1 man in the Iraqi stack. Smirking confidently, he leaned in, resting his hand on the Iraqi's shoulder, assuming the position to tap him to let him know to enter the room.

U.S. Army Staff Sgt. Brandon Blanton training the Iraqi ranger candidates on room clearing techniques, July, 2016. U.S. Army photo by Daniel Johnson.

That was it. The photo I was looking for. The photo the *Pentagon* was looking for. American Soldiers, hand in hand with the Iraqi Security Forces, training them. Through a stroke of luck, Blanton would become the literal poster boy for advising. When the U.S. Army launched Advise and Assist Brigades a few years later, his photo was the one used to sell it.

The fact that this was the only training of Iraqis directly going on in the entire brigade, and in a month A CO would be shifted from the mission to other things, was unimportant. When the article and footage of them were published, the story ended up in civilian news sources. Business Insider literally copied what I wrote word for word and published it, and the news that the 101st Airborne Division was training an Iraqi Ranger Unit made waves throughout the Army. There were comments from the media, defense experts, random guys on Facebook. A Company quickly became very famous, at least by rifle company standards, and Capt. Jacob was well taken care of, his name in conversations about building partner capacity.

The funny thing was when the 101st Airborne Division Command Sergeant Major saw all of this, he called down to A CO directly. He was incensed that they were talking to the civilian news media.

"But we aren't," came the reply from the company's leadership after getting on the line and letting the rant play out. "It was *your* public affairs guy who published all of this stuff. "The Sergeant Major was confused. An Army journalist had his stuff run in the civilian news media? This *just didn't happen*. How in the world was a 1st Lieutenant able to do *that?*

I don't even know the answer.

Chapter Seven - Baghdad

"The Iraqis crossed the Tigris L.T.," Maj. Sanders' voice, in a hushed tone, informed me over the phone. "The fight's changing and 600 more troops from Strike will be arriving in the country."

The ISF had bridged the Tigris on July 15th, supported by coalition aircraft and the artillerymen from 1-320th. There was also a new twist that Maj. Sanders forgot to mention: an advising team from 1-75 CAV, with a security element of infantry from 1-502 nearby, had been at the bridging site when the operation occurred. So close that they were close enough to see the ISIL spotters calling mortar fire down on their position. Oh, and close enough that as soon as the bridge was established, the advising team from 1-75 CAV *crossed over the river.* The mission creep had begun.

It always does.

"The Strike Quick Reaction Force is going to be arriving in a few weeks," Maj. Sanders continued. "All of the attention is about to shift up north."

"To do what exactly, ma'am?" I responded, dryly. It seemed like we had more than enough people at that moment. "Engineers, infantrymen, logistics personnel, that's a whole lot of extra people."

"We didn't think the Iraqis would make it this far by now," her response, short. "Since they have, CJTF wants to push towards Mosul. We need those extra people to open up Qayyarah West Airfield."

I was confused. Qayyarah West wasn't even in the conversation when we arrived in May.

"Qayyarah West Airfield is just south of Mosul." She continued. "The overland route from Taji takes too long and too much to secure. The ISF needs a new logistics hub, and we're going to help them get it up and running."

Maj. Sanders was excited, the change of tone evident in her voice. Something was up.

"Aren't there a whole bunch of bad guys in that area?" I asked, already knowing what her answer would be. "How's it all going to be secured?"

I could almost see her smiling.

"Well, you're going to see for *yourself* L.T.," she replied. "I need you up here by the beginning of August, so I need you to grab some last things from Taji and Baghdad. There should be some sling load training going on down there."

"Consider it a proof of concept."

The division prided itself on its sling load expertise, being able to move vehicles and guns under helicopters by attaching them to chains. If you had enough aircraft of the right size, you could bring a whole company of 100+ personnel within minutes, with vehicles and other equipment to boot.

"A proof of concept of *what*?" my reply, digging for answers. Something was going on.

"There's a lot of plans right now." She replied, the tone of her voice changing. It was like she had grown suddenly uncomfortable, almost as if she were trying to keep the conversation a secret.

But from *whom*?

"I have some tags you should put on your photos too; a lot of people are probably going to be looking to grab files from you."

More than they already have?

"I'm working on getting you to Baghdad to cover the operations there. Then I want you to create a video for the 101st's birthday."

I groaned.

"No more amateurish stuff," she continued. "Sgt. 1st Class Hoskins should be able to help you, and this is what I want...."

I pulled out a notepad to write down everything she was telling me: Videos of multiple Soldiers saying multiple lines, photos on the sling load training, and article on the advising in Baghdad, all done as quickly as possible.

"Does this mean I have a permanent slot? With 600 extra people coming and all?" I was coming up to my 90 days in the country mark; that meant I should have been getting sent back to Kuwait real soon if I wasn't finally added to the "Permanent" roster.

"No," she replied quickly and then paused as if she was waiting for something or someone.

To leave.

"I'm trying to get you a permanent slot," she continued, her voice low. "The Brigade X.O. won't budge. Just keep doing what you are doing and don't worry about it; you have to trust me on this one L.T."

With that the call ended, leaving me once again with more questions than answers.

In their run south, ISIL had spread to the Taji area and around the west of Baghdad, hitting the hotspots of Fallujah, Ramadi, and Abu Ghraib while conducting a series of bloody attacks. These were heavily Sunni areas, and the Iraqi government under Prime Minister Maliki was viewed as being more in line with Iranian and Shia interests than anything else.

With the Anbar province once again being a battleground, the coalition rolled in support to some of the old mainstays of the Iraq War: Al Anbar airbase, Taqqadum Airbase, and Baghdad. The area fell under the purview of the Iraqi Army's Baghdad Operations Command, being advised by none other than my old friends: Spader 6 and 1-26 Infantry.

They were based in the old green zone, at Camp Union III, right across the street from the U.S. Embassy. Literally. The old Green Zone looked impressive from the air as we approached in a UH-60, with its well-kept streets and palaces. It was the place to be back during OIF with all its freedoms.

Something told me that might have changed.

A sizable ugly stone building with a wall and barbed wire surrounding it like some old bunker in a WWII movie came into view as we descended to the landing zone.

The U.S. embassy.

Disembarking from the aircraft, I shuffled towards the waiting vehicles driven by Soldiers from 1-26. A whole convoy was required to move personnel from the embassy side to Union III, and it fell upon the Security Forces provided by the battalion. They didn't look exactly happy, and I couldn't blame them; no Soldier wanted to be at the "flagpole" with the Division Commander and his headquarters.

I dropped my bags into the vehicle and jumped in when a familiar voice called out.

"Long time no see sir!" a Soldier spoke up. "Where have you been?" I could recognize that New York accent from anywhere: Spc. Kelvin Barretto, a signal communications specialist. He had been there as I withered away in the assistant S6 position at Fort Campbell, working for a Captain who I despised and doing menial tasks. He was a good kid, motivated, in shape, and in it for the long haul. He was still motivated and in shape, but the in it for the long-haul part was in question, based on his voice.

"Good to see you!" I replied to Barretto. "Just hanging out all around. How's life for you?"

"Boring, sir," Barretto replied dryly. "Utterly boring. This place is like a prison." He paused, shaking his head. "My advice, get out of here as soon as you can."

With that dark statement, we began to drive, Barreto at the wheel. He had been excited to go to Iraq before we left and was one of the first people

117

picked by the chain of command to be on the deployment roster. What had happened; how did this place so greatly affect a highly motivated Soldier?

Camp Union III revealed itself as we drove across the street, as walled and fenced in as the embassy. Judging by the faces of the Soldiers on guard at the gate, Barretto wasn't the only person who had been affected. The vehicles rolled to a halt a few meters inside the entrance.

"This is your stop, sir," Barreto's words, shaking my hand. "It's good to see you again. We don't get many visitors."

"Why's that?"

"You'll see once you find Spader 6."

The vehicles drove off, and I was left with my stuff standing there in the night. An NCO appeared, walking towards me with a clipboard.

"Temporary or permanent?" he asked, not even glancing up from the clipboard or asking my name.

"Temporary," I replied quickly. I still had no idea where to go once I had arrived.

"Alright, go that way to get some housing." He pointed vaguely in the direction of some buildings, and walked off, leaving me to fend for myself. I looked in the direction he pointed; everything looked the same, and all the buildings seemed to be on top of each other. It was like I was inside a town in a glass ball. It was....

Depressing.

The temporary sleeping quarters were cold and unwelcoming too, almost if intentionally trying to scare outsiders away as soon as possible.

The camp could not have been more than three football fields big, if that, and when I started towards the division headquarters the next day, walking down the narrow "roads" felt more like tunnels than the outdoors. Even better-: a general walking towards me. I give a salute. Moments later, another general. Salute. Another general. And another.

I felt like there were more generals in this place than actual Soldiers. How many did we need for an operation with only 5,000 people? I would also learn from the 1-26 Soldiers on base that all that rank led to a whole lot of micromanaging of the Soldiers-the one big case that many of them referenced being what had happened when the unit tried to order body armor. When we first deployed to Iraq, we all were issued the older Interceptor Body Armor, meant for use in vehicles rather than dismounted operations or operations in the warm Iraq weather. Due to the Iraq and Afghanistan Wars, the Army had started issuing much more breathable and comfortable plate carriers for those deploying. Why *we* didn't get the same equipment issue was anybody's guess, and probably indicative of how ad-hoc this conflict was in the first place.

C CO's Soldiers and leadership had gotten together and raised money to order plate carriers to use, making sure that they had selected models that were in military standard. The high-ranking people in the division staff were doing so, so why not? The order went through, the Soldiers got their armor, and everyone was happy. Everyone except the random sergeant majors on division staff walking around who, once they saw the security forces wearing the plate carriers, made the call that they weren't regulation.

The kicker? The division staff kept on wearing the ones *they* ordered.

A tan building that looked more in place at a commercial park then Iraq stood near the front gate: the heart of the operations for the Combined Forces Land Component Command- Operation Inherent Resolve. Inside, personnel from 15 nations worked, overseen by Maj. Gen. Volesky and his headquarters. It was a labyrinth of offices with hallways that sometimes quite literally lead to nowhere. Most of the personnel were Majors and above, and I got some questioning looks as I tried to navigate my way to the PAO office.

Left, right, right, until I ended up in a small office in a back corner. Four desks, for the four people assigned. Not enough to orchestrate a public affairs effort that spanned two countries and thousands of personnel with dozens of different missions.

"How's it going?" I said as I walked in, waving to the three people sitting inside at the time. A Captain, a German officer, and from the looks of it, Sgt. 1st Class Hoskins. They glanced up at me, then at my uniform, which compared to everyone else around Union III was kind of bleached and worn due to all my time in the summer sun.

"Good to meet you face to face Sgt. 1st Class Hoskins," I offered to him as I walked further into the room.

The expressions changed to a mix of recognition, but still questioning

"Lt. Johnson?" Hoskins replied, looking closer at me. It was like he expected someone else; there weren't exactly a lot of lieutenants around that looked like me.

In more ways than one.

"What brings you down here? Good to meet you." He shook my hand with a grin, leaving whatever questions he had for another time.

"Maj. Sanders didn't let you know I was coming?"

"She probably did, but it may have slipped my mind." His reply. I looked around the office at the papers, charts, and documents strewn around, then observed the rest of the PAO section. They looked...tense. Like they hadn't been able to relax in months.

"She sent me down here to cover the Baghdad Operations Command and also hopefully get some tips from you."

"Tips? What do you need help with?"

"My photos and videos." My reply. He tilted his head at my vague request, almost as if he could not believe what I was asking. My instructions were clear: get help from the "masters." What type of advice that was, however, was the addendum that was missing.

"Auto color if you need to," Hoskins replied finally, choosing his words carefully. "You're not a bad shot, and premiere and photoshop can help clean up photos."

Typing on the keyboard, then a wave for me to come over to his desk. On the screen was one of my images I had submitted. An indoor shot that was washed out due to my attempt to use the camera to add brightness.

"Add some artificial light like a flash, so your ISO doesn't have to do it." He continued, pointing at the screen. "Oh and shoot dark."

"Dark?"

"If your image is overexposed, you can't fix it or bring out the colors. If you find just the right balance and err on the side of shooting with less ISO, you'll have a better time. There's also the rule of thirds…but start with that."

What the hell was the rule of thirds? I looked at Hoskins, nodding my head as if I now understood everything that was going on. Based on the expression on his face, he knew that this quick class, while helpful, didn't change the reality staring us in the face.

I was on my own.

He leaned in, giving me a nod.

"There is one thing; do you have any more of that GoPro footage?"

"I do." My reply, offhandedly. Gigabytes of footage had been sitting on my hard drive since my first trip, waiting for the opportunity to be used again. None had arisen. "I only used some of it for the first video."

There was a slight change in his expression. Something told me he wasn't the only one asking this question.

"People love that stuff!" he continued, glancing at his screen. "It's some of the hottest footage we've had. How many angles did you get?"

"Most of the crew started wearing them when they saw I was taking video. So almost all of them, I guess?"

"Do you think you can put it all together, give people a sort of multi-viewpoint look of a crew in action? It'll take some cutting but…" his voice was different. For once, there was a specific request for footage. Not a vague "take some video" or "write an article," but a desire for an exact type of coverage. Hoskins had been doing this for years, and he was *asking* me to produce something?

"I'll put something together, if I can." My reply.

"Yeah, let us know what you get."

Lt. Col. Thomas walked in the door with a stack of papers before throwing them down in a huff. I knew that look-: a time-consuming meeting that sucked up the already limited time she had during the day. Her eyes were red and stress lines were apparent; something told me she was being run ragged. She turned towards Sgt. 1st Class Hoskins and me, too exhausted to even look surprised.

"Maj. Sanders sent Lt. Johnson down to get some footage from the guys here at the BOC ma'am," Hoskins said quickly as she sat down. "And also, some tips."

"Lt. Johnson," Lt. Col. Thomas said from her desk, "Strike's man on the ground. Good to see you." There wasn't any sarcasm or emptiness in her statement; she seemed genuinely appreciative.

"Maj. Sanders sent you down here to cover the BOC? Good. You're doing a good job out there L.T. You're basically the only guy we have roaming around..." she shook her head as she spoke, looking at the only three personnel that she had available, obviously displeased with how limited her public affairs apparatus was.

In a perfect situation, Thomas would have had some extra human resources to help ease the load, like an assistant NCO or a photographer to do some footwork. She did have an extra photographer in Baghdad, but one rub-

That journalist was covering Maj. Gen. Volesky, and nothing else.

Her public affairs shortage was one created by policies, or opinions, that said that each general would have their own photographer/PAO. Cool and all, but when you add in General Volesky, and then his boss, and then whatever other bosses were floating around, you were left with-

Well. Me. And Maj. Sanders, to cover a unit spread over the entire country with thousands of personnel.

"I'm learning as I go ma'am" I admitted to Lt. Col. Thomas, sheepishly. "Sgt. 1st Class Hoskins and Maj. Sanders have been a great help."

I stopped, trying to form my next words carefully. There was another reason why I had been sent to their office: to find out what the overall P.A. plan was. I should have known something was up when Maj. Sanders requested that I ask.

"I do have a question, since I'm here." I continued, switching my voice to that of a poor young man trying to understand the world. "What do you need to collect? Or try to focus more on?"

Lt. Col. Thomas sat back for a second in thought, as if I was to first person to have asked her the question.

"There is something." her reply, her expression one of a chess player plotting their next five moves.

It was my turn to lean in.

"Tie us together with the training of Iraqi troops," she continued. "And take photos of Soldiers with Screaming Eagle patches."

Hoskins nodded in affirmative as I stood there processing, waiting for a speech or broad objectives or maybe even a large sheet of paper thrown my way. I waited.

We stared at each other.

It started to get awkward.

Then I finally understood.

Keep on publicizing us, and we'll keep on running it. Even without saying those words, I heard Lt. Col. Thomas clear as day.

There was no plan. We were making it up as we went along.

I was making it all up as we went along.

"Sounds good, ma'am," I replied lamely.

The entire public affairs apparatus of the U.S. Army was just blindly sending us out to report on what was going on, without telling us what they wanted to hear. Compared to the monolithic, all-powerful Pentagon portrayed in the movies and the media, this wasn't it. Everyone, from Maj. Sanders, to Lt. Col. Thomas, to the guys back in Florida at CENTCOM, and finally at the Pentagon itself would simply take whatever came their way.

Which was up to me, I guess.

Sgt. Addison Owen and I were in the same Company at Fort Campbell, and just like Spc. Baretto, he had been excited to come to Iraq the last time I had seen him.

"Good to see a 'new' face," he greeted me outside of the Security Force Company's sleeping area, an utterly forgettable building that could sleep 30+ on a floor. We warmly shook hands as I noticed Owen's tone of voice had changed since Fort Campbell, taking on an air of futility and boredom. He wasn't that much older than me, and yet this was already his third deployment, his first one being to Iraq when it was closing down.

The security force company on Camp Union III was drawn from Charlie Company, 1-26. They were one of the most trained companies in the battalion because they had trained at JRTC two times before the deployment, as the rest of the battalion went only once. For all their hard work, they were rewarded: 12-hour guard shifts inside the extremely small compound, ferrying people across the street or to the Baghdad operations command, and dealing with a bunch of high-ranking officers and enlisted who had nothing better to do than exercise their authority over the lowest ranking people in the camp.

The guys in C CO weren't happy.

"How have you been?" I asked as we stood in the little break area outside the barracks. Warm, quiet, you'd almost forget you were in Iraq.

"Just been stuck here sir," Owen replied, shaking his head. He was one of the Company's designated marksmen, pulled over from the battalion's scouts before the deployment to support Union III. "I just sit up on a roof most of the day and try to avoid the Sergeant Major or C.G. Most of us hate it here. It's like being back at Fort Campbell but in Iraq."

"What, all these generals around?"

He glanced sideways at me.

"You know it." He laughed. "I swear you can't go five feet without running into an officer- no offense." A quick shaking of his head in disappointment.

"I wouldn't mind it if this place wasn't so small. I'd rather be where the action is, honestly. At least the food is great, and the gym is well equipped. How have you been, you still in the battalion?"

"Not anymore. I now work for the *brigade staff.* I only come out to see the little people down at the battalions every now and then."

"You've forgotten about us already?"

"I operate at the *strategic* level."

I did my best haughty officer impression and we both started laughing. It felt good to forget about everything that was going on, even for a moment.

"What have you been up to?"

"Traveling around, taking photos. Same thing I did before."

"How'd you even pull that one off?"

"I have no idea."

"They bring Staff Sgt. Melendez out here too?"

"You guys must have hit it off *great* at JRTC."

"I mean, she did find me to get a photo. Made the U.S. Army Facebook page and everything."

"I helped her find you."

"But she *was* looking for me!"

He had a point there, I had to admit.

"She said she's getting out of the Army, that's why I'm here."

"She's getting out? I hope she doesn't, she's pretty good!"

"Better than me? That hurts."

"Your pictures on the battalion Facebook page *were* kind of whack sometimes…" He chuckled. "Like that video you posted of Spader 6 that made him look confused."

"I mean, he *was* confused at that moment."

BOOM.

A massive, dull explosion, rattling the windows and the ground. Owen glanced towards the sound, then at me, nonplussed.

"Probably a vehicle-borne IED," he said calmly. "Any explosion that I'm not in is a good one." For the briefest of moments, it seemed like he was in a different place, a subtle change in everything about him as he spoke those words.

He was speaking from experience.

The moment passed, and he put on a smirk.

"How do you like hanging with the bigwigs? They tell you what's going on?"

I thought about the fact that it seemed that Maj. Sanders was fighting the brigade staff to keep me in the country.

"They don't tell me much. I wouldn't consider myself part of their group to be honest."

There was a flurry of activity around us as Soldiers came outside, wondering what happened. That VBIED was the most exciting thing to happen at Union III in months.

"Do you guys get a lot of news down here?"

"Not really. It's almost like we're forgotten about down here. How is it up north?"

"Open, at least!"

"It's dangerous out there," Owen said, patting his rifle. "You need protection, like an assistant."

"And where would I find one of those?"

Owen smiled knowingly.

"I'm a scout who isn't being used. The brigade would rather have my skills protecting their PAO, don't you think? An officer shouldn't be out there by himself, carrying all of that equipment. *It's just not proper.* That's what us enlisted men are for!*"*

"That sounds reasonable," I agreed. "But I'm just a lieutenant in the United States Army. I don't think they care about me to allow such a *skilled asset* as you go."

We both laughed. It was partly because of the joke and partly because of the sad realization that a lot of people in charge probably didn't care about us at all.

The vehicles heading to the BOC were filled with yet more familiar faces from the old days.

"Johnson?" A lieutenant asked me as I settled into the seat of our vehicle, regarding me with a cocked eyebrow. "Where you been, man? And why are you heading to the BOC?"

"Going to get the story on Spader 6," I replied.

The lieutenant just shook his head. "You actually *want* to go there? Yeesh." Everyone else the vehicle had the same expression and reaction.

Our convoy snaked through the roads of the Green Zone, passing more palatial buildings. We were obviously still in a controlled area --- the signs of civilian life were few, bar some intersections where we found ourselves in more substantial traffic. Two giant swords appeared over the road, darkening everything around them in shadows; something about them seemed familiar, and then it hit me. As a child I had seen the objects on T.V., the voices of newscasters filling the air as they talked about the progress the coalition was making during the invasion of Iraq. Resistance was melting away; the U.S. military was outperforming expectations; the war would be over in months.

Considering I was now 25 and was a Soldier in Iraq, I would guess that the plan didn't work out.

We pulled up the ramp to a stately building that was no doubt a palace a few decades before. The Baghdad Operations Command in all its glory, the Iraqi guards out front waving us in without a word.

"They also wave in the Iranians the same way," the lieutenant said dryly. "The commander of the Quds force was on the BOC Floor recently. Wonder how long before *we* become the target." He shook his head ruefully as he grabbed his bags.

"Another shift in paradise. Follow me to Spader 6, *PAO.*"

The palace had been converted into an operations center, filled with consoles, maps, and communications equipment that blinked as Iraqi officers of a variety of different ranks milled around. We walked through the common area, towards a space in the back where Spader 6 and his advising team were headquartered. The office, if it could be called that, was unassuming, with computers, radios, and a few desks packed into an extremely cramped area that was about the size of a small living room. It was if they were intentionally put there to be out of sight, if not out of mind.

Intelligence, communications, fire support, and operations personnel filled out the advising group, working in a circle practically on top of each other. To continue the theme of no feng shui, their bosses worked on top of *them*. I felt like I was suffocating, and I had only been at the BOC for a couple of minutes. There was no small talk among the gathered personnel: no smiles, no jokes, no *anything*.

"Lt. Johnson." a Major walked out from an office behind the tables, regarding me from behind his glasses. He was the new executive officer for the battalion pulled down from the division staff early in the deployment and based on his taciturn expression and the fact that I could have sworn I saw some of the Soldiers shift away nervously when he appeared, he wasn't the one for jokes.

"We're going to do a shift change brief, and then the boss will be ready to talk." the X.O. continued, looking at the gathered group as if silently already evaluating what they were going to say. "Need anything else while you're here?"

I had no idea.

"Just one of the Soldiers for a video clip for the division's birthday." My voice spoke before my mind did.

"Who do you have in mind?"

Something told me that every conversation with the X.O. was this way: short, to the point, with whoever was speaking needing to be 100 % sure of what they were saying.

"One of the younger Soldiers," my reply. I paused. "Based on what Maj. Sanders said."

"We'll have one ready then." the X.O. replied, pointing towards someone to do just that. He looked towards everyone else.

"Shift change brief, now."

The slides came up as everyone gathered around recap the last 12 hours of operations. Air Strikes, bombings, assaults, current operations. Everything the next group coming in needed to know so they could take over for the next half day. The battalion X.O. led the meeting, ensuring that all the required information was spoken about, and if someone forgot something, he'd remind them. Forcefully.

Just a few weeks before at the end of June coalition airstrikes had destroyed over 175 ISIL vehicles fleeing the city of Fallujah. It was massive propaganda and tactical victory for the coalition and ISF, and based on what I was hearing, the BOC played a crucial role in coordinating the operation. The ruthless efficiency being showcased was a long way from when the unit started at Fort Campbell, that's for sure.

"Ready, Johnson?" Spader 6's familiar voice brought me out of my reverie as the briefing subsided. I glanced up at him and nodded, putting up a thankful smile as I walked into his office, closing the door behind me. My personal opinions of him or not, I could at least appreciate that he was a busy man; he wouldn't be wasting time speaking to me otherwise.

"You're doing good work out there," he said, giving me a firm handshake. I could read it on Spader 6's face: he was impressed that I had made it this far and wasn't stuck in Kuwait. I wouldn't mistake the look for *pride*, however, just one of…amazement? Confusion?

Ambivalence.

I said my thanks, understanding based on my experiences with him that I was useful, nothing more, nothing less. I had been invited not so he could talk to *me,* but the audience that he knew I could reach. If the Brigade Commander and those above him wanted to see how *successful the* advise and assist operation was, Spader 6 would show them.

"Thanks sir," my reply, sliding into the role I was expected to take. "I'm glad you allowed me to work with Maj. Sanders." I nodded my head slowly. "I'm trying to make sure the Blue Spaders are taken care of up there."

"I've seen." Spader 6's reply, a with a pleased expression. "I'm glad you're covering what we're doing."

We both played our bit, saying what should have been said. And not meaning a word of it. The words felt and sounded rehearsed, and we both knew it. As most of my conversations with the man, there was an air of uneasiness and awkwardness. It was as if we were aliens from different worlds; we weren't talking to each other, but *at.*

I pulled out my prepared questions, giving the whole "If you don't mind taking the time out of your day" spiel. He didn't.

"The Iraqis had been trying to retake Fallujah for about two years when we arrived." The colonel tilted his head towards the foyer, where we could both see the X.O. walking around, observing the Soldiers' computer screens.

"I heard about that big strike, sir," my reply, looking towards one of the maps, covered the walls of his office. "The BOC's work?"

He shifted his eyes towards me.

"You stay informed."

"It's my job, sir."

He continued, leaving that thread hanging.

"Several weeks after we got here, they decided to conduct concerted offensive operations. Within less than 30 days, the BOC had successfully isolated Fallujah, defeated pockets of ISIL fighters outside, and secured the city."

"That's a pretty fast turnaround." I offered, indicating that I was ready for the hook that we both knew was coming.

"I feel our advise and assist effort played a significant role in the Iraqi's army success."

Spader 6's proclamation was Army speak, which meant that it was exactly what the Pentagon wanted to see.

"The Iraqis are entirely in the lead," he continued, knowing exactly what I had been sent to get. The conversation continued, all the key points being hit, like clockwork. There was nothing shocking about what he was saying, and that was the almost sad part.

"When you look at what our team accomplished assisting the BOC with offensive operations in Fallujah, " he continued, teeing up the fly ball for me to catch. "The battle damage assessment results speak for themselves."

Battle damage assessments?

Body counts.

The easiest way in the military to say that your unit was making progress or that the war was being won. How many enemies killed, vehicles destroyed, fortifications reduced. Spader 6 was an infantryman and was now on his 4th trip to Iraq. He knew exactly what the point of BDA was.

Our bosses did too.

That data was gold. Maj. Sanders made me roll up the brigade's BDA to send up in the reports to the Brigade Commander. How many people our efforts were killing was a point of *pride.* Hell, it was *the* point. Who cares about the underlying structural issues that led us to return in the first place, or a plan for the areas re-captured that doesn't lead to an insurgency springing back up, right? I always wondered how we confirmed that all the "insurgents" killed were actually all insurgents, and that we hadn't killed civilians too.

Spader 6 continued talking about operations at the BOC, a true professional as always. He knew exactly what he was talking about and I admit it was refreshing to get some more extensive understanding of what was going on, even though that understanding led to even more questions.

The conversation between us died down, my questions adequately answered.

"Thank you for the time, sir," I began, smiling up at him. "This is everything I could need; it'll be too easy to get an article out of this." With that, I began to stand up.

"Before you go," Spader 6 said, motioning for me to stay for a little while longer, but it was odd. There was something different.

"I want to say that out of all the times I've been to Iraq, I feel like we're making the most difference this time."

He paused, an oddly human moment occurring. It was the inflection in his voice and the look on his face that threw me off — one of a man who had spent years of his life overseas fighting for the cause. One that lower ranking personnel usually don't get to see on their leaders.

I tilted my head. Difference? We were fighting the offshoot of a terrorist organization that literally came about because of our invasion of Iraq in 2003, which was itself based on bad intelligence, and then afterwards we made so many strategic blunders that there were whole series of books on the subject.

I remember reading a quote about the Vietnam War, where a week before the fall of Saigon in 1975, U.S. Army Col. Harry Summers was in a meeting with a Vietnamese counterpart in Hanoi as they conducted negotiations. In his words:

"'You know, you never beat us on the battlefield,' I told my North Vietnamese counterpart. He pondered that remark a moment and then replied, 'That may be so, but it is also irrelevant.'"

"In a narrow strategic sense, he was right. Whether they defeated us on the battlefield or not, they did win the war. But in another sense, he was dead wrong, for that fact was relevant indeed to the almost 3 1/2 million Americans who served in Southeast Asia during the war. Many of them still bear a burden they do not deserve and blame themselves for what went wrong there."

Col. Summers' words played in my head as I studied Spader 6, trying to understand what he was saying. Another war, or wars, another burden being carried by thousands of personnel who had hoped they were doing the right thing.

But were we making a difference?

Maybe I was the one who was cynical.

But we were looking across the table at each other in Iraq, after I had volunteered to be there when he wasn't trying to send me.

Maybe I was the one who didn't get it.

But here I was, against all odds.

I tried to analyze his words, to doubt them, but something told me he meant it. Over 15 years in the military, friends lost, birthdays missed, men killed.

You had to believe in it, right?

Or else you'd go crazy.

I thought about how he never gave me a platoon leader slot, ostensibly because of my lack of Ranger Tab, but then made sure the West Pointers in the same position got theirs.

I thought about the experiences the Soldiers and officers under him in the country right now were having, leaving them to feel abandoned. Furthermore, why was he telling me this? Why did he feel the need to stop me and speak those words; this time, it seemed like he was talking *to me*.

"Our success is due to the hard work those Soldiers are doing out there," Spader 6 continued, pointing outside. "Without them, we're nothing."

I couldn't buy it, and it showed on my face. Did he truly believe that? Or was it something he told himself? The fact that we were having this conversation in *2016*, part of a war with no name, made me question what he was saying; if everything we did in the Army was for some "purpose", and that purpose was never fulfilled, then what was the point? I was being told to disregard the reality staring me in the face, to not *question* it. I was supposed to believe it was   all worth the pain endured by personnel under our command, because if it wasn't, then why put them through it all?

I finally realized what it was that made every interaction with him uncomfortable for the both of us: beyond the military we had nothing in common. In outside life, we would never interact and would probably always have disdain for the other, and yet through coincidence or fate were confronted with someone who didn't fit our ideals of the world. Our problems with each other weren't about us; it was because at the fundamental level we were in two different realities. We would never be able to understand each other because the other person didn't make any sense.

In a world of order, regimen, discipline, and cohesion, that's a very frightening thought. Usually, those who question the unspoken rules and procedures would be excised from the group or organization. Like *he* had tried to do to me.

But if they weren't excised, and "achieved success" by doing things or behaving in a way that shouldn't have been possible, by turning a dead-end assignment into something big? All the while *questioning* your reality? Then what did that mean for *you,* and all the years you spent following the path laid out to you?

I left in silence unsure of what to say, leaving Spader 6 in his office. That was the last time we spoke until the summer of the next year when his change of command ceremony occurred, and I wished him well during the event.

Even then something was off, and as we spoke, we were still trying to get a read on the other.

We couldn't.

The last thing Spader 6 told me was that he hoped that I would go out there and get published someday.

The scary part was, based on the look on his face I recognized from Baghdad --- *is that a piece of him meant it.*

Chapter Eight – Escalation- August 2016

"We're going on an air assault L.T., and the battalion commander wants you there. Hell, we all do." The voice of Charlie Battery's new commander, unfamiliar to me, over the phone. I glanced around the headquarters tent, holding the phone a little closer.

"That's a lot of faith, sir."

"Yeah, but your name came up when we started planning this. We'd all appreciate the coverage. If you can, get down to KSB and we'll talk more. The guys have been asking about when you were coming back."

"I'll be there, sir."

August in Erbil. LSA Strike was fast becoming a legitimate camp, reinforcements arriving by the day for the next push. Maj. Sanders' directions as soon as I had come back were clear- talk to 1-320th to get on their next mission.

"And don't tell anyone," her guidance at the end of the conversation. "Don't let anyone know what you're doing."

She chose her next words carefully.

"Some people may start to get a little jealous."

"Of what? Me doing my job?"

"That's *exactly* it, L.T."

"A few months ago, nobody cared about me."

"A few months ago, your name wasn't ending up all over the internet."

"Doesn't that mean we're doing what we're supposed to do?"

"It does. But it also means people get grumpy because they feel like they're not getting any credit either."

I was starting to get frustrated.

"Of all things, PAO coverage and the PAO traveling around is bothering some people? We're in a combat zone, and this is what they care about?"

"Finally, L.T., you're starting to understand."

I could tell she sounded more pointed than usual. Even in the emails she CC'd me on; her tone had turned combative with some of the other brigade leadership. There were other little things too- odd comments from other officers that emphasized the fact that I seemed to be "traveling everywhere," or had "free reign." The fact that some of them tried to complain to her about the fact that I was laissez-faire, only for her to tell them point-blank that if they had a problem with me, they needed to talk *to me*.

Some did. One officer in Erbil tried to give me a speech about officer ship or something after one of my uniforms was torn. One of the *two* I had and was waiting to get replaced. She worked at the division headquarters element in Erbil and I could tell that she didn't enjoy being stuck there. I could read her dressing down of me for what it was: pure pettiness. Professional behavior, trying to take out your frustrations about your situation on someone of a lower rank. Ineffective, however, if they have a boss who's willing to back them up.

One conversation I had with the brigade information operations officer was especially telling. When I asked him if he was working with the PAO, he admitted that he wasn't. Well, enough, except I could practically see the words on his face; frustration, jealousy, disrespect- he didn't like that Maj. Sanders was practically running a solo information ops campaign and was succeeding. Strangely enough, I guess he couldn't talk to her to try to coordinate.

It's hard walking ten feet to someone else's desk in Camp Swift.

The veneer of cooperation was dropping among the headquarters, and people were separating into factions. There was politics at work here, and I was getting the feeling that it wasn't just about me. Small victories like making sure that I got exactly what I had *earned* were bigger than defeating ISIL for some people; it was only a matter of time before my boss would finally be outmaneuvered.

"Make the next few weeks count L.T." she continued, speaking in-between the lines. *Your time is almost up.*

"Who knows how the mission will change afterward."

"You came through. The guys are famous!"

Staff Sgt. Mont shook my hand warmly as the rest of the crew gathered around. It was good to see familiar faces, even if looked more haggard than the month before. Four months in and none of the Soldiers in the battery had been rotated out for rest and relaxation, *unlike* other artillery units in the theater who were only rotating units to Iraq for 90 days. You could tell that they were being worn thin; more weight loss, stress lines, and more dirt, along with a general frustration and fatigue.

Even Sabol and Trammel looked stressed out, the kids looking like they aged a year since the last time I saw them.

"My mom told me about the article," Trammel said, smiling. "Thanks for that, it was awesome."

"I only wrote about what you guys were doing."

"Speaking of that, we're trying to write a story too after seeing the article."

"Really?" my reply. "What's it about?"

"A story about three friends."

"In Iraq?"

"No, not Iraq. We're already here."

The suddenness of the answer caught me off guard, along with the expression on his face.

I waved at Pfc. Sabol, who came walking up. "Thanks for the GoPros man. People loved it!"

"Yeah, I saw!" he replied, pulling out some printouts. "I've got the clips saved. Maj. Sanders even quoted me in one of her articles. So cool to see that on the Central Command website."

There was something rewarding knowing that their stories were being told. Not just higher-ranking officers or NCOs, but *them.*

They were important.

"I know you have spotty connections, so I brought these." My words as I pulled out some screenshots of where everything was ending up. The front page of Army.Mil, clips on MSNBC, CBS, YouTube. By August Charlie Battery was perhaps the most well-known unit of its type in the entire military.

As if to emphasize this point, every time footage or a story about the battery appeared online, someone from the states who wasn't even affiliated with the brigade would send the clippings of the articles to the Soldiers. Families would do the same thing. Mont's father, a Navy Veteran himself, printed off a photo of his son from one of the articles and hung it in his office. That was the main objective of my mission in Iraq: families knowing what their Soldiers were going through.

"How'd the footage work out of the living conditions?" Sgt. 1st Class Young greeted me, giving me a fist bump. "I didn't see it online anywhere."

"They didn't want to release it," my reply looking down. "We were told, and I quote, 'That it would make the phones ring off the hook.'"

Young and Mont shared a look as if to say that the answer was what they expected.

"The holes are gone now anyway," Young continued, laughing. "They were filled in not long after you left." There was an amused look in his eye. "You wouldn't know anything about *that,* would you?"

"No idea. I'm just a guy who takes photos."

"Right…"

"What brings you back here?" Mont's question as the Soldiers looked through the screenshots, writing down links or taking pictures.

"I guess your commander wants me on the air assault that's about to happen," I smiled knowingly. "That you guys?"

"For once, it's not. That's Lt. Frank and first platoon. Gunny Joseph, smoke Burkett, and all of them."

I remembered Joseph's words from my first time to KSB.

"Well, Gunny Joseph did make me promise I'd come back and cover them."

"1st Platoon only got tapped for this because our gun's down." Mont replied, an edge of competitiveness sliding his voice. "You know we would hook you up, but Sgt. Burke's section from our platoon is the only one up right now." He pointed down the line to another artillery piece.

"How long has yours been out of commission?"

"Only recently," Mont shook his head. "Though the problems started about the time its hydraulics broke down last month, and we had to operate the entire piece manually. Of course, it'd shit the bed right when the Iraqis were crossing the Tigris."

"Weren't you guys out there all day?

"Yep."

"So, the entire smoke mission?"

"By hand." He shrugged nonchalantly.

"You...."

"Yeah, we had to crank it manually. But it all worked out." I wanted to ask more, but the fact that Mont seemed unconcerned about the fact they he and the crew had to manually operate the cannon dozens of times during the battle near the Tigris told me everything.

"These things are junk," he continued. "Hopefully, the next unit brings all new ones, another eight months of the way we've been putting through them, and they're bound to catastrophically malfunction."

A call came over the radio from the FDC --- preparation for a fire mission.

"You must be good luck or something," A Soldier said as he prepared to head over to Burke's gun. "It's been pretty quiet out here recently."

I shrugged and grabbed my stuff to head over there. I was smarter than my first trip; I was wearing a GoPro for video, and my Nikon for stills. There was no way I'd miss anything.

Hopefully.

Burke and his men were waiting in the fire pit, about the same since I last saw them. The most significant and most immediate difference between

Mont's and Burke's section was the age of their leaders. Burke was in his early 20s and had about half the years in the Army Mont had. Section chiefs were *supposed* to Staff Sgts. Due to a lack of manpower, or rather *mismanagement*, that wasn't in effect here.

"Long time no see," Burke greeted me and Sgt. 1st Class Young, who had also come to observe. "Not hanging with your buddies in 3rd section sir?"

There was some snickering among his crew.

"Well, the gun's down," I replied as I turned towards the pit exit, making a show of preparing to leave. "But if you want me to take photos of that... no problem."

The FDC calling down for a fire mission ended our back and forth.

Burke's screw sprang into action with the standard commands and movements. The target was a squad of ISIL fighters in the open, caught by intelligence, surveillance, and reconnaissance (ISR) assets as they moved position. Dust, rounds leaving the M777, loading. All the telltale sights and sounds of a fire mission at KSB.

But now, with the photos to prove it.

"I think we won!" One of the Soldiers called out as soon as the mission concluded. There was cheering and clapping, and I started looking through the photos. Good, good, goo-

Holy shit.

I clicked through the camera again, looking at the images both a split second before and after the shot. I had gotten lucky with a one in a million chance. The literal instant with the M777 firing with billowing smoke, the force of the round knocking dust off the walls and creating a surreal outline of dirt being blown off the Soldiers' bodies.

This was *it*.

I could just tell. This wasn't some magic intuition either- the past few months had been a learning lesson on what worked and what didn't. Experience is a great teacher, true, but I also had immediate feedback on my products, whether from Maj. Sanders, Sgt. 1st Class Hoskins, or the public at large. Each outing, good or bad, taught me something new.

Staff Sgt. Burke's crew firing an M777 at ISIL, August, 2016. U.S. Army photo by Daniel Johnson.

When the time came to post the photos, I used a new trick, based on what had happened before. Most photos on DVIDs go up as galleries, where they only show up on the image page in whatever random order the system loads them in. Cool and all, but there's hundreds of images posted on DVIDs each day, meaning your stuff gets lost in the sauce no matter how good it is.

Unless you attach it to a news story.

So, I created a short "article," just with the text saying that the photos illustrated a fire mission conducted at the Kara Soar Base. Cheating perhaps, but it also served another purpose; I could make my best photo the cover image of the news story, meaning that not only would there be less competition, but it would immediately draw clicks.

Which it did, in droves.

PBS used the photo as one of their cover images, and the subscribers to our DVIDs page skyrocketed, leading to the image ending up all over the internet. The United States Army would use it as their photo of the day, the Department of State and Department of Defense would use it as part of their official communications campaigns, and whenever Maj. Gen. Volesky, the Brigade Commander, or some other officer wrote something about our time in Iraq, they *ensured* the image was in there.

Hell, a few years later I found it floating around as part of a meme.

Capt. Joe Berlin was in his late 20s and had previously been working at the brigade TOC at Camp Swift before taking over Charlie Battery in July. The last commander's time was up, literally. Unlike war movies or military dramas, commanders leave units when their "Key Development" time is up. K.D. time is what you need to get promoted, and it varies by branch. For signal officers, it's a battalion signal officer and so on, for example.

For Artillery specifically, it was Battery Command. Since there was such a backlog of would-be commanders and not enough command slots, a Captain could wait a year plus before getting their shot. They only way to get one faster was to be *good.*

Berlin had previously been in the Ranger Regiment after earning his Ranger Tab as a lieutenant, a rarity for Artillery officers; with that "leg-up" his career was jump started. Once arrived at Campbell he was brought to Iraq, and now had jumped the pile to command the only artillery battery in action in the brigade.

Even better, he had a PAO that would publish the battery's exploits. When the time came to start planning this operation, one of Berlin's first questions was if Maj. Sanders could spare me to go along.

"Good to meet you, L.T." Capt. Berlin shook my hand warmly and firmly. "I'm glad to have you with us on this next mission."

"Thanks for inviting me, sir," My reply.

"We've been impressed with your work. It's good to see the brigade giving us some love." He paused, glancing at me. "They usually treat us like the red-headed stepchild. The battalion commander wants you on this next operation, an air assault across the river in so we can have the guns in position to support a Kurdish offensive. It's less risker than driving them out there; regular convoys don't draw too much attention. A convoy with artillery pieces will get a lot of interest though, just like at KSB when it was first established."

He pointed a finger at me.

"You're going in the first wave."

I couldn't hide the reaction on my face.

"We want coverage from the start to the end. We *know* you can pull it off. This is bigger than just Iraq L.T.; there's people all over the DoD who want to see how this goes." He looked around the TOC tent at the maps, battle positions, readouts. "Some people doubt that artillery is useful in this kind of war. We've been proving them wrong, and we're going to *keep* on doing it."

"I'll give it my best shot, sir."

Berlin looked at me, quizzically.

"How far would your 'best shot' go?"

"Front page of Army.Mil, footage on news channels, and some civilian entities looking at it, I guess."

He nodded his head, as if I were just confirming what he already knew.

"How fast can you have the images turned around? The second we get off this operation, people are going to be breathing down our necks."

"A day, sir."

Just saying the words felt surreal to me, and I thought he'd laugh.

No, *he* was taking me seriously.

"We want you at the sling load training for the preparation of the mission, and then the mission itself." Berlin said, walking around, gathering his things. "1st Platoon under Lt. Matthew Frank is down there right now getting ready. They're going to be your ride. The timeline is going to be tight on this- rehearsals start tomorrow."

I had first met 1st Lt. Matthew Frank at a bizarre, simulated training exercise in Georgia. To call it a war game would be putting it lightly, but Frank stayed on the floor above me at the barracks at the base. The first thing I noticed when I met him was his truck, an absolute beast of a vehicle that looked like it had been driven off the showroom lot.

"Where'd you get the truck, man?" had been my words to him one day as we returned from the sim center.

"Oh, that?" He waved towards the vehicle offhandedly. "Got that when we returned from Afghanistan last year. Figured we wouldn't be going anywhere for a while, so why not?"

He was in Iraq less than a year later with Charlie Battery.

In an Army where deployments for conventional units were hard to come by, Frank had gotten put on two in less than 36 months.

Frank's platoon was in another compound on the airfield, separated from our primary brigade footprint. As soon as Capt. Berlin dropped me off at LSA Strike I began trudging in their direction, and after some fumbling around, walking from tent to tent, I finally found them.

The interior greeted me with the smell of feet and the sound of movies hanging in the air. Soldiers with their socks off, shirts off, heck, even pants off, asleep. For once since May, expressions of pure relaxation. Going off the smell of food and assorted food bags lying around, I could tell they were taking advantage of the little P.X. on the airfield and the multiple dining facilities. Who could blame them?

They'd be right back to work in less than 12 hours.

"Look who it is," a familiar voice called out from one of the bunks. "Mont isn't here, you know." I looked towards the sound and recognized the face immediately. Gunny Joseph, lying on his bed listening to some music.

"I did promise to make you famous," my reply as we fist-bumped.

Joseph sat up with a smile. "You're coming with us?"

"I am the best cameraman in Iraq, aren't I?"

The Soldiers in the tent started to stir at our voices, glancing past our bunks. Without all their kit and dirt and grime from KSB in them, they all looked like the kids they were. 18-25-year-olds who wouldn't have looked out of place as students at Appalachian State. These kids had been raining shells on the most premier terrorist group on the planet, and some of them couldn't even drink alcohol legally. In a few days, they would be at the forefront of an operation that would be world news.

Crazy to think about.

"Good to see you didn't get lost, Johnson," the familiar voice of Lt. Frank called from across the tent, after having entered from the far side. "Glad to have the paparazzi on this operation."

The Soldiers began to get up and gathered around for our "war council."

"Paparazzi is so unrefined, Frank. I like to consider myself a *conflict journalist*, a man of the people.

"A man of the people? Great, didn't know we were in a class struggle."

"Not a class struggle, but the eternal struggle."

"Of?"

"Man, against himself."

"You're smart for an infantry officer," Frank teased. "What'd you study, English?"

"I did for a while, but I hated writing, so I switched."

"That's ironic. But then again, you are an infantryman watching us do the fighting, so…"

"Ready for the brief sir," one of the NCOs called out, his face expressing *"These LTs, man…"*

The platoon leadership gathered at the front and center of the map. Lt. Frank, Sgt. 1st Class, Juan Burkett, Staff Sgt. Joseph, and the two-section Chiefs: Staff Sgt. Johnathan Walker and Staff Sgt. Jeffrey Andrew. Along with the lower ranking Soldiers, about 20 personnel all told made up the platoon. Attached would also be an early warning radar section and FDC led by another L.T., infantrymen from 1-75 CAV to provide security for the L.Z., and the fire direction center, led by a Sgt. James Johnson.

"Just got done talking with Capt. Berlin," Frank began, tapping on the imagery in front of him. "The operation- Evergreen II- is a go. Details are about the same we talked about before. The Kurds are going to cross the Great Zab river to help isolate Mosul. We're going in on the far side of the Zab to provide support for their assault."

Frank's finger hovered over the river. "A few thousand Kurdish fighters are doing a contested river crossing here. Just like at the Tigris, we have to provide obscuration so they can get across." As if he had practiced the motion a thousand times, the platoon leader dragged his finger to draw the line of advance.

"Once they're across, they're going to move to take these villages east of Mosul to help isolate it. There are a few hundred ISIL fighters in the area, so we'll be providing fire support constantly."

"We're inserting early morning on August 12th, Blackhawks and Chinooks. First serial will be-" He pointed at himself, Burkett, and Joseph. "The pathfinder crew so we can mark the L.Z. for the guns to get dropped."

He pointed at the FDC crew and infantrymen. "Radar truck will also be on the first drop, along with security. Our ground assault convoy with extra ammo and personnel, along with a combat cameraman, will push through to help secure the area also once we arrive. Everyone else will come on the next two serials of birds."

"The Battery commander and my group will ride on one Blackhawk the first wave. Gunny Joseph, your crew will be on the other." Frank pointed to me. "This is Lt. Johnson, an *infantryman* assigned to the brigade PAO. Obviously, they're of little use out here and he wants to see the *King of Battle* in action."

There were some chuckles as some of the Soldiers regarded me.

"Brigade PAO, huh?" Staff Sgt. Walker, one of the section leaders, said, looking intently. His voice had a gravelly tone to it, akin to Christian Bale's Batman character. At 25, he wasn't all that much older than the Soldiers in his section.

"You're the guy who put Mont's face everywhere."

Recognition among more of the Soldiers, though some more ambivalent looks, and I could have sworn I saw someone cracking their knuckles like we were in a video game as the circle closed in around me.

"Your face will be everywhere too?" I said lamely, lest they thought I was playing favorites. Walker smirked at my line, and the room relaxed, as if that answer was the only one that I could have said before the battle music started.

"Where do you want to ride? Frank continued, looking towards me. You're coming on the first lift with us; the B.C. doesn't want you to miss anything."

"I'll ride with Gunny Joseph," I said, nodding towards the man, who smiled victoriously.

"Works for me. Stick with him during the rehearsals and mission. You are joining us for those?"

"Yep."

"Good, they'll start in a couple of hours."

The briefing ended abruptly as it started, the Soldiers' returning to their bunks. I wandered around for a bit before ending up in the center of the tent again. Staff Sgt. Walker was the first to approach me as I sat there.

"I heard you use GoPro footage." Turning towards his section, he nodded his head upwards. "We can get you a whole lot of that."

"I've been in the Army for over ten years. Hell, this isn't even my first rodeo in Iraq." Gunny Joseph's voice, trying to speak over the commotion of helicopter engines running. We sat in the middle of a field of Erbil, waiting for the birds to pick up their personnel and equipment and make their test run over our position.

"I was going to leave after my first contract, but Hurricane Katrina destroyed my home in New Orleans." He looked around, taking in the Erbil air. "The Army was all I had left, so I signed up again."

"Why do they call you Gunny?"

"Oh?" he gestured towards the rest of the platoon. "Infantry platoons have one platoon sergeant, we kind of have two. "Smoke" is the senior NCO, "Gunny" is the less senior position. I'm more in charge of the handling, accountability, transportation, and distribution of ammunition."

"Have you ever done something like this before?"

"Yeah." He paused, his expression changing. "My first deployment as an artilleryman, they used up to plus up infantry units. Route clearance, cordons, house to house patrols. It was something."

Joseph shot me a look. "I probably went to Pathfinder school when you were in high school."

"Did they have color photography back then?"

"This generation man…" he began.

"Well, now we're here together." I finished, smirking.

"Making me famous!"

The helicopters lifted off, carrying the artillery pieces below them. Sling Loading, what the 101st prided itself on being able to do. With two combat aviation brigades available to the division, it could move entire battalions and their equipment at one time, if need be. Unfortunately, when I arrived in 2014, one of the CABs was disbanded, which stretched the lift capability to the limit. That didn't stop the push for all Soldiers to go to Air Assault School where ostensibly Soldiers were taught how to conduct sling load operations.

Cool and all, except that the sling load portion was only three days out of the ten-day course. The division also had a sling load inspector's class, which was multiple weeks long but didn't give you the cool helicopter badge.

Guess which one was pushed more?

"Hook it up!" Joseph yelled, and two Soldiers rushed towards the bird, fighting the gusts of wind created by the blades. They dropped into the prone position, allowing the wind to wash over their bodies. Crawling under the aircraft, the two Soldiers flipped to their backs as they connected the hook, the crew chief on the helicopter giving them a thumbs up when they were good to go. Rolling out, they crawled away, getting into a low crouch when they were finally behind the gun.

The Chinook lifted off, slowly, the pilot feeling for anything out of the ordinary. A pause at the full extension of the rope, then the moment of truth: The gun left the Earth and stayed there.

"Looking good," Gunny remarked as the ropes beneath the helicopters extended fully, the M777s hanging in the air underneath the birds. In video games, pieces of equipment are attached to the aircraft itself, but we're not quite to that level of technology yet. Instead, they're attached by giant ropes called sling legs. Simple enough concept except that if you mess up the rigging the equipment can fall out of the sky, or, in the worst case, crash the helicopter.

Hence all these dry runs before we left. The Chinooks flew over the airfield giving their loads a test before turning towards the spot where Gunny and I sat.

"All right, L.T.," Gunny pulled out two red signaling flags. "Make sure to get my best side."

"With this many rehearsals, I'll be able to give you an entire gallery."

Staff Sgt. Darryl Joseph during rehearsals for the artillery raid, August, 2016. U.S. Army photo by Daniel Johnson

Capt. Berlin was adamant that we rehearse every part of the operation, day and night. With an extremely tight timeline like the one this operation had, a fuckup could cost lives or throw the entire offensive off synch.

It wasn't exactly a first-class experience being a passenger in the Blackhawks. Fully kitted up, the procedure to enter was two Soldiers, then all our bags and gear, then the rest of the serial. The pilots would count down at specified intervals, 5 minutes, 1 minute, 30 seconds, and then activate the green light. At that point we'd jump out and immediately go into the prone position with our rifles at the ready pulling security, and our bags would quite literally be thrown on top of us by the crew before they lifted off to get the next serial. The whole process only took seconds, because if the bird was taking fire, they sure weren't sticking around.

Who could blame them?

"This is a deliberate operation," Sgt. 1st Class Burkett said to me as the drowning of an aircraft taking off muddled his voice. "When we do these raids, we get in, do what we have to do, and get out before the enemy knows we're there."

"And if they do find out we're there?" I asked. Burkett shrugged nonchalantly. "That's what we'll have trenches for."

"With no overhead cover? What if we take a direct hit?"

"Then you pray."

The night was a different story then our relaxed day time rehearsals since we were at the point where we could do the operation in our sleep, and we

144

practically were. On one evening we had loaded up, did our lap around the airfield, and then disembarked, moving under our night vision goggles to our usual positions. The L.Z. was marked and the guns were hooked up. Too easy.

Kneeling next to Gunny Joseph, I could barely keep my eyes open. Everyone was exhausted and moving through pure muscle memory, which I guess was the point. In the distance I could hear the Chinook hooking up to the artillery piece to begin its run.

"Holy shit!" Gunny exclaimed as he happened to glance back at the tarmac. His body tensed up, and whatever exhaustion that he was feeling before immediately dissipated due to an adrenaline rush.

I turned my head to catch a peek.

The M777 was in the air, hanging lopsided a couple of dozen feet off the ground with the barrel pointing downwards. The Chinook struggled against the unbalanced weight, changing directions in the air constantly like an addled old man.

The bird started to stall and dip towards the Earth.

It was right over a pallet of high explosive rounds.

Click.

The front of the gun dropped.

Thud.

The back of the gun collided with the Earth as the Chinook gracefully slipped away.

Crash.

The rest of the gun landed in a heap, the sound of the impact echoing through the night. We were lucky- they had cut sling load away from the HE rounds.

Everyone on our side of the airfield looked towards the sound. Gunny shook his head and said what we were all thinking.

"That gun is fucked."

All action ceased immediately, Berlin and the rest of the leadership quickly rushing over to the piece. The rest of the Soldiers stayed in their positions, some falling asleep almost immediately. Maybe the rehearsals were over. Perhaps they could enjoy another day of relaxation in Erbil.

Aft hook failure was what the Lt. Col. in charge of the aviators called the accident. The crew had responded excellently to the situation, dropping the load before it brought them down. We were lucky: if they had been using the short sling-load ropes instead of the long ones that night, the Chinook probably wouldn't have made it and could have crashed into the Earth and the

HE rounds on the Tarmac. Most of us on the ground probably would have gotten killed too due to the HE rounds setting off.

A meeting was held at the gun, the figures gesticulating in the night. The aviation guys came down and joined in; head shakes, pointing towards the gun, which told us in the audience it was kaput. More back and forth, some calls. A head nod now from the higher ranked. Some more pointing in the telltale motion of orders being given.

Gunny Joseph jogged back over to our position.

"Commander said we're going to keep on rehearsing. They're bringing down another gun from KSB tonight."

"Tonight? That's quick as hell."

"They really want this thing to happen. The OP is still on for tomorrow night."

Chapter Nine-The Gun Raid

The wait is the worst part of the entire thing. All the time in the world to play out your worst fears, your greatest fantasies. Time for rumors to swirl about how the bad guys would be waiting for us on the LZ, or how would immediately bracket our raid site with IDF. Maybe we wouldn't even make it to the ground.

"The last time 1-320th did an Air Assault like this they got blown out of the sky," a random Soldier in a tent at LSA Strike. "This is bad luck." Of course, he had no skin in the game since he wouldn't be joining us on the mission but just had to let us know what he thought. I "thanked" him for his history lesson — another image to throw into the pile of the scenarios that continuously presented themselves.

All driven by the human obsession with the unknown. All playing out in our heads, if the muted silence among the group as we laid on our packs on the airfield was any indication. For a lot of us, the whole idea of flying into battle in the dead of night was something in video games and movies. Yet here we were.

Growing our force by 50%, sending Soldiers on offensive missions, and now sitting on the tarmac, kitted up, M4s loaded, ammunition stacked, about to fly into a random spot in the countryside and turn it into a chess piece in the ultimate game-strange what a non-combat "advising" operation entailed.

The evening turned into night, the bright lights in the city of Erbil visible in the distance. Civilian flights hummed in the twilight, bringing in tourists, civilians, adventurers.

A totally different reality.

30 minutes. Last-minute checks. NVGs, assault packs, food, water. Tension.

To think, a few years before I'd be moving back into Appalachian State about now.

5 minutes.

We massed on the edge of the tarmac, kneeling. Barely any sleep for the past few days, yet wide awake. I wish I could say we were excited, but we just wanted to get the whole thing over with.

The helicopters landed, red lights visible in the night as their cargo doors opened so we could enter. We marched forward, the only statement that I could remember hearing as we began our boarding sequence being "Finally."

Two flashes.

One was something outside of the aircraft, white, unnatural, discoloring the black night.

The next flash was red, UH-60's automatic defense system firing off its flares. It reacted to certain types of lighting without the need for human input --- the kind of light usually associated with anti-aircraft weapons. If it gets a read, it will fire automatically without the need for pilot input.

Thump-hiss. Thump-hiss.

Multiple sounds, the red fire from the flares filling the air suddenly like something in Star Wars.

A huge adrenaline rush, our bodies tensing up. Quick, immediate, so powerful that the "Oh shit!" and "Fuck!" came out of everyone's mouths almost subconsciously. The reflection of the flares highlighting everyone's faces in blood red as we shuddered, waiting for something that would indicate if our lives were over or if the game was still on.

The pilot banked and then began to descend towards the ground, off schedule, a signal that we needed to be dropped off - fast. The field rapidly approached, the terrain features becoming more apparent in the twilight the closer we got. Five, four, three, two, -

Green light. Gunny Joseph leaped into the night, the dust from the powerful rotors picking up the loose lying dirt and clouding his vision. The rest of us fell in behind him, hitting the ground with thuds and crawling forward. Our bags came out last, hitting us in the back of our heads as the crew chiefs pushed them out.

Just as quickly as we landed, the birds were gone. Gunny got up and looked around as we gathered our gear. I silently cursed the fucker who had almost jinxed us back in Erbil.

"We're in the wrong spot." Gunny continued to look around, spotting a hill. He leaned down to the rest of us. "Come on; the LZ is over there. Stay tight on me, L.T."

With that, he began to move into the night, leaving whatever the hell happened in the air behind. The adrenaline from the insertion and the fact that we were on the ground had made all our exhaustion dissipate. Joseph was moving fast, almost at a light jog, M4 at the low ready.

An explosion in the distance added ambient light as we crested the hill overlooking our original LZ. Gunny looked at the location for a moment and then turned back to us with a "This is it." He motioned to the assembled group kneeling below the top.

"Check that berm over there," he said calmly, pointing the Soldiers in the right direction. "Pop those chem lights and start shaking them." I pulled out my notepad, holding it along with my M4 to scribble notes about what was going on; I hoped that my writing would be legible the next day. We began moving forward, and a thought hit me as I remembered him sitting in his bunk in Erbil while everyone else was relaxing. He was studying the imagery of the raid site the entire time. The fact that we were dropped in a different location than planned initially *didn't even slow him down*- I guess the guy was Pathfinder qualified for a reason. That was the whole point of the course --- pathfinders provide navigational aid to incoming aircraft, and select, mark, improve, and control landing sites.

The Chinooks carrying the radar vehicle and communications equipment came in behind us as we moved forward. Like something out of Halo, one of them came in low bringing the radar truck, dropping it with a soft impact and kicking up dust. As the first Chinook turned off to return to base, the second Chinook landed, its ramp opening like a jaw. More artillerymen and Cav Scouts waddling out and over the side before getting in the prone. In less than a minute, that Chinook was off too as the Soldiers split up into two different groups. One headed for where the command post would be located, and the others jumped into the radar vehicle to start driving towards their pre-planned spot.

The marking team arrived at the berm and began to get down to business. Joseph moved purposefully as he and the Soldiers worked to make sure the LZ was visible from all directions, raising his voice only to be heard above the sound of Soldiers executing his orders. Well-rehearsed, it didn't take long for the group to complete their-

CRASH.

Grinding, mechanical in nature, echoing through the silence of the night. Everyone on the LZ paused to look towards the sound.

The radar vehicle had driven into a ditch and was now canted downward.

"Let the medics worry about that," Gunny's voice cut through our reverie. "Get back to work; we got more birds coming."

The marking team got back on task as Joseph walked the area once, then again, to make sure everything was correct. Down at the damaged vehicle, the medics pulled out the Soldier who was driving.

They asked her where she was hurt.

She told them it was a slight pain in her back.

While pointing at her head.

Two more Blackhawks soon arrived, dropping gracefully at the top of the hill, this time not releasing flares. More artillerymen and cavalry scouts jumped out, their silhouettes moving towards the security perimeter.

Thump. Thump. Thump.

The telltale rumble of Chinooks in the distance signifying that the guns were right behind.

"Do you have eyes on?" Joseph radioed to the pilots as they approached.

The response came back affirmative, and the helicopters made their approach, floating toward the landing zone. They got closer to the berms and then-

We were in a tornado. Dust, rocks, grass, ricocheting off our skin with enough force for you to hear to make it feel like you got stung by a bee. I tried to breathe but found myself swallowing and inhaling dirt. I wish I could come up with something to describe being 7,000 miles away from home, in the middle of the night, experiencing something I knew that would never happen to me again. From the second those flares went off, no movie, video game, rollercoaster ride, *anything*, could match that feeling.

That's why Soldiers keep on chasing it after they come home.

We got small, hugging the Earth to try to reduce the damage; it didn't help, and we soon found ourselves caked in moon dust.

We were ghosts in the night, both in appearance and action.

With a dull thud, the guns were released onto the ground and the CH-47s turned off into the night, leaving as quickly as they arrived. Working under the lime-green hue of their night vision goggles, the Soldiers moved their guns as they began setting up the systems, making adjustments, digging in, running lines.

"Got a problem with one of the guns." Lt. Frank on the radio. "Mechanical issue, we have to re-lay it."

"Roger," Gunny replied, shaking his head. He looked at me. "It's the same shit we had to rush down from KSB."

"At this rate, the whole battery will be down."

"You're telling me."

More Chinooks came in, ramps open. A second, smaller buzzing from inside the aircraft, and then suddenly a tiny 4-wheeler shooting out down the ramp, followed by more Soldiers. Its load delivered, the CH-47 peeled off as a few of the reinforcements grabbed on to the side of the vehicle and rode into the night.

Gun trucks from the ground assault convoy rumbled across the area, drone defense weapons in their interiors, as they moved to reinforce the perimeter. Down at the command post, communications specialists worked on establishing satellite communications. They pulled out a deflated container and began to air it up, like some sort of balloon. Within minutes it became a ball, about man-size: the GATR Ball, for missions like this, where the larger satellite vehicles were unable to be used. It didn't allow for a ton of data to be transferred, but it was enough for the FDC and CP.

Our hasty firebase began to take form, and aside from the one artillery piece, was mostly functional. Early warning radar, FDC, perimeter security, ammunition, just like we had practiced. Suddenly, we all started to crash, the adrenaline flooding out of our systems. Most of us collapsed by the guns, laying on the dirt.

I fell asleep next to a Soldier propped up on a crate of High Explosive Shells, figuring that if we did get blown up, at least I'd be well-rested.

By first light gun 2 was ready, and it was time to fire.

"Come on, let's go!"

I turned my head towards the sound, my vision clearing up. It was daytime, the sun rising over the hills to the east. Had long had I been asleep? Glancing down at my watch, I sighed.

One hour.

The Kurds were moving to cross the Great Zab River, and they needed smoke to cover their crossing. Artillerymen were readying their pieces, going through their crew drills. I pulled out my camera and GoPro and moved to a proper angle.

"Hey! Put this on your helmet!" I called one of the Soldiers, the loader. He had the best first-person angle. It took a couple of seconds before he put it in his helmet band, returning to his duties. Smoke missions are fired at a consistent rate to maintain coverage, utilizing white phosphorus. The rounds are designed to explode upon contact with the air and create a lasting smoke cloud, but winds dissipate it, hence the need for a steady cadence.

Boom......One round off. A pause for a while, then the next one loaded.

Boom.

The crews were at it for hours, ensuring that the obscuration was set.

It didn't take long for the heat to take its toll.

Soldiers would fall asleep in-between rounds, only being woken up by the next firing. I glanced down at Gunny at one moment.

He was asleep a few feet away from the gun. The sounds of the explosions didn't even stir him.

Soldiers from 1st Platoon, C Battery, 1320th FA, firing during the artillery raid, August, 2016. U.S. Army photo by Daniel Johnson.

Already exhausted and a little dehydrated from training the days before, the added body armor and helmets did little to help things in the 110+ degree weather. The guns are *hot,* like standing by a fire. Running the rounds that weighed 100LBs each was like adding kindling to it.

"We're black on water," Frank's voice, reporting to Capt. Berlin. We were gathered around the gun, looking at one of the few bottles left. He picked it up, then immediately put it back down.

"That shit is hot," he glanced over at Gunny, shaking his head.

"I'm not drinking that." Gunny put his hands up, refusing the bottle.

"I'll give it a sip," my reply, grabbing it and twisting the cap off slowly, bringing it up to drink.

I wanted to throw up. The liquid was 100 degrees, easy. Gunny watched me in a mix of amazement and disgust that I was forcing it down my throat. My throat and stomach started to bubble, forcing me to stop, spitting out the small amount I couldn't get down. By the afternoon the first Soldier had collapsed, falling over in the middle of running rounds. Those still standing were close to sharing his fate; their movements grew sluggish, their reactions detached. They were firing shells off pure muscle memory.

Berlin radioed up to the battalion that we needed water and ice now. The whole raid site was about to become a heat casualty.

"We'll get some out to you, keep working," was the reply.

Berlin wasn't pleased at that response, to say the least. Especially since more Soldiers were cramping up as he was on the call, including *him.*

A senior enlisted Soldier in 1-320th's HHC took matters into his own hands in Erbil, gathering water, ice, and some Soldiers. In a civilian vehicle, right in the middle of the offensive, they drove across the battlefield following the same route the ground assault convoy did to resupply the raid site.

Big difference though – they didn't have gun trucks with them.

The aviation assets in Erbil were also spun up for resupply and Gunny Joseph and Frank rode out to set up an LZ for a drop. Speedball resupply, where helicopters dropped in tightly packed packages filled with mission critical items to the Earth. The bird paused just long enough to drop their cargo out of the sky before turning off to return to Erbil for another run; below, them Gunny and Frank hastily loaded the ATV with water.

We drank that stuff like we had never tasted water before. Entire bottles gulped down in seconds.

"Gatorade power, put some Gatorade powder in there!" Gunny ordered, attempting to get us to replace our depleted electrolytes instead of draining our systems. I usually hated "Army Electrolyte Powder" as it was called.

That was the best damn Gatorade I've ever had.

When the sun set in the evening, it seemed to just ...fall behind the horizon at a rapid rate at speed. I could literally *see* it moving. I've been all over the world, and I haven't seen anything like it since. But then again, I also haven't ever been that dehydrated and exhausted.

After the resupply efforts, we were back a base level of hydration, if you could even call it that. The smoke missions had done their job and the Kurds and their enablers crossed the river in one day. Now, they consolidated and began to move on the villages on the road to Mosul. The call came down to the firebase and the smoke rounds were switched out for HE, to basically blast a path through ISIL defenses for the next few days.

"There are drones watching us." Lt. Frank, looking towards the perimeter from the guns. On the outskirts of the firebase, the Cav Scouts identified the telltale shapes floating in the air like evil spirits. Too small to be ours, too big to be animals.

"You think it's the Kurds?" my question, trying to come up with a safe reason.

"2-502 is with them, why would they need to watch us?"

We lied there in silence, staring into the night. Thoughts of getting attacked by unmanned vehicles played through our heads. I wish I could call it fear, but no-

It was resignation.

"It's kind of crazy that the robots are hunting us, for once." I offered to try to break the tension.

"Yeah." Frank paused, a look of realization and thoughtfulness coming over his face. "It was only a matter of time."

Silence. The uneasy feeling that just wouldn't go away, our minds running through a million scenarios. We were witnessing a changing world.

The UAVs were just close enough that they could see us, but just far enough that we couldn't do anything about them unless we filled the sky with lead. All either side could do was watch and wait.

And hope the other didn't make a move.

Daylight came. The offensive continued — Staff Sgt. James Johnson, the fire direction chief for Battery C, sat in the back of his fire direction center truck looking intently at his radio, waiting for a call for fire.

"This is where the magic happens," Johnson said as he concentrated on his console.

"You're an infantryman, sir, so let me dumb this down for you and explain how this all works." He flashed me a cocky smile as I shook my head.

"Observers, which can consist of assets from the ISF, unmanned aerial vehicles and other aircraft, acquire targets they need hit. Once the HQ receives the data, they push it to my team and me at the FDC." He patted his equipment like he was a car salesman trying to make a deal.

"All we need is a connection to the observers, even if the battalion HQ isn't involved."

Hence the reason why the battery was now in this location. As the Kurds advanced the targets shifted, engaging the ISIL fighters in the villages on the offensive's path. Though not as large as the rolling barrages of WWI or WWII, the idea was still the same. Keep the enemy suppressed or killed while the infantry advanced.

Frank came jogging by.

"Coalition troops got hit with some indirect fire; Battery Commander wants us to stay in full kit."

With that, he disappeared.

Johnson and I shared a look. Coalition troops?

2-502.

They had an advising element with the headquarters of the Kurdish Forces for the offensive. Then, as Frank said, they got hit.

Literally.

A mortar round exploded directly over the heads, raining them with shrapnel, metal bits bouncing off their body armor. They lucked out: a little lower and the concussive force may have done some severe damage.

Advise and assist, totally safe. No boots on the ground. Yeah, right.

Especially when reporters covering the offensive found the 2-502 Soldiers at the HQ, and then watched in amusement as they all turned their backs to the media and covered their faces like some sort of Special Forces element.

Back at the raid site, a few hundred feet away from the FDC, gun crews were moving around their weapon systems. They checked and rechecked minute details, made small adjustments, all while waiting to spring into action once the call was sent. A small lull in the action, enough time to try to relax in the shade of the trucks, though that didn't do much good. The weather was so warm that even the shade wasn't a respite.

Just then, the radio crackled, and Johnson grabbed his hand mic, listening to the data. He then began his battle drill, one he'd done many times before: The message to the gun line, "Gun 2, fire mission." A moment later. "Gun 1, fire mission."

"Sweep and Zone."

Sweep and Zone directed the crews to fire a pattern an "X" on the target and surrounding area. It was a massive display of firepower, and this call was for *fifty* rounds.

Down at Gun 2, the crew led by Staff Sgt. Johnathan Walker sprung up as the radio beeped; in seconds, they were at the firing position going through their crew drill.

"Come on," Walker yelled to the crew as they prepared rounds and took their positions. "Let's make money!"

His catch phrase before a fire mission, his gravelly voice rising above the din. One of the Soldiers nodded to him, making a negative motion.

"Shit."

Gun 2 was the one that had mechanical issues during the insertion, the one that had been rushed down from KSB. Now, during the biggest mission of the raid, rounds had to be fired degraded- utilizing no digital assistance. Scribbling in his notebook, Walker calculated the quadrant -- up and down -- and deflection -- left and right – required for each round. He had to do it 25

155

times, with no mechanical assistance, on the fly, in minutes, while suffering from exhaustion and dehydration.

He didn't make a single mistake.

The crew members looked through the sites and adjusted the gun as Walker yelled the fire data.

"Fire!" yelled the crew chief, and a Soldier gave the firing lanyard a slight tug. The gun responded to this small motion, shaking the Earth around the position as a high explosive shell was launched.

Staff Sgt. Jonathan Walker's section in action, with 1st Platoon, C Battery, 1320th FA, firing during the artillery raid, August, 2016. U.S. Army photo by Daniel Johnson.

"Let's get through this!" Walker yelled as he called off the quadrant and deflection for the next round. Driven by their chief, the Soldiers moved faster as the mission continued. The dash endured through round after round, the dust hanging in the air from the explosions adding to the salt from sweat stinging the Soldiers' eyes.

The ammo carriers were running rounds weighing over 90 pounds from the holding point to the gun, heaving the shells into the firing tube like turkey. Walkers' voice was growing hoarser as he yelled adjustments and commands, and behind the weapon, it felt like being in the middle of a pan, everything else dissipating in the distance.

Finally, an ending.

"Last round," the ammo bearer said as he walked up to Walker. With a nod, Walker readied for his last command of the mission.

"Ready -- FIRE!" he barked, bringing his hand down. After the last boom, the team began to celebrate, yelling and throwing their fists into the air.

"That was awesome guys," Frank said as he walked up and gave the Soldiers high-fives. At one point during the mission, he grabbed more rounds for them so they could keep going. "Everyone is impressed with what you did. You guys are making Mosul great again, one 155 round at a time."

There was a pause as he looked at me, and I stared back.

He shrugged. "You can put that in your article, it sounds cool."

"Are you sure?"

"Yeah, I want to be in there too."

"Alright then. If people end up commenting on it online, don't say I didn't warn you."

Unfortunately, our mutual friend Maj. Knoedler would not find it so cool, dressing down Frank afterwards and calling him immature, while at the same time praising him for his excellent work on the mission.

Guess you can't win them all.

Walker smiled at the praise and the performance of the men as he took off his helmet and he looked around the gun position.

"This is the life," he said, smiling. "This whole operation is what artillery is about; shoot, move, and communicate."

There wasn't much time for rest. Another sweep and zone would be called, and then more missions after that.

Seventy-two hours of continuous support, as Operation Evergreen II turned into a massive success: 12 villages seized, 150 square kilometers liberated, 12 miles of ground gained from the Great Zab river, and over 160 ISIL fighters eliminated.

Mosul was now cut off in the east.

The exfiltration was much more peaceful, and we didn't even hit the showers before we rushed to the DFAC still covered in white dust from being underneath the helicopters during insertion and extraction. The cook on the night shift recoiled in shock when he saw us; people who looked like extras in a zombie film. We looked like shit, but we were so hungry we didn't care.

Sodas, chicken, sauces, we gobbled it down like it was the best meal in our lives.

Looking back, it really was.

There was practically no time to rest; The guns were getting hooked up to vehicles and the artillerymen were leaving the next day to return to KSB. I found Gunny near the tent as he took a breather for a moment.

"Going to make us famous, sir?" he asked with a grin.

"I'll try," my reply. "That was something else."

Gunny shrugged in his usual calm way, leaning back and sighing, "This is what we train for. This is what we do."

"Glad I could see you do it."

"You're a good kid, L.T. We appreciate you being out there."

"It's my job, where else would I be?"

"We need more officers like you."

The fact that Joseph treated this whole thing like going to the grocery store stuck with me. We shook hands and I wished him luck.

When I returned to LSA Strike, I was asleep before I even hit the cot.

Ring.

What.

Ring.

My phone, someone calling me.

Ring.

"Hello?" my tired voice.

"*Sleeping L.T.?* Where's the footage at?" Maj. Sanders asked, almost sounding like she was about to jump through the phone.

"We just got back, ma'am." My reply, a losing battle, and I knew it.

"They want their footage. *I want that footage.* You knew what you were signing up for. I need it today."

"Yes, ma'am." My reply, crisp and clean, now fully awake. She wasn't joking around.

I pulled out my laptop and began to download the footage — a slow process due to the old shitty video camera I had. I worked on the photos as I waited, selecting ten good ones, three for the article, just like the bosses wanted. Cutting the video took a moment, but, thanks to the GoPros I gave out and the ones the Soldiers had, we got every angle. I even matched the GoPro videos with my vids, seamlessly going from 1st person view to 3rd, cutting and merging the sound right on top of each other.

The article didn't take too long, a stream of consciousness that was fresh in my mind since we had just returned hours ago. The hastily scrawled notes during the insertion, videos I had taken, sights, sounds, they were all thrown in.

I had it to Maj. Sanders within hours, and by that afternoon it was at the division headquarters being reviewed. As soon as we got it'd back, we'd-

"We're going to hold off on releasing this right now."

Great. The email from Sgt. 1st Class Hoskins said it all. No one wanted to touch this, at least publically. The whole flying out in the dead of night for an offensive operation was a little *much*.

Maj. Sanders was livid at the fact that we had provided exactly what the division wanted and now they were holding up the public release. I don't know what she and Lt. Col. Thomas said to each other over the phone, but they both dug in, hard. Finally, Thomas said she'd run my news release by Maj. Gen. Volesky *himself.* The fact that the Commander of CJFLCC-OIR would *personally* read my article was a little gratifying, if scary. I couldn't blame them; it was an abrupt change from "Totally safe, all Iraqis, no boots on the ground," which was already a pretty loose narrative. At least everyone had gotten the video, and the photos, and everything else they could use for their internal products — all except, oh I don't know, the actual news release about the Soldiers.

"Be patient L.T; I'll work on it." Maj. Sanders assured me. "But there are other things going on. I'm going to see about getting you to Qayyarah West."

Interlude II-App State- 2012

"You stop learning; you start dying."

Master Sgt. Wetmore's words were stuck in my head, an offhand statement he gave during one of his classes.

It stuck with me.

I was a much better student, pulling my grades from C and Bs to straight As. My physical fitness was up, and I could run a two-mile in just over 13 minutes asleep. Things were looking good, and all I had to do was finish strong and I'd get active duty and my branch of choice.

I just had to sink or swim.

Literally.

"Come on, Johnson," Wetmore's voice from the side of the pool as he watched me treading water. "It'll be harder in a full uniform!"

My arms were getting weak and I glanced at the wall clock.

Not even five minutes.

I needed ten to pass the real thing.

The Cadet Water Survival Test was a graduation requirement for all future commissioning officers. Blindfolded dive, rifle swim, equipment ditch. Ten-minute swim.

All in uniform and boots.

I finally tired out, and my feet touched the bottom. Wetmore shook his head. "Getting there, Johnson, getting there."

He looked at the clock, watching it count to 59, then 00.

"Begin again."

"Come on; you can do it!"

The swim teacher was cheering me on as I did my laps. Extra classes twice a week, plus the Friday morning at swim P.T. Wetmore conducted.

I hit the far wall, doing the transition to turn around, waving at one of the lifeguards I had a crush on.

She rolled her eyes.

Can't win them all, I guess.

Backstroke, forward stroke, flotation tube, flippers. Back and forth, back and forth, for an hour, late into the night. Some days it felt like I was going backward.

My swim class teachers had spouses in the military, and they kept on pushing me, motivating me, night after night. They didn't have to.

They did anyway.

Morning P.T., the gym, swim class, college classes, all of it blurring together.

People *believing* that I could be better, that I could learn, that I was worth putting their time into.

I couldn't betray that trust. I may not have been able to do it, but I had to at least *try*. I had to prove I was worth that faith in me, even when I didn't have confidence in myself.

This was it. The diving board was easy. The rifle swim was leisurely. The equipment ditch was natural.

Now I had to survive for 10 minutes.

"Ready!" The senior cadet called, looking at his watch.

"Begin!"

We all jumped in, some whooping and hollering like we were at a water park. My ACUs caught some water, and I began kicking and moving my arms.

One minute.

Good to go. Stay focused. I envied the guys who were laughing and talking like they were sitting on the couch, playing video games.

Four minutes.

My body was starting to feel it, and I began to glance at the wall clock. Fear began to creep in.

Six minutes.

I couldn't do it. Panic. Trying to keep my head above water. Seven minutes thirty seconds.

I grabbed the wall.

I failed.

Rage at myself as I hit the side. My best wasn't good enough- I wasn't good enough- my military career was over before it started.

"Get out of the pool, Johnson and go to the side," Wetmore ordered, pointing to a spot on the deck. I sat there and watched as everybody else passed.

I was the only loser.

As they got out of the pool, victorious, Wetmore waved them off and said he'd see us all in class. Once they all left, he turned to me. I hung my head low, waiting for the final words that I'd failed. I deserved them.

"Seven minutes and thirty seconds," he began, looking at me. "You gave up on yourself and panicked. *You* beat yourself."

I couldn't even look him in the eye.

"You know why the standard is ten minutes?"

"No, Sergeant Major."

"Because I wanted you all to train above the minimum. To *push* yourselves."

I finally looked up, in shock.

"All you had to do was five minutes to pass. You're a go."

With that, he walked off, the lesson completed.

It wasn't about the water or swimming. It was about that internal drive, because in the absence of all else, whether it was the threat of my career ending, getting dressed down, or being told I couldn't do it-

That would be all that mattered.

Chapter Ten-Shutdown - September 2016

LSA Strike had changed from a small outpost to a tent city as the reinforcements had arrived. Five hundred more Soldiers, from 1-26, 526 BSB, and 39th Engineers. For three months they had been waiting for the call at Campbell, and you could tell who had just arrived in Iraq because their Multicam was still green, not the washed-out tan from the sun damage.

"Hey, hey!" the voice of Sgt. Owen called out in the camp.

"I thought you were in Baghdad!" my reply as we shook hands.

"Nah, they said they need marksmen for this Q-West mission, so I got pulled up here."

"Glad to be out of Union III?"

"You know it. Not so many generals up here. This place is sweet."

He glanced at my faded uniform. "What have you been up to?"

"Just got back from an air assault artillery raid with 1-320th. It was...something."

A pause. Awkward silence. A skeptical look.

"You *do* get around sir. When do *I* get an article? I feel like I could be the face of the Army or something, like the photo taken of me at JRTC...." He laughed.

"As soon as we get the Q-West, hopefully."

"You're going? That's great!"

"Yep, that's the plan."

August 27th would be the most significant ground convoy operation so far during Operation Inherent Resolve, and there were ten days to get ready for it. Qayyarah West Airfield had been scouted a few weeks back: the bullet holes from a sniper in one of the MATVs bore testament to the danger of doing so.

The biggest issue was space in the vehicles, and the fact the leadership said every single person on the movement had to have a purpose-confirmed by said high level officials of course.

Maj. Sanders sent me to KSB to grab some footage to use at NFL games, and while there, I found the opening we were both looking for.

"We're down a guy," Staff Sgt. Villarreal, as I talked to them by their radar truck. The whole area was different; most of the gear now packed in a container that CW2 Miranda's crew would drag behind them.

"He got hurt and had to get evacuated, and we're not getting any replacements." He whispered as if he was conspiring, glancing around the area. "You could come along; you know you want to. We have a spot for you. You and Maj. Sanders are the only people from the headquarters company that seem to care about us."

"All we have to do is say you're riding with us." Chief Miranda concurred, nodding his head. It would be too easy, my name replacing another. No one would get mad because that seat was empty anyway; I would go in, get the footage, and when Q-West was finally stabilized, catch the next thing smoking out of there.

"How long do you think it would be?" I asked.

"About a month most likely," Villarreal replied. "Until more movements start going back and forth. Rough living, rocket attacks. You know, the usual. In a rush to get back?"

"To just sit around in Erbil? Not particularly."

"No holes underground this time too," Miranda continued. "We hope."

"It would be pretty good footage, worthy of someone of your *caliber,*" Villarreal continued, egging me on. "What other place would you rather be?"

"Back home, playing videogames, I guess?"

"But you're the one who volunteered to come. And this is much more intense than any video game can ever hope to be, good or bad."

"Ah, touché."

"I *am* very high caliber," I agreed, nodding my head, his words having the desired effect. "The footage would be pretty good..."

"Maj. Sanders will love it too," Villarreal finished, as all three of us were now smiling like Cheshire cats at the brilliance of this plan.

"I'll call Maj. Sanders on your phone. Let her know what's going on." I began to move towards the trucks.

"What's up L.T.?"

"Looks like I got a spot to Q-West ma'am." I nodded at Miranda and Villarreal. "Chief Miranda's radar crew has an open spot since one of their Soldiers was injured."

"*Really.*" I knew that voice, the wheels were turning. There was a pause for a moment. "Stay flexible L.T. I'll do the groundwork to get you on the movement. Wait until I call you. This is our chance. Documenting the occupation of Q-West is right up our alley."

I gave a thumbs-up to Villarreal and Miranda; we were all practically already there. All I had to do was grab my gear from Erbil. Maj. Sanders did her part, ensuring that my name was on the manifest and that there would be no surprises. The battalion approved it.

Then the brigade X.O., doing a line-by-line review of the manifest, saw my name.

Everything had come to a head.

As an Infantry Officer, I was "supposed" to go to Ranger School, graduate, and do my platoon leader time. Then, it'd be time for me to suck in the operations shop, maybe get company executive officer time, and then, *perhaps* I'd get selected to go to Iraq.

No one was supposed to be able to get around paying their dues.

Maj. Sanders hid the fact that I was on the air assault until after it had happened, and now I was going on the largest ground convoy since Inherent Resolve had begun?

"Have you done any K.D. time yet?" the question from Maj. Sanders, as I prepared my gear in Erbil. I had finally gotten my extra bags from Kuwait, giving me two additional uniforms to wear.

Her question had come out of the left field and confused me. I responded that I hadn't, which was the whole reason I was working with her in the first place. My mind raced with possibilities.

Maybe they're thinking of putting me into an infantry platoon leader slot?

Had she been working on something like that this entire time? It was exceedingly common for a switch to happen mid tour or even before a unit left if an officer got all the months he/she needed.

"We need to talk," her reply, short, concise. "Come to Camp Swift as soon as possible."

I sighed inwardly. I had been in Iraq for just about 90 days, so the gig was up.

"Should I begin packing my stuff for a trip back?"

"No, it doesn't have to do with that."

Then what does it have to do with? I wondered, the question eating at me up to the moment I arrived at her location:

Camp Swift.

The small, enclosed compound that housed our brigade headquarters. Connected to the Nineveh Command, which was responsible for the Mosul region, it was one of the few places where the Kurds, Iraqis, and Americans all worked in one location. Swift was the heart of the advise and assist operation, where the brigade staff did whatever it was they did. Even though

I was technically on the staff, I avoided Swift as much as I could. Out of sight, out of mind, which had worked for the past three months.

The interior of Swift was like the BOC, but *worse*. Brigade staff are prominent elements, with Majors, Captains, Lieutenants, and whoever else gets drafted in as part of their rosters. To make matters worse, members of battalion staffs were there too. All of this in a building about the size of an apartment; the Brigade Commander slept in the office there in a tiny room. Outside wasn't much better, a small gravel area with sleeping tents. Beyond that, guard positions and a giant wall. The whole thing made Camp Union III feel gigantic.

As I navigated through the building, I could feel eyes on me, and not all in a friendly way. I turned left, finding my boss sitting at a cramped workstation, surrounded by personnel busily tapping away at their computers.

"We're going behind the building," she said as soon as she saw me, picking up her patrol cap.

"More privacy," she said a little quieter to me, as she walked past.

What the hell was going on? We reached the back door, pausing to go into a little corner out of view of the main path.

"You're not going to Qayyarah West." she began, looking closer to me to judge my reaction. I nodded; I was not surprised mission needs came first. It was a long shot anyway.

"In fact," she continued, her tone of voice changing. "The Brigade X.O. had a talk with me about your career as an infantry officer."

I couldn't hide my reaction to that.

"Strange of him to care about me," My reply, sarcasm beginning to drip. "They're sending me down to a platoon then?" I already knew the answer.

"Not quite."

My eyes narrowed.

"The S3 cell here at Camp Swift."

"And doing PowerPoint slides in some room helps me how? Helps the *mission,* how?"

Silence. For once, she honestly had no answer. She looked conflicted, and it hit me that she had been going above and beyond to protect me this entire time; she wasn't my enemy here. It was the people above her, and this, at the end of the day, was the military.

I shook my head, understanding.

"Ma'am, if they feel like I'm wasting a slot here or whatever, I have no issue going back to Kuwait, or home. You've more than kept your side of the deal, and I appreciate it. I don't want to cause you any grief." I felt a sense of relief now that I knew what I was facing. I had gotten much further than I thought, and if the goal was to get rid of me, I'd make it easy.

"No, you're here now. You're not going home that easy. I won't let that happen."

Why?

The question I wanted to ask since she had agreed to take me to Iraq in the first place. The one I wanted to ask when she threw me at covering stuff even though she knew I didn't have any idea what was going on. The one that would have told me her reason for defending me against other officers, the XO, the *commander,* when she easily could have sold me out.

But she hadn't. What had I done to be worth the extra stress; to earn that level of respect? *Me,* of all people.

Her voice changed again, more natural now. Something told me the lines about my career had been forced by ...others.

"Officers don't run around taking photos." She looked back towards the headquarters building. "You've been going out on the missions, doing what everyone else wants to do."

"My job?"

"When the X.O. saw your name on the roster to go to Qayyarah West, that was the last straw."

I tensed up in anger. "These guys have done it before. What the hell is the problem with me doing exactly what I'm supposed to be doing? They don't want to send me home, but they want to keep me here in the S3 section to slave away?"

"We both know why. There isn't any real reason L.T." She sighed heavily.

"So, this is all about them being mad that a loser like me is doing something they aren't."

At that moment, all my trust disappeared. Not in Maj. Sanders, but in everything that the Army said it stood for. Five months ago, I was considered a *joke.* I wasn't *good enough.* I wasn't *worth the time,* effort. to even keep in the Army. I was on the path to elimination from service.

Now, people who had been in the Army for years with exemplary service and courage, who I was told to look up to, were jealous of *me?* First, I wasn't good enough, but now that I was "doing good", that was a problem? In the middle of a war zone, this was an issue? Not that fact that Soldiers felt abandoned, that they didn't know what was going on, that they were being asked to suffer while their leaders weren't?

I was seething. My own leaders didn't care about the important stuff that affected people's lives-

So why the fuck were we here?

"They've been gunning for you since day one."

"Why?"

"Because you make them uncomfortable."

I stepped back. "These guys are hardcore killers or whatever, and *I* make them uncomfortable? They why don't they leave me alone?"

She visibly weighed her next words. "It's like they can't read you. They don't know what you're going to do or what you're about. It's like you're *judging* them. The fact that you don't seem to care or respect anything or anybody yet are doing what you're doing bothers a lot of people."

"I respect people who have earned it."

"They feel like they've earned it.

"Yeah, but feelings and behaviors are different things. Feelings don't change the fact that we're sitting here in *2016*. This is all about egos. Didn't know I was serving with people still in elementary school. And yet, they expect me to respect them because of some rank?"

Spader 6 and I talking past each other. The stilted conversations.

"Why are you here L.T.?"

"In Iraq, or in the Army."

"Both is the question.

"I kind of fell into the Army, but I'm here because how dare I wear this rank or uniform if I'm not going through what the Soldiers are?"

"Do you *believe* in any of this?"

"It's *irrelevant* what I believe because the Soldiers are still out there. They volunteered to serve their country, not be used and abused by the "leaders" who they trust to look after their well-being."

"You're *odd for someone in the military* L.T.; even I'll say that." She laughed. "Something tells me you would have ended up in the peace corps in another life. It's not often that an officer volunteers to do an enlisted person's job without a concern how it looks." She focused on me.

"You may be at risk for not getting promoted."

"I knew that when I volunteered, ma'am." My response. "*It doesn't matter.* Maybe they can volunteer to do an E-5's job, if they feel so strongly about it. Or is that the problem, I'm willing to do something that's 'beneath' me while others aren't.*"

She paused, leaving the answer unsaid. "You don't care do you?"

"I'm not in the Army to get promoted."

There was a knowing smile.

"They thought you would back down and roll with it, L.T. I had a feeling you wouldn't." She glanced towards the door again, making sure no one was nearby.

"Listen, there's going to be some changes soon in some key positions."

"Meaning?"

"I'll speak with the Brigade Signal Officer. Since you're branch detailed from the signal corps, maybe we can have you work in the brigade S6 for now."

"Then, what happens?"

"What happens is that you keep your head down. Don't make any waves. Be patient, and I'll work it out. Until then, your reporting days are over."

The "mighty" Strike Brigade of the 101st Airborne Division.

Where doing your job gets you in trouble.

The convoy to Qayyarah West pushed off on Aug 26. and went off without a hitch. Dozens of vehicles snaking their way towards the airfield, carrying hundreds of personnel. Upon arrival at their small cantonment, the work of clearing and rebuilding the airfield began in earnest.

It would take months.

A U.S. Airman assigned to the 1st Expeditionary Civil Engineering Group levels poured concrete in a trench during runway repair operations at Qayyarah West airfield, Iraq, Oct. 8, 2017. U.S. Army photo by Spc. Christopher Brecht.

I watched the reports of the operation from my new position in Erbil, *assistant to the assistant* brigade S6. Every day, I reported to the signal tent as ordered.

Then I did absolutely nothing for the next 12 hours. Why? Because there was nothing for me to do. Signal operations, once established, are usually stable It was a quiet place to spend nine months, and I couldn't complain about the working or living conditions; I was just furious that I was put there because of officer politics.

Ironic, because I was getting more views on my work than any other journalist in the U.S. Army. I had figured out DVIDs and how to ensure my stuff was on the top of the pile: have all photos attached to an article, even if it was just a few words. Put a good photo at the front of that article. Tag one of the hometowns as Washington D.C. and New York City. Then boom.

It was probably one of the reasons for the strong reaction to the Gun Raid article.

The division and the higher headquarters played hands-off for weeks on the whole deal. The media still wasn't being let in to see what was going on, so they were taking it upon themselves to find out. They spotted the convoy going to Qayyarah West; they located the engineers around Qayyarah West; they spotted American Soldiers in all these weird locations that they weren't supposed to be in. Still, an official explanation was something CJTF-OIR was loathing to do. That is, until CJTF-OIR's PAO dropped this tidbit unexpectedly:

"Over the past several weeks east of Mosul, Iraq, coalition forces supported Peshmerga forces who were conducting Operation Evergreen II." He said during one of his usual briefings, which were usually dull but needed to at least be able to say that *some* information was put out.

"The coalition used helicopters to lift the artillery into position and then exfiltrated the guns when the operation was complete. The firing solutions this offered provided maximum flexibility for the commander on the ground."

The cat was out of the bag; there was no excuse not to release the article now.

"Here are the Colonel's remarks." My email to Maj. Sanders, who immediately set the fire even though I didn't technically work for her.

"What's the hold-up?" Maj. Sanders to Lt. Col. Thomas and Sgt. 1st Class Hoskins.

The article went up again — edits by Sgt. 1st Class Hoskins. No problem. Edits by Lt. Col. Thomas, which I had never seen before. Silence for a bit, as Maj. Gen. Volesky read the article personally. Add some stuff here and there. Done.

CJTF-OIR now. Edits from the usual guy up there. Then out of the blue, inputs from people who I didn't know existed. Was that a full bird Colonel? Who the heck was Maj. Christopher Parker, who left a comment about *my perfect use of the semicolon*? I had never gotten so much scrutiny before, and it was kind of odd.

Finally, the article went up, Gunny Joseph being the cover image. The video followed soon after, and as usual, Hoskins sent up the link.

The Pentagon ran it as featured news on Army.Mil the next day. The Association of the United States Army would use my footage as a key point in their presentations, which meant that everyone from the Chairman of the Joint Chiefs of Staff to defense contractors got to see it.

The newspapers started emailing CJTF-OIR *within 24 hours*, with major news stations taking the video and using it in their news B-roll. The footage was so good that a few of them used almost the whole thing; like the Rachael Maddow show on MSNBC, my eyes in disbelief as she talked over the footage about the war in Iraq.

The Soldiers of 1-320th were delighted and when I met Gunny and the rest of the 1st Platoon back in Erbil later in September, I let them know how the article was doing.

"Guess it was good," Frank offered, with a grin. "People back home have messaged me about it. Something about my sleeves being rolled up in a photo."

"Told you, I was more than the paparazzi!"

"Whatever, whatever." He shrugged, while subtly shaking his head in agreement on how positive things had turned out.

"Told you it'd be worth it." Gunny Joseph said when we met up again. "See, did Mont and his crew get you something like this?"

"They did actually."

"Whatever." He laughed, then got serious for a second. "You're one of the good ones, sir. You...understand. A lot of officers don't."

"I'm-"I struggled to find the words. "I'm just doing my job."

"A lot of people don't even do *that.*"

In a time where people were questioning the usefulness of artillery on the modern battlefield, a release about an in and out insertion behind enemy lines to blast targets as the infantry advanced was in demand. The article was shared back home at Fort Campbell, with family members tagging their children, spouses, siblings. Then, it ended in weird places all over the internet, beyond even newsrooms.

If our job in the public affairs section was to publicize the unit in a way that encouraged media organizations to want to cover what the Soldiers were doing, we accomplished that in spades. Everything was great, except for the fact that news organizations were still being refused access.

I was excited one day soon after while doing my weekly rollup to see one of my images used by the Washington Post. My excitement turned into despair however, when I clicked on the link.

"U.S. forces are using white phosphorus munitions in Iraq but it's unclear exactly how" the title read, ominously, with one of my photos featured prominently. CJTF-OIR's PAO gave a thorough response about the pictures to the Washington Post:

"The 48-hour operation, called Evergreen II, involved 2,000 Kurdish fighters as they fought to secure the Gwer River bridge in the northern Iraqi town of Gwer. The white phosphorus smoke rounds were used to obscure Kurdish forces moving on enemy positions on the opposite bank of the Great Zab River."

With such a clear-cut answer, it almost defeated the whole need of the article. But that wasn't the point; the word was the Post ran the article because there were some hard feelings on the whole being shut out of what we were doing. While I could understand the frustration, to say that CJTF-OIR was *livid* would be selling the reaction shortly. As far as I understand, the Washington Post was blackballed for a month or two after that and it took some serious convincing to get them back in the good graces. Especially after how other "news" entities ran with the story.

On Youtube, I saw a link to a video with one of my photos. Maybe it was a thumbnail? Clicking on it, I was in for an unpleasant surprise.

"U.S. Soldiers are using white phosphorus in Iraq for unknown reasons," the anchors of Russian Today said as my photos, in high definition and enlarged to fit the T.V. screen behind them, cycled through. The white phosphorus shells were highlighted with a filter akin to a flashlight.

I was shocked. Mostly because I took the photos in JPEG and we always had issues enlarging them while these guys not only blew them up, but made them look *better*. There was also the fact that the Washington Post article had given them the perfect ammunition, the anchors being so good that they basically used quotes from the article while skillfully moving viewers towards the conclusion that we were lying through our teeth.

It was my first taste of actual information warfare. The whole idea that I was just taking photos for the simple reason of letting families back home know what their Soldiers were up to dissipated in that instant.

This was a war of ideas.

This was something I hadn't prepared for and now I was right in the middle of it, if the media arm of the Russian government of was paying attention to what I was doing.

I knew from that point that whatever I posted from then was hot. Stories from the Soldiers' perspective were what everyone wanted. By late September, we didn't have to send the media press releases or invites. They were emailing CJTF-OIR, requesting access specifically to 1-320th or 1-75, and then would *specifically say* the articles were the reason why.

One reporter literally attached a link to the Gun Raid article when he asked for access, saying that stories of that type were in *high demand.* It got to the point where the Associated Press used one of my photos without me even needing to submit it.

A U.S. Army captain speaks to his counterpart in the Iraqi army earlier this month. U.S. and Iraqi forces are preparing for an offensive on the Islamic State stronghold of Mosul. PHOTO 1ST LT. DANIEL JOHNSON/US ARMY/ASSOCIATED PRESS

Capt. Gerard Spinney speaking to a member of the ISF at Camp Swift, August, 2016. U.S. Army photo by Daniel Johnson

This was everything we wanted since we started in May. The brigade could be pleased-

Oh, wait.

"Working in the S6 now, Lt. Johnson?" The Brigade X.O.'s voice interrupted my vital work of tracking stocks for investing. He was leaving

Iraq, moving on to bigger and better things in Washington D.C., another step on climbing the rank ladder. It was odd, though.

The S6 tents weren't exactly in his path, and I was sitting *near the back,* yet he had somehow walked in and noticed me.

Yeah, right.

I looked up, and I saw that fucking smirk. The one people give when they feel superior about putting others in their "rightful" place.

"Yes sir," I replied, gritting through my teeth. He stayed there for a few seconds, looking down at me as I sat as if savoring the moment. I tensed up, and I could tell he was enjoying making me rage inwardly. Finally, he nodded and then walked off, no doubt content that I had been taken care of.

I can't make this shit up. I can still see him standing there, representing everything wrong with leadership in the Army. At that moment, I realized something-

We were all fucked.

If that was what got promoted to the top?

We were all super fucked.

Chapter Eleven- TAAs and PAAs

1st Lt. Jeffrey Cooper was assigned to 2-502 Infantry, and was originally from Mill Creek, Washington.

He was 25 years old when he was killed in a vehicle rollover while supporting Operation Inherent Resolve.

Cooper had served his country since 17, enlisting in the Coast Guard as a Reservist while still in high school. While part of that branch, he was part of the Coast Guard's effort to clean up the Gulf Oil Spill in 2010, a massive effort that brought together over 45,000 personnel and ships from agencies and organizations across the nation.

When he graduated college in 2013, Cooper decided to transfer to the U.S. Army and attended Officer Candidate School at Fort Benning, Georgia. His father, who was a Sgt. 1st Class in the Army Reserve, recruited him. OCS is one of the three commissioning paths, alongside ROTC and the service academies, where candidates are assessed from day one of the course against their peers. Branch, or job selection, for officers is competitive. Branches like the Infantry, Aviation, or Armor are highly sought after, and OCS graduates get the lowest number of slots for branches due to the process proceeding through West Pointers and ROTC cadets first.

Cooper chose and was selected to be an infantry officer, and then was assigned to Fort Campbell and the 101st. When the time came for the brigade to deploy to Iraq, he joined his battalion in Kuwait. As September arrived, he had spent the past few months getting new personnel into Iraq, transporting them from their landing area and ensuring that they made their flight into the country.

The mission required a ton of traveling on Kuwaiti roads; the route to and from the airbase area was notoriously ragged and had caused fatalities among coalition personnel before. On Sept. 10, 2016, Cooper's group was transporting two personnel who had just arrived in the country in a Mitsubishi Pajero, the civilian vehicle commonly used by U.S. forces in the Middle East. A tire blew while they drove, flipping the vehicle over, and even though Cooper was wearing his seatbelt, it failed. He sustained fatal injuries and three other soldiers were wounded, two of them the personnel who had just arrived in the country.

A communications blackout signified a friendly casualty. The last thing anyone wanted was for a Soldier's family member to come home, open

Facebook, and get the news broken to them in a Facebook Wall post or Snapchat. Before we had left, everyone had updated their family's contact information to ensure that if something *did* happen, the casualty notification team could find them. Only once that occurred would the Soldier's name be released to the media and other personnel.

Maj. Sanders' call came early that afternoon.

"L.T.," she began solemnly. "I trust you heard the news."

"Yes, ma'am." My response as I walked over to my cot and began pulling out my laptop.

"We need his photo to send to the division. Lt. Jeffrey Cooper, 2-502. Send it to me when you find it."

The military had also learned over the past 15 years that when a Soldier was killed or died the media would pull any photo they could find. The photos could be benign, or it could be a guy flashing a gang symbol with his patrol cap on backwards. It became Army policy that every deploying Soldier would take a photo before they left to ensure that wouldn't happen. I had about 1200 of them on my Mac, all taken by either myself or Staff Sgt. Melendez. Once I had the image, I sent it to Maj. Sanders, who handled the rest.

1st Lt. Cooper's funeral service was to be held in Erbil, and the brigade leadership decided that we would tape it so that his family could have the footage. The event was held in the headquarters building of the effort in Erbil, a large open auditorium with everyone in attendance, including Maj. Gen. Volesky.

1st Lt. Jeffrey Cooper's memorial in Erbil, September, 2016. Photo by Daniel Johnson.

Lt. Cooper's friends and coworkers spoke of him, their memories, and how they would miss him.

Then came the roll call.

"Spc. Rodric."

"Here, First Sergeant!"

"Lt. Christiano."

"Here, First Sergeant!"

"Sgt. Cooper."

"Here, First Sergeant!"

"Lt. Cooper."

Silence.

"Lt. Jeffrey Cooper."

Silence.

"Lt. Jeffrey D. Cooper."

The only response was the salute from the rifle detail outside.

With the seizure of Qayyarah West and Operation Evergreen II, 2BCTs' role was now unclear. The ISF had advanced further than expected, and what we could provide to them was the question of the hour. The next big thing was literally on the horizon:

Mosul.

The prize that everyone wanted a piece of. The only question was how. The argument was that advising from the Makhmur area entirely wasn't going to work now that the fight had gone well over the Tigris; the division and brigade wanted to get closer, so they came up with a plan to start setting up bases closer to Mosul. Ostensibly, it would allow the ISF to get their support and strikes processed quicker.

And I would be stuck in a groundhog-day, until we all went home. It was frustrating trying to process the fact that I was getting punished for simply doing what I was supposed to do. Frustrating to realize that if my own leaders really didn't care about the mission, but instead how it made them look --- that there was really no point to any of this. If even during an armed conflict they were acting like children, then what did that mean about everything we did? Everything we were doing?

The sinking feeling that had started in my body that first day in Erbil was growing worse. I had been screwed with before back at Campbell, but that was nothing compared to this: the knowledge that even with lives on the line, the calculus wasn't one that showed any care about any of us. All the conversations I had with personnel across the country played in my head, the feelings of abandonment, the distrust.

The powerlessness.

All the little actions that by themselves seemed minor: lack of supplies, lack of support, two-faced standards with awards and uniforms, an aggressive tendency to mission creep, to play down risks, to disregard, to target a lieutenant for just doing his job, totaled up to the sum feeling that we didn't matter, and that our lives were not in the best hands.

An already dangerous situation, with an added layer of anxiety about the very people who were supposed to look after you. It doesn't just happen in combat zones either, it happens in garrison with insane training schedules, multiple JRTC rotations, late workdays. It happens when a Soldier needs help but doesn't get it from their leadership or is targeted because *they have*. It happens when Soldiers die or are injured because of command decisions that push them past their limits or into dangerous conditions.

Why try anymore? It didn't matter. Why not give in and just survive? There was no point in fighting the system. They would always win; in fact, they had *already* won. The Brigade XO had every reason to smirk, he *had* put me in my place. They had all the power over all of us, and they would get

178

away with whatever they pleased. The longer I sat there, the more frustrated I got, and the more frustrated I got, the harder it became to even see the point of showing up to the S6 office instead of being anywhere else all day. I had gotten screwed, why do the right thing?

I had gotten screwed.

But this was bigger than me, wasn't it? Using that excuse, I'd prove myself worthless to all those people who for some reason, put their trust in me. I'd prove that I was as worthless as the people who tried to keep me down thought.

I'd prove that I was just as worthless as *them*.

No, I wasn't going to let them have that satisfaction, even if I spent the rest of my career stuck at that desk. There was no external point to it, but I could do my duty and continue to show up, because it was what would have been expected of any Soldier in the same position. I couldn't control the situation, but I could control my reaction.

If they couldn't break my internal motivation, what power did they have over me, really?

I watched the rest of September go by from that tent.

"Advise, assist, accompany," Maj. Sanders told me in one of our conversations as I whittled away in the S6 section. "We'll be there to display that we're behind the ISF the entire time, steeling their resolve, occupying Tactical Assembly Areas and Position Areas for Artillery. They're going to serve as our advising headquarters, and now and then we may accompany them on their operations."

"Aren't those different names for Combat Outposts and Firebases?" I replied, dryly. I'd never heard of a TAA or PAA before. It seemed like one of those terms somebody up high was coming up with to play down what was going on.

"We're not calling them that L.T." I could see her shaking her head through the phone.

"Alright, but accompanying sounds kind of like a combat word, or a word that leads to combat, which we're *totally* not doing."

"The mission's evolved, and so have we. You should know this; you were part of an operation that saw you fly out into the dead of night to assist an offensive."

I still didn't buy it. Advise, assist, and accompany was what Special Forces personnel on the ground were currently doing. It was their bread and butter and judging by the wide swaths of ground that had been taken recently, the very American sounding voices that were calling in fire sometimes, and the fact that gun raid was partly in support of Canadian and American SOF, they were doing a pretty good job at it.

Which made this whole AAA for us mission seem...odd. Advising at the HQ level made sense. Steeling the resolve of the Iraqi forces? What the hell does that even mean? What if U.S. Soldiers got engaged? What if the Iraqis suffered a counterattack and couldn't hold the line? If the whole point was just to sit there and watch, the threat didn't quite seem worth the cost. If it was a combat operation with 101st Soldiers providing extra firepower, so be it. If it was an advising operation with 101st Soldiers staying back and letting Iraqis take care of business, so be it.

But the in-between world where Soldiers would end up standing there running the risk of indirect fire, direct fire, and drones, sounded odd. It seemed like something someone came up with so they could get credit for liberating Mosul.

"Multiple avenues to Mosul L.T." Maj. Sanders continued. "Multiple different advising missions, with multiple TAAs. The big push is going to come through the east, from the village of Karmalis, towards Bartallah. 2-502 will be on that."

Which meant, of course, that C Battery and most of the firepower would be on that axis of advance. The Karmalis-Bartallah approach was also augmented with a whole company from 1-26 Infantry, Company A, quietly pushed into Iraq from Fort Campbell in early October. The U.S was well above the officially given troop cap of 5,000 at this point, moving more personnel in for the counteroffensive.

"From the South, the Iraqi Police, and the PMF. That'll be 1-75 and 39BEB from Q-West."

Great. Another name for the Iranians or Iranian backed Shia Militias. They didn't like us, but they didn't like ISIL more. Not that we didn't get some reminders that an enemy of your enemy is *still* an enemy.

From the North, there were another few Iraqi Divisions, striking from the Mosul Dam, their advisors being 1-502 Infantry.

By mid-October, Maj. Gen. Volesky and the 101st HQ element began to get replaced by Maj. Gen. Joseph Martin and personnel from the 1st Infantry Division. Martin was a little more proactive in the public affairs sphere than Volesky was, and he wanted to start giving reporters more access than they had before, even down with interviews with Soldiers.

Qayyarah West would be the beta test for the whole idea, and the first time since OIR began news organizations would be allowed to see coalition operations firsthand. CJTF-OIR was pushing forward a spokesman from Kuwait to run the media operations there.

At the same time, the combat camera personnel would now be utilized more in line with their skill set- they would continuously rotate through the PAAs and TAAs, grabbing images for public release. They would also get more of an opportunity to do image collection with the special mission units in theater.

Then there was me.

"Now that certain people have left," Maj. Sanders said, hinting at our...mutual friend. "You're going to hit all the TAAs and PAAs. While you're doing that, I'll handle the media. I'm hooking you in with 1-502 first, so head over to their TOC."

I was shocked. "You mean I'm *free?*" She had come through.

It's sad, looking back, that I had almost expected her *not* to.

"No, you're just visiting those locations for the brigade S6 to see how things are going." She sounded mischievous.

"Roger," my reply, barely giving a goodbye before getting off the phone and heading to the next tent over.

It was packed, serving as a liaison area for all the battalions at this point; Erbil was kind of the last point before you headed out to the TAAs or PAAs and it looked like it. Fresh 2nd Lieutenants just arrived in the country, early re-deployers, and Soldiers from different countries.

Now that the Ranger training and other missions down south were complete, most of 1-502 would be heading to the Mosul Dam. Their commander was Lt. Col. Shawn Umbrell, who *liked* the idea of me coming along. In 2005, he had been the commander of the headquarters company of 1-502nd in 2BCT during its time in Iraq.

Sent to secure the restive Triangle of Death, the brigade soon found itself fighting for its life among the towns and terrain in the area, battling a ferocious insurgency. 1-502 was especially hit hard, with 19 Soldiers from the battalion being killed in action during the deployment, 10 of them from B CO. On that same deployment on Mar 12, 2006, 5 Soldiers from B 1-502nd would gang-rape and kill of 14-year-old Iraqi girl Abeer Qassim Hamza al-Janabi, and then murder her family in one of the most heinous war crimes of the conflict.

At first, there was a cover-up by lower-level leadership about the murder of the Iraqi family., Pfc. Justin Watt, however, upon hearing of the crimes notified military authorities about what had occurred.

The result was explosive, with Watt receiving death threats and B CO for all intents and purposes being shut down. The battalion and brigade wanted to move on from the incident and that deployment. Still, the well-renowned book "Black Hearts" by reporter Jim Frederick ensured that the event was firmly etched in the national and military consciousness; it spoke of how the failure of our strategy in Iraq at the time, fighting a war on the cheap, led to the conditions that allowed five Soldiers to murder an entire family, and then *almost get away with it.*

There weren't a lot of people from that deployment left in the Army in 2016, and Lt. Col. Shawn Umbrell was one of them.

Lt. Col. Shawn Umbrell in Taji visiting Ranger BPC, July, 2016. U.S. Army photo by Daniel Johnson.

His career had continued, and he quickly rose through the ranks after that tour, hitting key developmental positions and even commanding an ROTC battalion at the University of Kentucky. In Army culture, Lieutenant Colonels who went to command an ROTC battalion were usually seen to be at the end of their career, officers who had made it far but not quite far enough. Three years in a cushy assignment training the future leaders of the Army, and then they could go home in peace with a nice fat retirement paycheck. Umbrell obviously didn't want that, and now here he was commanding the same battalion he had been a Captain in 12 years before in Iraq.

A lot of officers in his battalion were in middle school during that 2005 deployment. In a bizarre twist, that was either intentional or not, a large amount of the lieutenants in the battalion were also *his former ROTC cadets*. That usually doesn't happen and created the hilarious situation of the KU guys being together for seven years, serving under the guy who probably taught them how to wear the uniform. It was like the West Point Club that was in 1-26, where Spader 6 only invited officers who had went to WP over to his house for dinner.

Wait, no, it was *much less* elitist than that.

That Umbrell had experience teaching on a college campus was readily apparent in my encounters with him- calm, understanding, down to Earth. He was the type of commander to judge you by your performance, not schooling, or where you came from. He gave the officers under him a fair shake, even the infantry ones without Ranger Tabs if they could perform. I genuinely liked the man.

"Our recon has confirmed that everything is in place." Capt. Jacob, during one of our last briefings before departing for Mosul Dam. Some of the Soldiers had driven up to the site, just barely missing getting engaged by some ISIL fighters who were eliminated by an airstrike right before they attacked the 1-502 element. The mission had confirmed the key details: the ISF was in position, and the L.Z. could support the insertion. I would be going in on the first night with most of the advisers, a drop that would have everyone ready for operations the next day.

"First night we'll occupy the position and set up security," Jacob continued, indicating the extra manpower from A CO in that had come from Taji. "We're going to continue to dig in as soon as we arrive." Jacob pointed at the perimeter layout- barbed wire, interlocking fields of fire. The perfect patrol base/COP. Resupply was going to have to be done by air due to the risk of ISIL activity on the roads

Umbrell nodded. He motioned for the next briefer.

Medical, signal, fires, all portions thoroughly discussed, illustrating a well thought out plan of operations. It had to be; the battalion would kind of be out on a limb. Lt. Col. Umbrell calmly emphasized the importance of what they were doing.

"We're here because our allies need us and trust our professionalism." He said during one pause. "They're putting their faith in us- we're going to live up to that in everything we do."

Straight to the point and practical; In a few seconds, he had hit the "provide purpose, direction, and motivation." As rushed as it felt, it seemed everything was in place for once: good leadership, a clear plan of action, a blessing from the top.

Erbil was a flurry of activity as we got ready to move out. Convoys, supply pickups, new personnel moving in. 1st Armored Division, Marines, Naval Personnel, Army Reserve, National Guard; a mishmash of uniforms all over the base.

October came, the first respite from the blazing heat of the summer. The advance party occupied the TAA near Mosul Dam. The rest of us heading there loaded our gear on vehicles to be dropped off at the location.

Another insertion, another adventure. As dawn came on the day before we were going in, I was glad that I would hopefully be seeing Erbil for the last time. I walked to the 1-502nd tent to check-in and make sure that I didn't miss any hard times; it was busy with personnel typing on computers or looking at feeds from ISR

"Lt. Johnson!" The battalion S3 greeted me. He had been extremely helpful over the past few days. "We've been looking for you."

"Did I miss something, sir?"

"No. Word just came down from the Brigade HQ You're not going with us."

"You need to get to Qayyarah West as soon as possible."

"Good to meet you, sir," I said, extending my hand to the figure before me, freshly arrived from Kuwait.

Maj. Christopher Parker, schoolteacher, U.S. Army Reserve Soldier.

And now the face of the war in Northern Iraq. Or at least the only face that reporters were able to talk to outside of the generals and guys in Baghdad. He was part of the CJTF-OIR PAO section, the echelon above even our division headquarters in Baghdad. The 3-Star general said he wanted the media to start having access to operations at Q-West, a joint media operations cell, and a press conference at the location.

And to accomplish all of this, they sent *one* man. It was an odd decision not to send at least an extra Soldier with him, but considering that there was stuff going on everywhere, they probably couldn't spare the personnel. At least, that's what they said.

"Lt. Johnson." He replied with a smile. "You're my ride?"

"I am, sir," I replied as I grabbed some of his bags and moved it to the vehicle.

It was a short drive from his landing spot to LSA Strike.

"You've been doing good work, L.T.," Parker said as we drove. "That Gun Raid article was amazing. It was so good I wish we had been able to put some media on the mission."

"You're the one who commented on my semicolon."

"It was a *good* semicolon."

I smiled. I admit it did feel good getting some praise.

Parker was a steady hand in public affairs, and he had the schoolteacher look. Youngish looking for his age, obviously active, glasses that he sometimes looked over when asking questions. He was an enlisted broadcaster back in the 90s, taking part in the NATO operation in Bosnia. I could tell just talking to him that he was good at what he did --- he had to be, being sent to Iraq all by himself. He also had been in *my* shoes at one point, a kid trying to figure out how to tell a story in the middle of a conflict zone.

"Are you trying to branch PAO?"

"Kind of sir...I'm an infantry officer."

"So, this is an additional duty?"

"My only one."

"And you're running around Iraq by yourself? How'd that happen?"

"I volunteered?"

Maj. Parker tilted his head, looking interested.

"You haven't even been to DINFOs?"

"Nope. I've just been kind of winging it."

There was silence for a bit.

"It all makes sense now. I knew your stuff was a bit...different. But it works."

I had to get him on the next thing smoking to Qayyarah West; the media gates had opened, and every major news station and paper wanted to get the first crack at the story. ABC, CNN, NBC, CBS, all of them were piled in on top of each other. There was only one problem in the division's eyes: CJTF-OIR, by sending Maj. Parker to run the show, was now calling the shots on what message would be put out, without input from the division HQ.

After almost five months and the opportunity everyone had been waiting for had been jumped on by the guys in Kuwait. CJTF-OIR was even activating a contingency public affairs team from the states of over five personnel for the counteroffensive.

Until then it would be Parker running the media show at Q-West. He was the point of contact, the access, the man to be. All except that, at no fault of his own, he didn't have the contacts and relationships with the units on the ground to help. Only we did. Since I was going to be hopping around the TAAs and Maj. Sanders would be running around with the BDE Commander, it would be a tough task. Which is why he smartly asked for help as soon as he arrived.

And which was why with only two pairs of clothes and my camera equipment, I was running around trying to get on the next convoy to Q-West after my ride to Mosul Dam got cancelled.

"I tried to tell them you were the only asset I had," Maj. Sanders on the phone, her voice cracking in a fury "All of the people at CJTF-OIR, at Division, and they called *us?"*

I couldn't blame her. The whole plan for coverage of the Mosul offensive was out the window, and I also didn't want to trade being stuck in Erbil for being held at the airfield. But I was just a lieutenant, so who cares what I thought.

Maj. Sanders released a few choice words in anger at the whole situation.

"They *fucked* us over. You're the *only* asset I can trust in this entire country, and now *they're* telling me where to send you? *To help some guy from Kuwait* who hasn't been here the entire time."

She went silent for a moment, collecting her thoughts. Finally, she continued, her voice cold.

"The tasking came straight down from the top. I've got you a spot in a convoy heading from KSB on the 17th. Don't miss it. I've got some things to say to Maj. Parker."

With that, the call ended.

At least she wasn't mad at me.

Considering I had no clothes, the issue of my bags still being at the Mosul Dam was very pertinent. I was able to grab a helicopter out there, speeding through the night to the L.Z. where a Soldier from 1-502nd met us and threw my bags on the bird.

Of course, it being me, I found out once I was dropped off at a refueling point in Erbil that the bags belonged to *another* Johnson.

Par for the course.

Chapter Twelve -Q West– October 2016

Capt. Alex Carlier, the commander of the company that was responsible for transporting personnel to Qayyarah West, stood in the center of the amassed group reading the names on his manifest list. The movement had personnel from the U.S. Marine Corps, U.S. Air Force, and French Army.

Carlier, from Columbus, Ohio, was 29 and was on his second deployment in his career with his first being to Afghanistan. He had taken command of the company early in July right before the surveillance and then the occupation of Q-West had been conducted.

A CO of the 39th BEB, also known as the Beasts due to their radio call sign, was a combined route clearance operation company (CARCO). The CARCO was made up of a mixed element of engineers from 39th BEB and infantrymen from 1-502; since arriving in Iraq in May, the two separate units had been working together in one company. The engineers provided the route clearance expertise and assets while the infantrymen provided security. They had been shot at, had mortars called down upon them, and had other close calls that would continue through the fall into when they finally went home.

It was October 17th- the official start date of the Mosul Counteroffensive. The time had come for all the disparate Iraqi forces and their advisers to start making the dash towards the city; it wouldn't be fully secure until *9 months* later, July of 2017.

"We're hitting it from multiple directions; that's part of the reason you hear those detonations in the background." said Carlier. "The ISF are pushing forward, but there's still a big threat from indirect fire until they gain enough ground. Alright, let's get moving." With that we headed for our Mine Resistant All-Terrain Vehicles (MATVs), some Soldiers stopping off for a prayer session held by the chaplain before we departed.

MATVs aren't made for comfort, the cramped inside of the vehicle barely holding six fully equipped Soldiers. There are no windows to speak of aside from the driver's seat and the gunner's turret so the only thing to do is sit there and try to sleep, stare at each other, or listen to whatever music that was playing over the intercom; today it was some eclectic mix of rock and rap.

I glanced out the front window and saw the sky begin to darken even though it should have been getting brighter. We stopped a little while later, the ramp dropping to reveal we were in a small set of houses alongside the road. As Carlier departed with some Soldiers to talk to the Iraqi officer who was leading the convoy, I got a chance to look at the horizon.

Black smoke.

The oil fields were on fire.

Giant plumes were belching towards the sky, shrouding our path forward in an unnatural darkness. The Gulf War veterans had told stories about driving through Kuwait as fires raged. But actually seeing it in real life?

It was surreal.

The fires seemed even *worse* towards our destination, with the explosions that occasionally rattled the ground seeming to also originate in that direction. Carlier returned from his conversation with the escort, signifying that it was almost time to move again.

"Our escort is a Colonel in the ISF," he said to me as he arrived, pointing back at the vehicle. "Daesh has taken a lot from him. They stole his car, and then they slaughtered many of his family in cold blood."

Pausing for a moment, Carlier looked at the vehicles in front of him stretching down the road, the darkened skies, the sounds of war in the distance.

"ISIL is an abomination," he said finally.

It wasn't long before we started moving again.

In the gunner's position on top of the vehicle, a young Soldier named Spc. Shawn Carman scanned his sector. Carman, a New Jersey native, was on his first deployment and his first trip outside of the United States. He had agreed to tape the movement with his GoPro and pass the footage to me once we arrived, both of us figuring that if anyone was to see what was going on, it would be him.

Small human shapes began to appear as we passed through a village. Kurdish children, by the dozen, full smiling faces and laughing. There was something about the scene that immediately lightened the mood and the Soldiers in the vehicle smiled and waved back.

"Here you go, Carman," Carlier said, stealthily passing some balls up to the young Soldier. The official rule, at this phase of the operation, was that we weren't supposed to be interacting with the local civilians. This isn't hearts and minds they said, we're advising, not trying to win over the populace. Yeah, if you were in a war zone and saw children coming out, legitimately happy to see you, that wouldn't last too long.

The Soldiers had gotten together and gathered balls and other goodies for the kids. Since no one high ranking was around, no one would notice the drop-offs occurring from gunners in the turrets. Balls went flying from the gunner's hatches in of the vehicles, Kurdish family heads enjoying the scene and smirking as the kids grabbed the stuff and started playing.

"It's like we're on a parade," Carman said through the headset, a tone of legitimate joy in his voice. "Best part of this trip is seeing the kids."

Raising a family in a war zone; trying to be a child in a war zone.

We'd leave after nine months; they'd have to deal with this for the rest of their lives. All because of forces beyond their control, some of them being our own foreign policy.

Carlier received a message on his computer and looked down. Reports on the progress of the operation. "It's a bad day to be Daesh today," he said to his crew. "The colonel even said that civilians have been rising up as the ISF pushes forward.".

The air was so thick with pollution that it seemed like we were pulling into a black hole. With the creaking of the ramp dropping, our new home was revealed to us: Qayyarah West Airfield, now the one of the largest coalition bases in Iraq.

We filed out from the vehicles, moving around in the dusk to grab our bags. I tried to orient myself to my new surroundings as I did so: tents, black smoke, artillery firing, a wall. It all jumbled together. There was a mix of uniforms and even languages as everyone gathered up and headed to their assigned areas to prepare to get down to business the next day.

I had no idea where I was supposed to go.

"Which way to the TOC, sir?" I asked Capt. Carlier, who helpfully pointed me in the right direction towards a group of tents in the shadows. I began to march that way, my footsteps echoing off the loose gravel that served as a "road" for vehicles. There wasn't a lot to the camp, with everything practically visible from one location in the center which served as trunk for the branches that were the sleep areas, artillery locations, and tenant unit HQs..

I steered myself towards the tent with the most antennas and people around, figuring that it was the main HQ. As I turned the corner-

The Brigade Commander was here? What the hell?

For a second, we both jumped back in surprise upon seeing each other, silence hanging in the air for a few moments. Then the look of surprise on his face turned to anger.

Here we go.

"Where have you been?" he asked, an accusatory tone on the words.

"Huh?" my reply, caught off guard. He wasn't having it

"That Major from CJTF has been looking for you for the past couple days. I keep on getting asked where you're at. Have you been sleeping in or something?"

He obviously wasn't happy, but after the whole experience where members of his own staff tried to fuck me over petty childishness, he wasn't exactly on my best friend's list either. Maybe I was being too hard on him, but then again, aren't leaders "responsible for everything their subordinates do or fail to do", or is that only applicable to lieutenants and below.

"I just got here, sir, literally." My response, a little testy. Did he think I was hiding out?

"You need to find him so they can stop bothering me."

"Where is he?" I asked, shaking my head. Was I supposed to be able to track people automatically? "I have no idea, if you could point me the right way."

"I don't know. Check over at the JOC side." The response was short, brief, upset.

"Alright," I nodded and walked off, leaving him to fume. At least I knew which direction to go.

As I turned, a voice called my name, and I glanced in its direction, seeing a friendly face: the 2nd Lt. who was the unit public affairs representative for the 39th BEB. The UPAR program was still in place when we were in Iraq, and she was assigned the duties alongside her usual ones as a platoon leader. This usually wouldn't have been too much of a problem…except for one issue.

"I'm glad you're here!" she said. "I've been working with Maj. Parker on trying to do media escorts, but I have *no idea* what's going on. NBC came yesterday, and it was crazy."

I started to reply that she had more experience with media escorts than me at that point. Still, I held my tongue, figuring it wouldn't help the situation.

"Trying to do the media stuff and my regular job has been a little, much," she continued, waving me over. "Come on; I'll take you over to the Iraqi side where Maj. Parker works." We turned towards the edge of the coalition area, signified by a wall and large gate with a guard tower next to it. Figures could be seen moving inside the window.

"Two going out!" the UPAR yelled up to the Soldiers in the guard tower.

"Roger!" A helmeted figure replied before he disappeared then reappeared on the ground to open the gate. Grinding noises could be heard as he did so and the UPAR and I soon stepped through the opening, the gate grinding closed behind us. In front of us were two wooden buildings isolated in the middle of an open area — our destination.

"I don't like coming here by myself." She said to me as we strode towards the JOC in the night, the only light coming from a small flashlight she carried.

"The Iraqi side is *creepy.*"

Creepy? That was an odd phrase. I knew enough of the UPAR to realize she wasn't bothered easily, but something was unnerving her, and just my luck, whatever it was would be my problem soon enough. We approached the back of the tent, passing through bunkers that would serve as protection against IDF. I looked back towards the barely visible guard tower and saw that it didn't have a great view of the area, as lifeless as it was.

The UPAR punched in the code on the door, quickly opening it. We entered a bare open space that held a couple of desks and smelled like wood. A Soldier sat at one watching what looked to be camera feeds.

Maj. Parker was at another.

With Maj. Sanders.

"Glad you made it L.T.," she said calmly as if nothing was amiss, turning away from her discussion with Parker. Neither of them looked happy to see each other.

Great.

"Doing battlefield circulation with the Brigade Commander?" my question.

"The Brigade Commander is going to run operations at Q-West for a while," her reply. "He only brought a small part of his staff, so I came along."

Brought? Or did they carry *them*selves? With Maj. Sanders, I knew it was the latter. There was something else at work here, considering that the commander was choosing Qayyarah West seemingly at random.

"It's getting kind of cramped at Camp Swift," she continued, filling me in. She glanced at Parker. "Maj. Gen. Volesky moved his staff down there for some reason."

Of course. The issue now was that Maj. Sanders and Maj. Parker were trying to do the same thing for two different sets of people-to say that the relationship started strained would be an understatement.

I figured I might as well try my hand to get out of Q-West before I got caught in a tug of war between Majors.

"Since you two are here, why am I here then?"

Maj. Sanders and Maj. Parker glanced at each other. Obviously, there was some disagreement there.

191

"You're here to assist me…" Maj. Parker started.

"With setting up the media visits. Beyond that, not much else." Maj. Sanders finished.

I could tell this would be painful for a moment.

Our PAO "headquarters" would be that small little room at the back of the JOC, out of sight and out of mind. Maj. Sanders, Maj. Parker, myself, the combat cameraman, and the civil affairs liaison for the area.

The civil affairs liaison was a Staff Sgt. Miller; he was a veteran of some hard fighting in Afghanistan and now had the task of trying to coordinate efforts, all by himself, for the Qayyarah West area. It was a massive task, one that found him watching dozens of intelligence feeds with chat rooms filling his screen as he tried to keep pace with what was going on. He didn't want anything to do with whatever our public affairs mission was but soon found himself drafted in due to the shortage of personnel.

To get to the area where the media were staying, we had to leave the already pitifully secured JOC, walk down the road and past an open gate that practically spilled out into Iraq, then through a tent city of a living area that held the media tent.

Which was right next to tents occupied by Shia Paramilitary Forces backed by Iran. How did we know? Staff Sgt. Miller asked me to snap a picture of one of the symbols on an Humvee there, and when he looked it up, it confirmed our suspicions.

Therein lay the critical fact about the southern axis of the advance into Mosul: The ISF Golden Division, the Iraqi Army's most elite fighters, were coming from the east. Other units were coming from the north. But from the South? The Iraqi Federal Police and PMFs, who might have well been flying Iranian flags. To say that they didn't like us was an understatement. Their goals ostensibly aligned with ours, however, and who could blame them?

We were basically giving Iraq over to Iran.

"Ready to go?" Maj. Parker, grabbing his pistol, with Maj. Sanders right next to him. She wasn't going to let him coordinate anything without being there too. I sighed, grabbing my M4, along with the combat cameraman.

"We need your help too Staff Sgt. Miller." Miller looked up from his computer screen, obviously annoyed. He understood that it wasn't an order, but a request. I could see him weighing the options before eventually deciding to come along.

"Alright," he said, grabbing his rifle. "But I can't help you all the time. So that you know, we'll be totally exposed over there." He looked around the building. "This spot is already bad enough with no security, but over there? I know for a fact that most of those guys are shady." He patted his rifle. "Hopefully, you make it quick."

We all walked out, three M4s and two pistols: all the firepower that we could muster. Pausing just around the corner from the JOC we chambered rounds, the only thing needed to fire now being switching our selector from safe to semi.

Maj. Parker and Maj. Sanders took the lead, the combat cameraman and I behind, Miller watching the rear. As we turned the corner to the media tent one look at the area told me that this probably wasn't the safest idea. Dozens of Iraqis, milling around, all armed. Some of them relaxed and friendly when they saw us. Others not so much, warily watching our moves. The Majors quickly walked into the tent, leaving the rest of us outside to take up a position. Staff Sgt. Miller faced the rear, the combat cameraman and I took the front, getting behind some cover. I glanced at the tent and a reporter popped out, obviously comfortable with the situation. Who could blame him, considering who it was?

I blinked my eyes in disbelief. Richard Engle of NBC. The guy who I watched at 12 years old on T.V. as he reported on the bombing of Baghdad to begin the Iraq War. Here he was still reporting, and here I was no longer in middle school but a Soldier in the conflict. Engle was embedding with the Iraqi units who were pushing forward as part of his reporting on the offensive, and after months of everyone trying to get access, he had been one of the first to visit coalition troops at Q-West. It was a hot scoop, and he was on to other ones in the area.

Maj. Sanders and Parker eventually popped out of the media tent after what seemed like forever.

"I'll be there escorting the media too." Maj. Sanders said, pointing back to the tent.

"I can handle it myself." Parker's reply, shaking his head. "That's *what they sent me down here for.*"

"You're here from CJTF-OIR. I'm here to make sure Strike is taken care of."

They continued to argue-converse all the way back to the JOC.

Soldiers moving equipment in the interior of sleep tents at Qayyarah West, October, 2016. Photo by Daniel Johnson

Ring Ring Ring.

Incoming! Incoming! Incoming!

Drop to the ground, and then get to the nearest bunker. Eventually dropping to the ground and going to the nearest bunker became more of an annoyance than anything, or something you just skipped. After enough times, the sound of the incoming alarm didn't even cause an adrenaline rush.

ISIL fighters were well within the range of the airfield and multiple times a day Chief Miranda and his radar crew would detect rounds rapidly approaching our location.

Boom.

The sound of a round impacting outside, much different than the movies.

Wait for it. Wait for it.

Look at everyone's faces, some serene, some tense.

Wonder what would happen if the bunker you were in took a direct hit.

All clear.

At least the indirect fire nterception system could work. Proof of that came when it blew up an incoming rocket right over the sleeping area, raining the ground below with shrapnel.

Back to business, until another round was launched at us.

These were the conditions that the personnel working on rebuilding the airfield had to endure for months before finally finishing in October. That, along with the unexploded ordinance that littered the area, and corpses laying around in some of the rubble, rotting and decomposing for months. Some of them were discovered quickly. Some of them weren't, and some of them were but were left in place like the one that sat out for months just outside the cantonment area, it's location well known by anyone who had gotten to do some exploring. It eventually disappeared, buried by someone: a dirty job, considering the body had been sitting there from August to October.

Maj. Sanders and Parker were a pretty good team, once they got past the initial awkwardness. It helped that they both genuinely wanted to do the right thing.

"You know, I get the feeling your boss doesn't like me," Maj. Parker to me one night, after Maj. Sanders had left for the night to rack out for the next day. I could tell by the look on his face that it wasn't just the standard "shit talk," but that he just didn't get why he was met with hostility.

He nodded his head towards me for my opinion.

"I don't think she has anything against you personally, sir," my response, looking back at everything we'd experienced the past few months. The failures, the successes. "She just really cares about making sure the unit gets spotlighted, and she's kind of miffed that CJTF-OIR sent down a spokesman when she's been trying to get media coverage for months."

"I'm not trying to steal her thunder," Parker's reply, shaking his head.

"I don't think you are sir. It's just that we've been left out on a limb for the past few months, and now everybody suddenly wants a piece because we're near Mosul." I threw my hands up. "I mean, she had to rely on *me* until about a month ago."

Maj. Parker looked thoughtful. I don't know if my words had any effect, but I could tell that the two warmed up to each other pretty quickly.

The media got the world tour during their visits. First, Maj. Parker and Maj. Sanders took them to the JOC to see where Soldiers from 1-75 CAV and Marines from the Special Marine Air-Ground Task Force were advising the fight. This was the first time anyone had really gotten a look at an actual advising cell in action, with its ton of computer screens, officers pacing dramatically around the floor, ISR feeds, the Iraqis requesting for fires, our guys calling in fires, gigantic battle maps, etc.

Next, the reporters were taken through the gate that separated the coalition side and the Iraqi side before meeting MATVs that chauffeured them around the base. Cue Maj. Parker talking about how Iraqi forces are taking the lead, American troops are in the rear, how this is their fight. Hit the HIMARs unit, which had called their area Rocket City (a big hit with the media) where their young platoon leader or grizzled platoon sergeant talked about hitting targets in Mosul with pinpoint accuracy. Next up the Paladin units, who said the same thing. Technological overmatch at its finest, *our boys and girls weren't in danger at all.*

Maj. Parker left out the part for future visitors that the Paladins promptly left Qayyarah West not long after the offensive began, speeding off one evening to bring fire support closer to the front line. There was also that they got attacked while doing so, but those were *minor* details.

After the artillery, it was to the airfield, now operated by the United States Air Force's 821st Contingency response group. The CRG was a highly specialized group that focused on training and rapidly deploying personnel to open airfields and establish, sustain, and coordinate air operations. Commanded by a Full Bird Colonel, Rhett Champagne, they ran their own show on Qayyarah West with their own security forces and cantonment area.

After the tour of the airfield, the reporters were sped back to the Iraqi side for closing remarks by Maj. Parker. All benign stuff, but finally it was proof of what we were doing in the country. The big media groups were happy, except for one small detail.

They couldn't use any names at all, save for Maj. Parker, Maj. Sanders, and the Colonels. Acting as if we were some elite Black Ops unit, the guidance from the top was that they were to be referred to by their branch identifiers, like Marine, Sailor, or Soldier. The media could post some small details about them, like how long they had been in, but beyond that, nothing.

"This doesn't make any sense," my words during a discussion with Maj. Sanders and Parker back in our "office." "Even with Special Forces Soldiers invaded Afghanistan, they at least had nicknames like 'Bob" or Joe.'"

"That's the rule L.T." Maj. Parker's reply, he himself also a little frustrated by the situation. Like any public relations guy, he was the nearest thing for the media to complain about the policy, and like a lot of P.R. people, he didn't agree with the procedure in the first place.

"But I can write an article with names, names attached to faces, hometowns and everything, literally from the same interview? If I think it's schizophrenic from the inside, imagine how it looks to *everyone else.*"

"Once General Volesky leaves," Maj. Sanders interjecting. "We'll have a little more freedom." She shrugged, but from the tone of her voice, I could tell she didn't feel that relaxed.

"It's like he doesn't want anyone else's name out there," I asked, feeling out the room.

Maj. Sanders and Parker were silent, and I took that as my confirmation.

Volesky was staying in the country until the last possible moment, the joint press conference at Q-West airfield that Maj. Parker had been sent to prep. The commander of CENTCOM, at that time, Gen. Joseph Votel, along with the commander of CJTF-OIR- Lt. Gen. Townsend, would fly in with a large group of Pentagon reporters, hold a conference on the airfield, and then have a media pool at the brand new JMOC.

The JMOC that currently had 2 personnel assigned to it and was just an empty tent surrounded by Shia Militia.

Chapter Thirteen- Poisoned Air

Rotten eggs.

The smell of sulfur hit me at the same moment I noticed the total lack of visibility outside the sleep tent; the air was already toxic, but this *was different*. It was thick. The sensation filled my body as I tried quick breaths, working for full ones. It wasn't possible.

The air was so bad that we literally couldn't breathe, and I ducked back inside, reaching for the M40 Gas mask issued to us in case that ISIL used chemical agents such as mustard or nerve affecting ones. Kind of useless without the while suit in those cases, but at least the filtration device worked against particulates.

Like sulfur-dioxide.

Mask on, hold the filter, full breath to ensure there was a seal. Just like we trained.

I never thought I would have to do it in real life.

I stepped forward again, this time able to breathe clearly. As I glanced around the gloom, I noticed others doing the same thing, gas masks covering their faces as they moved towards their positions. French forces on the base had caught wind of the danger, *literally*, first. Their chemical weapons early detection systems immediately and automatically set off an alarm that notified the entire chain of command that Qayyarah West was under a Chemical, Biological, Radiological, and Nuclear Operations (CBRN) attack. Chief Miranda and his team set off their warning alarm soon after, klaxons echoing loudly in the unnatural fog.

ISIL had set the al-Mishraq sulfur plant on fire, blowing clouds of sulfur dioxide towards Coalition forces to delay their advance. The very definition of chemical warfare, described by the DOD as – "All aspects of military operations involving the employment of lethal and incapacitating chemical munitions/agents and the warning and protective -measures associated with such offensive operations". We weren't prepared.

The M40 gas mask filters last for less than 10 hours, due to the train of thought being that the military forces don't try to *stay* in a CBRN environment- all equipment is meant to keep Soldiers survivable until they reach a decontamination point well outside the affected area. Soldiers on duty in the guard towers at Q-West worked 12-hour shifts, however; and by the time their rotation was over, they would have already been inhaling the fumes for hours.

The air was so thick that black collections of Sulphur, dust, and oil began to gather on our uniforms. In the time it took me to walk from the sleeping area to the JOC, my uniform looked like I had jumped into a box of filth. I hastily unlocked the door, barreling into the back room, only to see Maj. Parker and Staff Sgt. Miller already there.

"The air quality isn't affecting coalition operations," Maj. Parker was going over the talking points.

"Really, sir?" my response, the mask giving my voice a nasal tone. I glanced over to Staff Sgt. Miller, who was sitting at his desk. He just shook his head.

"I can confirm, sir, the air quality here is that bad." Miller was leaning into his phone as he talked to someone from Baghdad. More calls kept coming and his instant messaging program on the computer was filled with so much text it was like he was on a raid in an online game. The second the French chemical weapons alarm went off, every high-ranking officer from Baghdad to Washington wanted to know what the hell was going on.

"Air is black," Miller continued, dragging and typing into more message boxes. "Nothing can fly. The civilians who live right next to the sulfur field are in trouble."

Parker's phone rang, and he was now on the phone with someone talking back and forth.

"Coalition Forces are not being affected by the sulfur," he repeated, multiple times to multiple people. The media it seemed like. CJTF-OIR had pushed out the talking points

"The Combined Joint Task Force - Operation Inherent Resolve is assessing the potential risk to personnel at Camp Swift and Qayyarah West Airfield, located about 50 miles south of Mosul, as a result of nearby burning oil wells and a sulfur plant fire."

A female lieutenant who worked for brigade staff walked in the door. She immediately started coughing.

"The coalition has taken air samples, and the analysis is ongoing to determine what, if any, health concerns may result from the fires, which officials said were set by Islamic State of Iraq and the Levant terrorists. As a precaution, coalition personnel at sites affected by the smoke have been directed to limit their activity outdoors. Some service members have voluntarily chosen to don protective masks for their comfort." I glanced at the door as more people arrived, most in gas masks. The ones who didn't or who had defective filters were suffering the same coughing fit the earlier arrivals did.

"The use of chemical weapons by the Islamic State of Iraq and the Levant underscores why the international coalition is assisting the Iraqi government in degrading and ultimately destroying ISIL, which continues to kill indiscriminately and operate completely unencumbered by any legal or moral restraint."

More calls, Staff Sgt. Miller and Maj. Parker going to the front to talk to JOC personnel. Satellite images of a gigantic plume of sulfur on news sites. Reports of civilians being sickened, dying. An atmospheric scientist tweeting that if the sulfur dioxide was released from a volcano instead of the plant, it would already be among the most massive eruptions of 2016.

Maj. Parker returned, looking concerned.

"The media is clearing out for now, one of the reporters collapsed in their tent from the air."

The air was toxic as shit, no matter what the talking points about how we were "unaffected" were trying to say.

A study done later would show that we were in one of the absolute worst areas to be during the event, AEGL-2 where, "the airborne concentration (expressed as ppm or mg/m3) of a substance above which it is predicted that the general population, including susceptible individuals, could experience irreversible or other serious, long-lasting adverse health effects or an impaired ability to escape." Over 1,000 civilians in the surrounding area would need medical treatment for suffocation symptoms.

The Al-Mishraq plant *was the exact same one* that was sabotaged in 2003 by Iraqi forces. Some of the Soldiers now at Qayyarah West had been there, their lungs irrevocably damaged, and it all had happened to them *again*. If the air remained toxic for too long, we'd become a prime example of how an environmental chemical could disable a military force.

As the days went on, I started to see stuff I'd never thought I would.

Days dark as night, the night like a black hole. CW2 Miranda, gas mask on, in the radar shelter, hunkered down, knowing that he was breathing in toxic air. Soldiers standing on guard, their postures obviously sullen, knowing there was no escape — coughing fits, giant balls of dirt in the air, on equipment.

It went on. A few days in and some Soldiers had already switched to rags to try to filter the air because their M40 masks were now pointless. Skin conditions begin to break out due to the soot. People who had never had an issue before developed eczema, rashes, and started to have black nasal discharges, which to be honest, I didn't think was possible until I saw it. My skin starting to itch every-time warm air hit me, a condition that started at Qayyarah West and wouldn't end until I got home. No matter how many times I washed my uniforms, it just wouldn't go away; I'd never had a skin condition in my life up to that point.

One morning I walked up on the unit's chemical officer who was outside with his gas mask on, checking pieces of paper hanging in the air. He turned towards me and gestured towards the line.

"I'm taking air samples," he said. "The battalion commander wants me to do a few a day to brief him on the air quality."

He paused, and then said words I'd never thought I'd hear.

"I wish I had my chemical platoon to help me."

I had met Soldiers from his chemical platoon. They were spread all over Iraq doing random stuff. Why? Because there'd be no way they'd be needed, right? I would later learn that it had been expected by other intelligence units in the AO that ISIL would blow the plant to slow our advance. Heck, it *had happened before.* For some reason, that message wasn't put out in the proper channels so our supply personnel could make the necessary movements to get more equipment in.

The Marines at Qayyarah West from 3rd Battalion, 7th Marine Regiment, Special Purpose Marine Air-Ground Task Force –led by Maj. Ryan Hunt, would help us out. Hunt had hand-picked his team due to the possible CBRN threat in northern Iraq. Soon after the cloud hit, the Marines were working with the 39th BEB to run tests and then, they were able to get thousands of extra filters shipped to the base faster than our supply lines could. You could see them around the airfield setting up more sensors to get a better reading or passing out filters to the personnel who needed it as soon as a supply run came in. The air might have still been toxic, but at least the guys in the guard towers could breathe easier.

On the public affairs side, the visit by the generals to hold their long-awaited press conference was canceled due to the bad weather. Even when the air cleared up enough to allow for flights it was decided that it would be a bad look to bring the media to a toxic area. The rest of us would just have to suck it up; literally. Good to know just how expendable we were.

"Hey, Lt. Johnson!" the voice of the unit's supply sergeant called out. "You need to come sign for your plate carrier!"

"Plate carrier?" my reply, confused. I hadn't heard a word about a plate carrier in months and expected we'd never get them. Much lighter and comfortable then our IBAs, plate carriers were made for dismounted operations and operations in warm weather.

Like Iraq was in the summer.

I followed the supply sergeant to the TOC, where he pulled out the vest --- clean, smaller, and immediately identifiable as something that would be much better than what I was wearing now.

"You're one of the last ones since you've been traveling around," the supply sergeant continued as he pulled out the paperwork.

"No worries," my reply. "Thanks for telling me, when did the brigade get these?"

"In the summer."

"The summer?"

"Yeah. Camp Swift got first crack at them of course.'

I thought back to the guys from 1-320th almost collapsing from dehydration during the Gun Raid, their IBAs making the situation that much worse. And yet high-ranking NCOs and officers had got the kit first? Guess there must have been a lot of dismounted operations going on.

For the mere minutes or hours they did whatever circulation they did.

A bridging advise and assist mission, our engineers meeting with some Iraqis at the Tigris. Snapping sounds in the air; Staff Sgt. Miller noticed it first. Walking over to some Soldiers who were pulling security, he told them they were getting shot at.

"Really?" their reply, as they glanced towards the position Miller had pinpointed the shot were coming from. They held their fire- the rule was that if you didn't see the target, you couldn't shoot. They crouched in their positions until the shooter eventually left, thankfully without causing any casualties.

A walk on a patrol, the sound of a gunshot filling the air. Not out of the ordinary at Q-West. The telltale sign of a close miss was, however.

Bzzzzt-. Like a humming. The distinct sound of a bullet being fired in your direction, with the snap at it passed us making us duck. It was like we could *feel* it.

"Shit-"

"Fuck"

"That was close!"

Everyone reacted at the same time, crouching down involuntarily. Our postures changed as we took aggressive stances. One thought-

Who the fuck shot at us?

I knew we couldn't trust the PMF.

An Iraqi Soldier turning the corner. Him stepping back, glancing at us.

It's weird how people can sense the tension in the air.

"Relax!" he said, putting his hands up as if to ward us off. We did-slightly.

The Iraqi Police outside the JOC, groups of them harassing the Soldiers on guard. Walking close, trying to grab pieces of their uniforms, teasing them. The kids trying to play it off, their fingers just barely off the triggers. At points they were mere inches from brawling.

"Nice watch," one of the Iraqis, to me, as I approached.

He reached to grab it.

I pushed him off.

A sly smile on his face.

"Why so tense? We're friends!"

"We're not." My reply.

Laughing from his buddies, the type of laughing you hear from people who know they understand the inside joke, and that you don't.

Guard duty, Maj. Parker in the tent, talking to the media. The road was a little livelier at this time of day. Parked in front of us was a vehicle with PMF markings that were tied directly to groups that had targeted American Soldiers before. Staff Sgt. Miller noticed it immediately, and his whole demeanor changed. This was a man who had been in dangerous situations before, and when the situation even made *him* feel uncomfortable, it began to make me even more nervous.

Movement, a truck coming towards us. Three guys in the back. Lean, fit, their gear tightly put together like actual fighters, well-armed and well equipped.

Something was *wrong* with them.

One in the back turned to us, an expression on his face that immediately caused me to focus on him and nothing else. It wasn't even aggression, anger, excitement.

It's the look you give when you're looking at an object, not a human.

That empty stare of killing intent.

I wonder if he saw me looking at him the same way, because he was keeping his eyes on me, too.

It's hard to explain the feeling.

Tension, sweating, heart beating, everything dissipating but that truck. Slide into some more cover. Get ready. Shit.

Don't do anything until you see hostile intent.

The truck got closer.

It was like I could see him perfectly clear, as if I was standing right next to him.

He shifted slightly towards me, a sign that my mind took as him about to make his move.

The truck spun, almost impossibly. It was a rushed maneuver, almost as if the driver was trying to avoid an accident waiting to happen. From the rear of the vehicle, the figures glanced back at us as they retreated.

"What the *fuck* was that?" Staff Sgt. Miller, beside me now, his voice different; the one of a man who was ready to fight. It surprised me, I didn't even know he was there. He had seen and felt it too, his feet unconsciously carrying him towards that truck as soon as he saw it.

We both knew that this was dangerous, and he knew that whoever those guys were, they weren't friends. We beat feet back to the JOC as soon as Maj. Parker returned.

"This look right to you?" an Air Force Captain, glancing at the radar screen near the Airfield. The media was talking to Col. Champagne, and I decided to check out the area. I looked at what the Captain was pointing at: lines filled the screen, pointing towards Qayyarah West.

"The ISF have advanced to here," he continued, pointing towards the front lines. They were making good ground, well supported by coalition firepower. Yet...

"Why would they be firing back all the way to here?" He pointed to the airfield. The lines told the tale. Our allies seemed to be firing backward towards us.

"Our guys in the guard tower have had some near misses. Someone's been taking potshots at them." The Captain shook his head. "I don't trust the PMF guys at all."

Who could blame him?

A dull explosion, one that sounded different. No indirect fire alarm and yet that sounded *close*. I walked over to the Security forces tent to check-in.

"It blew the axle right off." the Soldier on shift said, shaking his head. There was a huddle in the tent, the commander and the first sergeant checking in and occasionally making calls to higher to inform them of what happened.

"What blew the axle off?" My question.

"One of our patrols hit an explosive out there. They were lucky it wasn't any bigger. It blew the axle off an MATV, and now we have to recover it."

"Strange, weren't there just thousands of Iraqi troops staging here? How come they didn't run over it?" A glance from the Soldier, his face saying, "I can take a guess". The Soldiers in the vehicle had been thrown around, and no doubt probably had TBIs, so they were rushed to the aid station on base.

"So, they're going to get purple hearts for getting wounded, right?" TBIs and their effects on personnel who suffered the injuries were being more understood by the day. Life-long headaches, stress, depression, anger, that could pop up at any time --- the very definition of a physical injury. The DoD allowed the award of the Purple Heart even if a servicemember was not treated by a medical officer, if a medical officer certified that the injury would have required treatment by a medical officer had one been available.

These guys had been treated. It was a no brainer.

Silence. A look of ambivalence.

We both knew that wasn't going to happen, not in this brigade. The company commander and first sergeant could write up awards all day, but the approval authority lay well-beyond them. The guidance was to keep the incident on the down low, out of sight, out of mind.

I hope that those guys can get treatment in the future.

After the sulfur had cleared a little, the generals held their joint press conference at Qayyarah West. They brought a whole crew with them, members of the Pentagon Press Corps.

They all landed at the airfield, cameras live and broadcasting to the world. Lt. Gen. Townsend and Gen. Votel saying the right words, giving a speech about how the Iraqis were advancing while we were in support.

After their bit of proclamation, the gaggle moved to the JOC for more talking about how the operation was succeeding. Cue pointing at maps and people sitting around the table. Finally, they moved over to the tent --- I mean Joint Media Operations center, opening for questions. It had been set up well; there was even a big sign hanging with the Strike Heart and 39th BEB Insignia. The CENTCOM PAO was happy, which meant the CJTF-OIR PAO was delighted, which meant Lt. Col. Thomas was happy, which meant that Maj. Sanders was happy.

This was Maj. Gen. Volesky's last ride with the 101st --- not long after he returned to Fort Campbell, his division command time would be complete and new person would be installed. Out of his 30 months in command of the

Division, 15 of them had been deployed. If you count pre-deployment training and reintegration, Volesky spent more time away from the Division and "his" elements" than with it.

The Brigade Commander returned to Camp Swift as soon as Volesky left, taking Maj. Sanders and the rest of the staff with him. They were going to start doing more battlefield circulation with the media especially since the main bottleneck was gone. Maj. Parker would soon be on his way to Kuwait, his job done, with a replacement PAO team from the states relieving him.

I was still stuck, however.

U.S. Army Spc. Briana Henderson, 39th Brigade Engineer Battalion, and other Soldiers from the unit. pulling security during a bridging advise and assist mission, November, 2016. U.S. Army photo by Daniel Johnson.

Smoke rose in the distance from the burning oil fields as I stepped out the door to the tent. Sgt. Owen stood there staring into the distance, obviously ruminating on something

"Still glad to be out of Camp Union III?" I asked jokingly.

"Yeah. That place sucked." His reply.

"The Iraqis started landing planes on the airfield a few days ago." I offered, joining him on his watch. "Long way from the days where there were only a hundred of us in 1-26."

He chuckled. The smoke from the oil fires continue to belch into the air. I'd never see something like this again.

"It was pretty bare out here when we occupied the airfield in August," Owen said, waving towards some of the Soldiers walking around. "It was just desert and blown-up buildings around our security perimeter. I told the new guys before they came out here that it might be a little rough. We were lucky; it could have been much worse."

"Mortar fire and toxic air is your idea of a sunny day?"

I at least got a smirk with that one.

At 27 years of age, Owen, a California native, was the only person in his immediate family to enlist. He had already spent over two years of his life deployed in the Middle East, having been to both Afghanistan and Iraq in the years before OIR.

"You know, I've wondered. Why did it take them 6+ years to award you the purple heart? What made you join the Army?"

"It sounds cheesy, but I joined the Army because I wanted to serve my country. That aspect of the military really drew me in, and it was always something I planned on doing."

A short while after joining, he found himself in Iraq with the 1st Cavalry Division patrolling the city of Basra. The Iraq war was winding down, and for 12 months the 1st CAV operated in the area working to bring stability. Foot patrols, meet and greets, terrain denial. An endeavor fraught with danger, no matter if you called it "Stability Operations", Advise and assist, or COIN.

"There was a lot of activity since we were by the border," he continued. "We were getting hit with rockets, regular improvised explosive devices, and explosively formed penetrators. It sucked trying to find whoever was attacking us. They didn't want to stick around to try to fight."

The explosively formed penetrator, commonly known to U.S. troops as the EFP, was one of the deadliest weapons used by insurgents during Operation Iraqi Freedom. The tactic of choice was to set the charge to explode under or on the side of vehicles as they traveled by. It was created by Iranian Forces operating in Iraq to harass the coalition, planted along known routes to cause damage to convoys. They made their reappearance once again in 2017, an EFP killing Spc. Alexander Missildine, age 20, from the 10th Mountain Division. There were no reports of ISIL ever using those types of weapons; Shia paramilitary forces *did* though.

During one patrol, the vehicle Owen was riding in was struck by an EFP.

"It hit us from the side," Owen said calmly, making a motion with his hands to indicate where the weapon impacted from. "I was in the lead vehicle, a Caiman mine-resistant ambush-protected truck. Luckily, no one was killed."

He sighed, thinking back to the event. "I was wounded in the attack. Suffered a spinal compression and traumatic brain injury and spent two weeks at the troop medical center before returning to my unit. I didn't want to be away from them for longer than I needed to. I finished out the full 12 months."

"Did they lose your paperwork? That's a pretty clear-cut case of being wounded."

He glanced at me, shaking his head in an exasperated manner.

"They said my paperwork got lost once it got past the battalion level." He laughed. "Lost for six years though? Hah. I had just gotten back from Afghanistan with this brigade when the issue was finally fixed."

Suddenly, he stood up taller, pride in his voice, as memories flooded back.

"My battalion commander during that deployment, Lt. Col. Andrew Poznick, was the epitome of a great leader, and everyone knew how much he cared about us. He was always pushing leaders to take care of their Soldiers and he encouraged everyone to get help and talk to someone if they needed it, even if it was him directly."

A pause. A subtle sagging of the shoulders as the pride seemed to dissipate, replaced by something else.

Sadness.

"Unfortunately, he lost his battle with his own PTSD in March of this year, shortly before 1-26 deployed."

"I'll write an article on you," my offer. "You deserve one. Why'd you leave the medical center early?"

"My friends were out there," an immediate response. Honest. "I have friends that are here now. And if we come back again someday, I want to be there with them too."

Owen receiving the purple heart in 2015. U.S. Army photo by Sgt. 1st Class Sierra Melendez.

Owen's words told the story. I sent it up to the new NCOIC for CJFLCC public affairs.

The process wasn't exactly straightforward. Unlike at Erbil, we didn't have the WIFI PUCs to quickly upload images from the MAC. I had to take the photos, put the memory card in my military computer, and hope that I hadn't taken a *really* bad photo because I could only use Microsoft Paint.

The new NCOIC was different from SFC Hoskins. Hoskins was a Photojournalist; the new one was a broadcaster. Two different ways of doing business. There was a slight miscommunication however --- if I said that what I was writing was for local papers, the new NCOIC didn't care as much. He was worried about news about Inherent Resolve, not Soldier profiles.

I may have *forgotten* to tell him that Big Army and media organizations were going directly to the 2nd Brigade's DVIDs page.

I posted the story online.

Sgt. Owen sent me a photo of the article a few days later.

The Department of Defense had posted it as feature news on the front page of their website, under their long-running "Face of Defense" series, highlighting him as *the* person that the Pentagon felt represented the service men and women of the country. It wasn't just for American audiences however, but also to show the world.

News sites even commented on the story and how it showed just how long we had been at war to have a Soldier get wounded seven years before and then come back to Iraq *again*. Sadly, he was one of many. Owen's words on his battalion commander also illustrated the point --- all of this had a cost, even after we returned home.

Especially after we returned home.

Interlude III-Fort Campbell -2015

"Your son will go far," Wetmore's words at my class's commissioning ceremony, to my parents. "He's a good kid; he'll make a difference."

But I *hadn't*. I had failed him. I had failed everyone that had put any faith in me.

I brought the paperwork to Capt. Ryan Rivas, the assistant operations officer at 1-26. University of Florida graduate, Afghanistan Veteran, and soon to be civilian.

You would think he would be in the Army forever though, due to his work ethic. He still showed up every morning for physical training, still worked hard, and always *cared.* Funny how the military loses so many officers of his caliber right at Captain.

"You've got to be kidding me." He looked at the documents. "This is what the S-6 came up with?"

I shrugged. "Trust me, I know. I'm just an assistant."

He laughed bitterly, then pulled up the order he was working on. "I'll let him explain it to Spader 6 then."

I watched him as he typed while poring over the document for any little error, and then looked at the calendar.

He had less than a few weeks left.

"I don't get it, man," I interrupted. He glanced at me comically, as if I had interrupted him mere moments before he unlocked the secret to eternal life.

"What is it, *Johnson.*" His response, drawing out my last name as if we were in a sitcom.

"You actually care, you would make a good company commander, and yet you're choosing to leave."

Rivas looked at me, half sad, half amused.

"That's precisely the reason I'm leaving."

"Yet, you're working just as hard as always."

"Because the external reason doesn't matter. Until the last day, I'm going to do my job because it's the right thing to do."

He turned to me, analyzing.

"You get shit on every day, and yet you keep on trying. Why?"

I hesitated.

"Because it's your *duty*. I've been watching you for a while man; you keep on coming in here every day."

"The Soldiers are trying, why can't I?" I offered lamely.

He smiled.

"That's exactly it. It's just who you are. Don't let anybody change that man."

He pointed to his desk and all the papers. "Ryan Rivas the platoon leader, Ryan Rivas the S3, Ryan Rivas the commander, it *doesn't* matter. I'm not going to put my work on someone else." Rivas nodded towards the hallway.

"There's enough of that around here."

Silence hung in the air as I tried to process his words. I thought back to the time I requested for him to pin on my new rank when I got promoted to 1st Lt., which he was glad to do.

Spader Six told him no, saying that, "What did I think this was?" The one of the few times I saw Rivas generally frustrated, because, you know, it *was my promotion ceremony*, and he was honored to be a part of it. The fact that Capt. Rivas took the time to try to help me out when as often as he could in the twilight of his military service is something I'll be forever grateful for.

He moved to put his headphones in, then stopped.

"You're a good guy Johnson. Don't let any of this change you. You motivate *me* sometimes. Whether you become a platoon leader or not, make Captain or go home, don't let these guys define you. A job doesn't make you who you are. You do."

With that, he went back to work, his task not yet complete, shooing me away as he did so. True to his word he gave 100% until his last day, where with a, "Not a bad way to spend your 20s," he shut down his computer and walked off, starting law school a few months later.

Chapter Fourteen, Different Realities- November 2016

The cloud of the election was over *everything and* watching how contentious it was through the summer and into the fall from Iraq made it seem like we were watching it from another planet. The election was probably the biggest reason Iraq was getting so much media attention at the time.

It had ISIL, public enemy #1, responsible for terrorist attacks that happened across the world. It had the U.S. Army back on the ground in Iraq after the Obama administration was dragged back into a conflict he had run on ending. It had Donald Trump and Hillary Clinton, who had different views on foreign affairs. Over the summer, we started to notice the bot networks of social media that were signal boosting certain types of *fake* news stories. It was obvious, with the same types of accounts posting the exact same message repeatedly, all part of an attempt at information warfare. Like with the white phosphorus before, all these actions were being undertaken by non-legitimate actors to sow chaos, confusion, and mistrust. We thought it wouldn't have too much of an effect.

Because if it did, that meant that the messages had found a *very* receptive audience.

As the presidential election and holidays inched closer, more tours were scheduled. Some news organizations even pitched having a feed on Q-West during the election for some live reaction shots. That wasn't going to happen since none of us knew what emotions the election would elicit on November 8th.

I couldn't sleep. Any chance I got, I refreshed the page on the internet, painfully watching it load. The results were coming in. November 9th in Iraq. November 8th, back at home.

Trump wins Ohio.

Okay, that's a given.

Trump wins Florida.

Eh, to be expected.

I finally get to bed, waking up the next morning to check the results. Surely, Clinton would win.

Trump wins Pennsylvania.

Holy shit.

Wait, didn't Obama win these states in his elections? What happened?

Breakfast. A rush to the chow tent to watch television in there.

Hilary Clinton has conceded. Donald Trump is now President-Elect of the United States. I glanced around. Some were happy at the results; some were not. I looked towards a Soldier I knew.

He's grinning in victory.

For some reason, I'm not shocked at the results.

In the bathroom, I ran into another African American Soldier.

"You know, I'm not even surprised after President Obama," he said with the calmness of a man who's been through all the ringer's life has to offer. He looked at me sadly. "It's just the way this country is, man."

He gave me an understanding nod, patting me on the shoulder before walking out.

At home, racist graffiti in Durham. College students driving through campuses yelling hate speech. White high school students marching through halls shouting, "White Power." All of this in the year 2016.

The cold hard feeling that in no small portion of the population, I and people who look like me are less than human.

Risking our necks for these people?

You had to be fucking kidding me.

First, I was angry, and then it turned into an all too familiar feeling for millions of minorities in the country: acceptance.

Just like thousands before me, who swore an oath to defend the nation and its ideals, even if it, or the people in it didn't always live up to those expectations. Even when enemy POWs were treated better than them, even when they were fighting for democracy halfway across the world while not being able to vote at home, even when they volunteered to fight for a new nation where they were considered 3/5ths of a man.

What else could I do? I could take solace that more people voted for Hillary Clinton than for Trump, while also being dismayed that so many people voted for him in the first place and a lot of people chose not to vote at all.

The world was going to be different once we came back. We were people out of time, separated from reality for almost a year. And all we could do was watch.

Thanksgiving came, and with it, the curtain call of my time at Qayyarah West. The Associated Press was coming to run footage of all the personnel getting chow and enjoying-, *surviving* the holidays. Even better, it was going to be a live stream, brought to people across the world by the magic of satellite technology that wasn't 2MBPS.

The chow hall was going to be cooking the best food and the media would get to see it. The news organizations wanted to get B-roll of the whole thing: the chow line, the food being served, Soldiers eating hearty meals. Good stuff for the folks back home. The AP guys were pros, dropping the video cameras to get POV shots, hitting the right angles in the kitchen, and setting up the video camera in the chow tent for the live feed, posted on local news sites in the states to reactions. (The views reached into the 10s of thousands.)

The meal was great, and there was more than enough food for seconds. The smell of oil, of Sulphur, in the air. Soldiers massing up to send messages to their family back home. People moving out for missions. Then, back to the bunker and the cot, another night in Iraq.

Only a little bit left to go.

"National Geographic is coming to Iraq for a documentary." Maj. Sanders, informing me that the information she had sent just a few minutes before was real. "They *specifically* mentioned that they wanted to see 1-320th and 1-75 CAV. I guess someone read your work."

"Really?" my reply as I clicked through the messages on my computer back in Erbil, trying to get deeper into my cold-weather gear.

Pttt. Pttt. Pttt.

The sound of rain hitting the tent overhead, the first time we'd seen weather like it in six months. I glanced down at my boots, heavy due to the thick mud that covered them. It turned out that during the summer nobody thought about the fact that LSA Strike was in a mini flood plain.

They also didn't think about ensuring our sleeping areas were weatherproof either, if the two tents that collapsed early one morning during a rain shower were any indication.

I looked at the email traffic and its massive CC line from the Pentagon down. This was no joke; NATGEO was requesting to see units in the brigade specifically.

"National Geographic is getting full access," Maj. Sanders continued. "They're going to get everything except the Special Forces. It's not going to be an embed, but they are going to be able to stay for an extended amount of time."

A media escort I could get behind. "So, we'll have to stick with them then?"

"Yep." Her tone was one of legitimate excitement. "That's not an issue; we have enough PAO assets in the country now to take care of that now. This is what we've been waiting for, and finally, everything and everyone is in place."

The series would be a documentary about the war on terror; NATGEO was getting unparalleled access to service-members across the world and the operations in Iraq were the first stop. CJFLCC headquarters in Baghdad was giving Maj. Sanders all the leeway on this operation since our brigade was one NATGEO specifically requested. They were more than happy with her plan of action.

"We'll need to get them to the PAAs and our advising sites." she continued. "I can't be at all of them, but I trust you can help out with some of our units. I want to get Bartallah, Qayyarah West, and the artillerymen in action. We don't have long to do this L.T.; if they get here in December, we'll have less than a month."

I could tell what she meant just by looking outside. Deployers, re-deployers, people loading containers, tents being emptied and filled- the tell-tale sign of a shift in operations. The first guys from the 82nd Airborne Division had started to arrive, the advance party for the rest of the brigade that would mostly be on the ground by the new year. We also got reinforcements in the way of even *more* late deployers from Fort Campbell, some of whom were staying in the country for only a couple weeks to 30 days.

In the Army, you wear your resume on your uniform. Air assault? Ranger? Deployment? With whom? Combat action badge? Combat Infantryman Badge? But how? What about the cases where you got wounded but got no combat badge? Or got your combat badge for mortar fire a mile away? Or under the same criteria and the same events you got nothing while the one next to you did, like at KSB?

It was absurd. Being a "slick sleeve" was seen as embarrassing, or made others question your competence. But here's the thing- the criteria for receiving one is that you simply step foot in an active combat zone. If you were in Qatar or Kuwait, the goal was to get to Iraq or Afghanistan for at least a day so you could qualify for the right shoulder patch. Then you'd simply catch the next thing smoking and fly out.

It was *encouraged*, at least for officers. 1-75 Cav rotated their lieutenants out about every 90 days, and even the liaison officers the brigade had in Kuwait were flown in for a couple of days. Even as late as December, with the 82nd Airborne starting to arrive, lieutenants from the brigade were *still* arriving in Iraq to "help them in their career."

Appearance trumps everything, I guess.

I didn't get it; a Soldier working intelligence could be just as useful to the fight at Fort Campbell or D.C. as being in Taji or Erbil. A person who spent one day in Iraq wasn't magically more competent than a person who hadn't.

Or, a better leader, based on my experiences.

"I'm going to send you home early January to set up the ground there," Maj. Sanders continued. My ears perked up. It was a strange feeling, realizing that all of this would be coming to an end. "NATGEO wants to be there for the Brigade Commander's coming home, so I'll need you to work with Staff Sgt. Melendez."

"Then, we go on post-deployment leave?"

"No. Not until after the re-deployment ball."

"For two weeks or thirty days?"

She hesitated. "I'll get back to you on that."

Most units in the Army would give Soldiers returning from an overseas tour 30 days off in leave (vacation) afterward. (Mid-Tour leave during deployments switched to this method as they turned from 12-15-month tours down to 9) The process usually consisted of returning home, in-processing back at base, and then as soon as that was done, riding off into the sunset.

Our brigade leadership wanted to do it differently; no one would be allowed to take post-deployment leave until well in February, a month after we returned. Then, it'd only be two weeks.

Once families back at home got wind of the plan to only give Soldiers about 12 days off instead of 30, the response was overwhelmingly in the negative: phone calls, Facebook Messages, texts. The unit's thought process was never truly explained, but a look at the calendar explained a lot; there was an upcoming exercise at Fort Bliss, Texas, that summer just about five months after everyone returned. The brigade leadership finally relented after all the complaints. Soldiers could take 30 days of leave upon coming back from Fort Campbell.

Strangely enough, most of the brigade leadership wouldn't be in place for the exercise at all, since they would all be moving to new duty stations upon our return.

We'd still have to wait around a month though.

"Where do you want to go, L.T.?" Maj. Sanders question, with the unspoken words that time was, finally, running short.

"I guess I'll head towards Mosul and 2-502, there hasn't been any coverage up there recently. Whatever I write will probably get run everywhere."

"You sound like you have a connection up top," her response.

"I don't know ma'am," my reply. "But at this point, it's just a fact of life. I can guarantee it'll be worth your while."

"And then after that?" her reply.

"Christmas with the artillerymen." My reply, immediately.

"Again?" she sighed. "You've written two articles on them already!"

"And this one will go just as well," I was almost begging.

"Alright," she relented. "It'll be your last rodeo, so might as well. You'll be on one of the first flights home after the New Year. Time to start thinking about reality L.T."

"It'll be here sooner than you know it."

"Looks like you're not stuck in Taji anymore." I greeted Lt. Brooker, who looked just as stoic as always, even in the change of scenery at Erbil.

"The new battalion commander of 526 BSB moved me up here." She paused, looking at my camera. "Looks like you're still running around. You're going out to Bartallah?"

"You know it."

"To do…?"

I shrugged. "Win the war one high fidelity image at a time, of course."

"You and your 'high fidelity',"

"I mean, have you seen those pics, the people in the Pentagon love them!"

"Blah blah blah pentagon, blah blah blah front page. How come the photos we asked you to take on that recon were so blurry?"

"You guys wanted me to take a picture of the PMF flag while trying to take a picture of *you!*"

"And you failed us."

"What can I say? It's a character trait/flaw."

"Trait *slash* flaw?

"And or flaw doesn't have the same ring to it."

She smirked, but didn't fully crack.

"Always so serious." I tsked while shaking my head. "You and your plans and calendars. You should just go with the flow."

It was her turn to tsk. "That sounds stressful. Have you even thought about what you're going to do once you get back?"

"No." I paused. "I never thought about that part. It'll all buff out."

"You always say that, but what if it doesn't?"

I didn't know the answer to that.

"You'll never give me credit!"

"Because you give yourself enough of it." She was shaking her head at me with a smile now and seemed to be in a better mood now that she felt like she was participating in the greater mission. I was glad to see it, it was a great feeling to see other people with purpose, who cared.

Especially compared to *some* people.

"We'll leave in a bit to go out there," she continued. "You cleared it with the battalion commander of course?"

"Maj. Sanders did I think."

"Sounds good. Hopefully, you get the battalion right this time." She continued, with an expression of victory, reminding me of the time I had mistakenly confused 1-502 and 2-502 in an article. I rolled my eyes at her self-assured smirk. That was all in the past, but no one let me forget it.

My goal was to reach Bartallah and ...I didn't know. To be honest, the battalion commander didn't know I was riding that far. Better to ask for forgiveness than permission as the saying goes.

We left in the morning in civilian vehicles, tops off, dark eyepro on. Kurdistan opened before us as we moved west through the battlegrounds of the past few months, the land still bearing the scars.

Our in-between point was a town that was a repurposed gas station that was less village, and more a literal outpost that was occupied by coalition troops before the final push towards Mosul began. There we made the switch to actual tactical vehicles, our up armored MATVs.

Then we were off, down the road, towards Bartallah. It was a quiet ride in the back of the vehicle with the SECFOR Soldiers of 2-502. Shifts at Bartallah were conducted in rotations between them and the 1-26 Soldiers-four days on, four days off. The 2-502 guys had been in the country since May, starting out all the way down at Al Assad before being pulled up north for this detail. One that would find them quite literally in Mosul taking indirect fire and dodging drones before it was all said and done.

The vehicle stopped. The ramp opened. I stepped out and-

There was nothing there.

I glanced around.

We were quite literally in a field next to houses in a village, the perimeter being ...the two trucks we had just gotten out of.

The 2-502 Soldiers marched towards one of the houses, and their platoon leader waved at me.

"This way," he motioned for me to follow him before pointing at the house. "This is our place."

I followed the Soldiers into the building, our bags in our hands, walking past the battalion commander, who gave a, "I didn't know about this."

Too late.

The sight of the actual interior of a house, living room, kitchen and all, was off-putting. It felt so...foreign after so many months of seeing bunkers, tents, and trenches. Inside the house, on the bottom floor, was the "Advise and Assist" cell. Personnel from 2-502 and other entities that made sure the Iraqis were getting the fire support they needed. It wasn't much of a jump from the front line, mere kilometers away, to the location, and you could literally see Mosul from the roof of the house.

The Soldiers moved up the stairs, bags in hand, one of them patting me on the shoulder.

"Welcome to the Frat House!" his words as he brushed past, up and then into a bedroom.

Soldiers returning from patrol entering the "frat house", December, 2016. U.S. Army photo by Daniel Johnson.

I had no idea what was going on, so like anybody who was lost, I followed the person in front of me up the stairs, dropping off my bags with the others. I looked for anyone I could recognize when I spotted some familiar faces.

Sgt. 1st Class Brian Bailey and the commander of A CO, 1-26 infantry. I knew both from Fort Campbell, and thank god they knew me, or I probably would have gotten thrown out of the house by the battalion commander right then. They turned to look at me, Bailey looking shocked at my seeming materialization out of thin air.

"Where have you been?" his question, as if I had told him I was going to the gas station and had taken an hour.

The commander tilted his head.

"Maj. Sanders should have let me know you were coming," he looked confused. "I would have taken you out with us. We just rotated our guys out too for a break.

He looked at Bailey.

"You got him?"

"I do," Bailey replied, smiling.

The commander patted me on the shoulder and walked down the stairs to catch his ride, leaving me with Bailey.

"I didn't know you were here!" We shook hands warmly. "What's this, deployment number nine?"

"Yep, it is." His reply. When I had met Sgt. 1st Class Bailey, I was hanging around the 1-26 S6 section doing nothing. He had come to the unit after returning from the Afghan 2014 deployment and I had spoken to him about his experiences since I'm a big fan of history. One day I showed him a picture of Afghanistan I had seen as a kid --- three Soldiers in the mountains of Afghanistan, a Chinook landing in the background.

"That's me in the picture." He said, pointing at one of the figures.

I was shocked.

"No way."

"I'll prove it to you."

He did some digging online and showed me the entire Time magazine article with multiple photos of his platoon.

Bailey had joined the Army in the 90s, before the Global War on Terror. Following the 9/11 attacks, as a Pfc., he had arrived at Fort Campbell.

"Who wants to deploy right now?" asked the Soldier who ran the replacement company. Bailey and one other man raised their hands; they were separated from the group and a few weeks later, they were in Afghanistan.

And now here he was again, 17 years later, in Iraq. The funny thing was, not only was he in the initial push into Afghanistan with the 101st in 02, he was also part of the initial push into Iraq a year later, and then the *initial* occupation of Mosul.

Considering he was part of another operation to secure the city and we could see it from the house, I wonder how strong his sense of Deja vu was.

"I'll show you around town," he offered, grabbing his kit.

"I need some fresh air, anyways."

Bailey led me onto the street, pointing at the buildings surrounding us. There was a lot of other traffic consisting of Iraqis and the Cool Guys, who were based next door to the "frat house."

The gym, which consisted of a bench press bar and some weights, was right next to a building in with unexploded ordnance, occupying a small enclosure behind the house. To get there you had to walk through a narrow alleyway that led past abandoned homes; toys, pieces of furniture, trash --- they all filled the interiors as the telltale signs of a hasty escape. The road outside wasn't much better, filled with debris and obstacles from the battle.

"The battalion commander wants us to do a P.T. test," Bailey said, looking towards the perimeter. "They don't believe me when I tell them it's just not possible."

A Soldier pushed past us, walking towards the gun trucks just meters away.

"What, they want you to clear out a 2-mile route and then have the gun trucks pull security as you run?"

Bailey's glance said it all. *Don't give them any ideas.*

I looked out again at the town: it felt like the image of a google image search of "war-torn."

"If they'd visit us out here, they'd see what was going on," Bailey continued, shaking his head. "They haven't come once, and I don't get why they think we're lying. How can someone in Baghdad tell me what I'm seeing on the ground isn't true?"

Bartallah was a Christian Village, or had been, before ISIL had invaded forcing the citizens out. A large stone church stood in the center of the blocks of houses as the most recognizable landmark in town, Bailey pointing it out as we began our loop.

"When we arrived, most of the town was still booby-trapped with IEDs." He nodded towards an empty structure, its windows busted out. "Some of the buildings still are. EOD is still working on clearing the village."

In early October, they had set off an explosive round a mere 50m from the 1-26/2-502 Soldiers, the force of the blast literally throwing them off their feet and producing a telltale smoke cloud that could be seen for miles.

We passed through an aid station where Iraqis from the front line were brought in for care. The station was ostensibly operated by only Special Forces medics because the rule was that the conventional medics couldn't get involved.

Considering that the medics volunteered to be in the military, then volunteered to be a combat medic, and now found themselves confronted with human suffering, that *rule* was bent all the time.

"I'm only going to assist them," was how one of them put it to me before he went to start his shift. The Iraqis brought there were in bad shape and the medic's eyes showed the strain of the stress of trying to save as many lives as they could, without the support they would have had on a coalition base.

You could tell when an Iraqi passed on, his last moments being on a cot in a blown-out village. His friends would fire a volley in the air in remembrance.

It was a familiar sound.

"When we first got here, the aid station was the only place Iraqi civilians could think to bring their injured." Bailey stopped and looked at the building for a long moment.

"They brought some children once who were injured in a strike. Some of them died in our arms."

"Every time I deploy something happens that tests me. I had hoped this one would be different. We had to stop accepting civilian casualties after that."

Bailey's face was…. stoic? Pensive? Sad? I couldn't read the multiple emotions that seemed to be flickering as we progressed through the town.

Ahead of us we spotted a vehicle surrounded by ISF Soldiers who were milling around. That wasn't unusual. What was unusual was the blindfolded man on the side of the car, visibly shaking and quivering as he responded to what appeared to be questions.

Bailey motioned for me to keep quiet as he got closer to the interrogation, taking a position to the side of the interrogator, who gave him a nod.

More questions, a short response. Anger on the Iraqi Soldier's part. The posture of a man who's accusing another. The blindfolded man stepped back as if trying to escape. A second Iraqi Soldier was nearby to stop his progress.

Bailey walked over, his voice low.

"They caught this guy in one of the villages." He pointed at the two. I realized that he understood Arabic, a skill he kept on the downlow. "They're asking him where he's from, and they can already tell he's not a local."

"So, he's lying to them,"

Bailey shook his head.

"That's what they're thinking."

I knew enough to know what happened to "liars" around here.

We were looking at a dead man. Even not understanding a word he was saying, I could hear the universal language of fear.

We continued.

Chapter Fifteen-Going Home - December 2016

"Chow Time," one of the SECFOR Soldiers said as he almost sprinted down the stairs past me.

The sun had set, and I followed, wondering what he could be so excited about. As soon as I reached the bottom, the front door cracked open, revealing Sgt. 1st Class Bailey standing there, grinning.

"I was able to trade for some food." He announced, holding up some bags of steak.

"Who wants to cook it?"

A few grill masters volunteered and started to fire up the grill that had either been left there or brought, (I still don't know), behind the house. It wasn't long before the sweet smell of barbecued food started to fill the air, a welcome respite from the usually thick one that hung around Mosul.

I joined them in the back, and we all laughed about being home soon, spirits high. We'd soon have all the barbecue we could, our own beds, and gyms not on top of bombs.

"Long time no see," a familiar voice called out. Besides Sgt. 1st Class Bailey, I didn't really know anyone else at the location, until I glanced towards the caller.

"Whoa," my exclamation, memories flooding back. "Been a while since Air Assault school!"

I shook hands with Staff Sgt. Brian Stillman, who was the class leader (as much as he didn't want to do it) of our class at Air Assault school. The ten toughest days in the Army- I'd consider it more of the ten wackiest. He handled the responsibility like a champ; his sarcastic remarks held until the cadre were out of earshot.

"How have things been?" my question. "You look a lot less stressed than at school!"

"Things are less crazy here, believe it or not." he laughed. "We got up to Erbil before we got pulled up here for the offensive. Our element was up on that mountain over there when the whole thing started," Stillman continued, pointing towards the ridgeline.

Front row seats to the massive display of firepower that kicked off the attack. He recounted how his Platoon had found themselves moving towards Bartallah, to secure it for the 2-502nd forward HQ. As their element and others moved in, an IED struck an up-armored vehicle, clearly visible to the rest of the convoy. Naval EOD tech Chief Petty Officer Jason Finan was killed in action, the first American casualty in the battle of Mosul.

Stillman was on his 2nd deployment unlike most of the Soldiers in his squad, many of them who hadn't even been out of the U.S. until coming to Iraq. Still in his late 20s, he was a seasoned veteran compared to a lot of us.

The scent of fully cooked meat began filling the air as we talked, signifying that the foood was ready. Served with some rice, the fact that it didn't have any seasoning or sauce on it was irrelevant.; everyone dug into it like it was the best meal on Earth.

Even the battalion commander joined in, looking more relaxed than I had ever and would ever see him as he hastily grabbed a plate in the kitchen. For a moment, I could tell that he was thinking about life once we returned home, his friends, his family. The moment ended quickly however, as he immediately got called back into the advising cell due to troops in contact.

The conversation turned to home, what would be the same, what would be different. Life goals, whether to stay in the Army or not, anniversaries that were coming up, and the upcoming holiday season. Nothing's changed, the older guys would say. We'd find that people hadn't done anything since we left.

"It's just part of the job," Stillman said, disinterested. "At least we get to save money on Christmas. It's probably harder on those who have a wife and kids at home, but if you're single-"

"This is my real family now," another Soldier cut in, his voice joking. His face was serious.

Looking back at the previous eight months and all that had happened, there was no way that everything would be the same, right? I dug into my piece of steak, trying to separate myself from the out of body feeling that I was experiencing; having a cookout in the middle of a warzone, people dying only a few yards away, the room next door filled with people calling in hellfire on their enemies (sometimes from killer robots) with kids no different than the ones I hung out in the dorms with or complained about how hard college life was, but instead were armed to the teeth.

Techno music suddenly began blaring in the air, reverberating off the walls. I glanced up in its direction.

"Oh yeah," Stillman said. "That happens every night. One of the special forces guys is a DJ or something."

Steak dinner to a techno mix. Only in Iraq.

I joined Bailey on the roof of the house, the rooftops of Mosul visible in the distance.

"Getting everything you need?" His question.

"Yeah, I am." I nodded down towards the two trucks guarding the street. "This isn't what I expected, to be honest."

"It never is."

The silence hung in the air, louder than everything else. I felt out of place standing there on that roof with a man who had been doing this long before I even thought about the Army. Eight, almost nine months felt like enough experiences for a lifetime.

But eight or nine *years?*

"You know," Bailey continued, his eyes roaming the streets of the city. "In 2003, my unit used to drive through here all the time. I don't think any of us thought we'd be trying to retake this area 13 years later."

Nine deployments.

7 and a half years spent overseas fighting in the Global War on Terror.

Mosul, Tal Afar, Kandahar, Marjah --- names that were foreign to most of the population but were all too personal for him, and thousands like him.

"In Boston, maybe one in 10 people know someone in the military," he continued. "For a lot of people back home, the military experience is foreign to them. A lot of them don't understand *this*."

Months later, as I was reading an article on PTSD and its effects, I came upon a passage that brought up a point about the Iliad: the myth wasn't just a story about gods and crazy adventures. It was a tale of Soldiers coming home from a war to a world that was alien and strange to them, to people who found *them* foreign and strange. They were no longer *standard* members of their society, but something else.

But why? Why, even if with the adverse effects of warfare, did people volunteer?

Why did *I* volunteer?

There was a common theme I heard through multiple conversations with Soldiers about why they serve --- the opportunity to do something greater than themselves. It was the reason Bailey had raised his hand to go to war that fall day back in 2001.

"Making that decision put me at the beginning of all of this." He spoke. "I joined because of a desire to be something better than what I was at the time."

He paused, thinking for a moment.

"I stayed because of the people."

Not wanting to fail them.

That was *it*.

"I chose this life. I've had a lot of experiences -- some good, some horrific. It's truly an honor that the Army allows me to be who I am and lead soldiers. I get to see real effects on my environment and participate in events that will be remembered in history. I'm thankful for that every day."

Bailey finished, and the silence once again deafened the air. His statement was simple, one that carried him through 20 years of military service, through the loss of friends, through seeing humanity at its most-base.

It was a sense of purpose, not of the flag-raising patriotism of saluting the troops events at football games, or the Facebook posts of the weird American Soldier memes, but a simple dedication to friends, to the mission, whether those above you cared or not. It's something that everyone, in the military or otherwise, is capable of.

Security Patrol in Bartallah, December, 2016. U.S. Army photo by Daniel Johnson.

Bailey and the mixed 2-502/1-26 element would soon find themselves pushing forward, closer to the front line and into increasing danger; the kids who were on their first trip out of the country finding themselves hearing the zip of bullets flying past their heads as they "steeled" the resolve of Iraqi Forces. Multiple times they would be forced to disengage because the situation was just that *hot,* a part of Inherent Resolve's *inherent* dangers that would not be spoken about to families or anyone else. The difference between life and death was sometimes mere feet, like when a mortar round landed directly on the roof over the element's sleeping quarters at a schoolhouse in East Mosul.

They would face everything ranging from being harassed by drones that dropped grenades, to mortars landing directly on locations Soldiers had been standing just moments before, to driving through areas with a high risk of IED attack.

All in the last two weeks the brigade was in the country.

Why?

So that our leaders could say that they had got the Iraqis through East Mosul before we had re-deployed.

The headaches started after I left Bartallah. Lying on a cot, waiting for the movement to Erbil, hitting my hand on my head to stop the throbbing. It was a dull pain- something different than I had ever felt. I felt like I wasn't even there.

The first noticeable signs of depersonalization.

I was feeling---different. It was hard to explain. Like nothing mattered, like I was watching myself in a movie. I thought then that it was just due to the anxiety of returning home... The fallout of the presidential election, having to set everything back up, having to fix my car. Things we hadn't thought about for 9 months, since the only purpose and focus had been what was going on in Iraq. But even returning home in January wasn't a given.

"They're thinking about extending us," Maj. Sanders warned me during a call when I returned to Erbil.

They're thinking about extending us, or we're thinking about extending us? My silent thoughts.

"Why?" my verbal question.

"We're making good progress in the Mosul campaign, and we want to keep up the momentum. It would be about three more months."

I shook my head. Extensions hadn't been used since the high days of OIF, when the Army didn't have the personnel for operations, and units were engaged in combat constantly. Sometimes the extension happened *after* the first element from a unit had returned home; some Soldiers had the horrific experience of being on the plane, landing at their home duty station, thinking they were free, and then watching as their plane turned around on the runway and headed back into hell.

At least back then, the Army could stretch the logic and say those Soldiers were critical for combat operations. But for an advising mission? With the first elements of the replacement brigade already on the ground? Yeah. Right. The only people angling for an extension would be those in our local chain of command.

It gave them more time to attach their names to the retaking of Mosul.

Someone's OER bullet, or the thing they would use to get the next promotion, with no tactical use at all. It's not like the Iraqis were going to be in the country for, oh, I don't know, forever. I doubt they truly gave a shit who was aiding them if it kept on coming.

I submitted the article on Sgt. 1st Class Bailey to CJTF-OIR as the cloud of our brigade trying to get us extended hung over all of us. No one really thought it would do well, and in fact, didn't really want to run it. I convinced them it was for local Fort Campbell use only.

The Department of Defense used it as their Face of Defense feature, prominently displayed on their home page.

Media outlets ran the story, and some even began trying to contact Sgt. 1st Class Bailey due to his words. He was the prime example of sacrifices made by thousands of Soldiers during the Global War on Terror; a conflict that had stretched on for so long that he was now patrolling in Iraq with Soldiers who had been *Kindergartners* when he was fighting in the mountains of the Hindu Kush. Spader 6 emailed me with the link to the DoD article, saying how it was great I was highlighting leaders in 1-26. I thanked him but also sent him the link to the article about Sgt. Owen, which, based on the total lack of response, was a surprise.

I submitted footage of a security patrol Bailey and the other Soldiers did in Bartallah up to CJTF-OIR too. Local security was the basis of maintaining a proper defense, and the fact that one of the advising locations happened to be in a village didn't change that. Other opinions differed, however.

"A good video, but," the CJTF PAO NCOIC began. "We can't release this video. It would give the appearance that we're boots on the ground in villages."

I was incensed. It wasn't an appearance; it was *what was actually happening*. Trying to hide the reality of what was going on wouldn't help at all, considering that there were already plans for the media to visit Bartallah. With Christmas only weeks away, both the Associated Press and National Geographic would be in country looking for spots to hit and Maj. Sanders felt that the story of a Christmas service in Bartallah would really emphasize the message of terrain being liberated by ISIL.

I disagreed.

It was an important piece, but I knew that the imagery that would *sell* would be the artillerymen raining down rounds on targets in Mosul during the holiday season. All these months, all these media entities running around, and they still hadn't got that footage. Everybody wanted it-why not give it to them?

"You've already covered the guns, L.T." Maj. Sanders demurred. "People are kind of mad they're getting all this attention." I audibly sighed loud enough for her to hear it. "I know they're your buddies and all."

"But it sounds like a misuse of resources ma'am," my reply, trying not to say aloud that a church service sounded more boring than operations at the artillery base. "A combat cameraman could easily get great photos there-"

"And you could get great photos at the firebase."

An impasse, except that she was calling that shots, and it sounded like she already had her mind made up.

"How about this," she continued, her voice taking on the "' I've got an idea tone," "You go up to PAA 14, and NATGEO will get that footage for the documentary. I'll take the AP down to Bartallah for the Christmas ceremony."

"That'll work." My reply. As if me saying no would change anything.

"I also need you up there because President Obama is going to call one of the Soldiers for the holidays."

"Really?!" Of all the places the President of the United States could call to wish Soldiers a happy holiday, he was selecting 1-320th in Iraq. I wonder what brought the unit to his attention.

"Yep." Her reply. "I need you to do the usual." She paused for a long moment, the silence hanging in the air. "It's your last stop L.T. After that, back to Erbil, then to Kuwait."

"Is this the part where you say you're proud of me and all of my good work?"

"And make your head even bigger? No."

"But I will say, you're loyal. I'll give you that. You're a goofball L.T."

Was that... audible fondness? At long last?

"Now, get to work."

Yes.

Yes, it was.

When 1st Lt. Austen Boroff arrived in Iraq that October from Fort Campbell to replace Lt. Frank, she was the only female Soldier in the battery. She was also the first female in 1-320th's history to lead an artillery platoon in a combat zone. 2015-2016 had seen the start of the gender integration of women into combat roles in the U.S. Army, and now the implementations were occurring in a deployed unit, perhaps for the first time. For years, women had been told they couldn't do specific jobs, that the stressors of combat would be too much. She was proving those doubters wrong.

Boroff had a family history of military service. A New Jersey native, both she and her brother had attended West Point where she was part of the school's first all-female cadet command team, a fact that was noted by President Barack Obama at her year group's graduation in 2014. The year Boroff graduated from West Point, the U.S. Army opened previously closed platoon leader and fire support officer positions to female artillery officers as part of its combat arms gender integration program. She was selected for the Artillery Branch, and at Fort Campbell, she had gone to Air Assault and Pathfinder school before attempting to be one of the first women to attend Ranger School.

C Battery had split into multiple PAAs at the start of the offensive, one overlooking Mosul and another on the low ground near the Great Zab River. As part of the substantial amount of firepower provided on that avenue of advance (Apaches, Paladins, drones, attack aircraft including A-10s), the Iraqis had advanced *fast.* Their best units, the Golden Division and CTS, led the advance. The advance wasn't so fast that ISIL didn't have time to launch some small attacks on the PAAs, such as a drive by shooting or rocket attacks, but quick enough that the entire battery was able to collapse to PAA 14, which occupied the high ground far above Mosul. In the dead of winter, with no life support such as heat or tents. Add that to the fact that the rainy "season" had begun in the country and, PAA-14 turned into KSB 2.5- but with more ice.

The artillerymen once again occupied bunkers mere meters from their artillery pieces and found themselves trying to stay dry and warm at night. It was almost like they were *intentionally* being forgotten about; whether it was awards like the Combat Action Badge, living conditions, rotations for R&R, plate carriers, or anything else, they seemed to always be last on the list. Odd, considering they had been doing damage to ISIL all summer, through horrid conditions, rain, snow, or shine.

"Lt. Johnson," 1-320th's Liaison Officer at LSA Strike greeted me, shaking my hand. "Been wondering when you were going to head up there to PAA 14. We got a ride leaving pretty soon."

"Works for me," my reply. Get footage of the Soldiers during Christmas time, write the story, and have it turned in and publish before the new year. A tight timeline but if I didn't get it out before the holiday season was "over", it would get lost in the sauce. News had to be, well, *new.*

"What are you heading up there for?"

"To get videos and photos to be used by the Pentagon major media companies like MSNBC, CNN, the Associated Press."

I said it with a straight face, even though the words sounded just as unreal to me as they did to him.

He shook his head.

"Jeez, man, they need to be paying you more for getting all that."

Well, shit, I *still* wasn't getting my hostile fire pay.

The route to PAA 14 was out of Erbil, then north through the Nineveh Plain towards the ever-visible mountains on the horizon. It was an idyllic part of Kurdistan, with small villages with children, grasslands, and no telltale scars of battle. The only thing that ruined its picturesque peace was the city of Mosul burning in the distance. At the edge of the plain, we finally hit the base of the mountains, a large stone structure coming into view on the side of one of them.

"That's St. Matthew's Monastery," the driver said, pointing it at like we were on a bus tour in Europe. "It's about 1,650 years old, and ISIL almost blew it up before the United States came in. It was home to a lot of civilians in the area for a long time when the invasion happened." The Ottoman and Persian Empires, Mongol invaders, and now ISIL, yet the structure still stood the test of time. For a moment, I tried to forget about the conflict and enjoy the sight.

It didn't work.

Up a dirt mountain road, higher and higher until we reached the peak, the city of Mosul visible in the distance, like a small miniature. The perfect vantage point to hit whatever target you wanted, which by the sound of artillery firing, was exactly what C Battery was doing.

"Lt. Johnson," Staff Sgt. Johnson was one of the first people to greet me when I got out of the vehicle. He had a wide smile. "If it isn't the man who made me famous. You did a good job explaining me at the console, controlling the fight."

"Controlling the fight, huh?" my joking reply.

"We thought you went home!"

"Without seeing you guys up here? You know I wouldn't do that."

I glanced around the camp. In front of me was the "gym", which was literally a rowing machine and some weights on top of some wood to keep it from getting wet. Beyond that, the FDC and Company command post, both of which looked about the same as KSB. The guns were on-line, just like KSB, their barrels sticking out of the camouflage netting.

"Figured you come out when we had the tents." Staff Sgt. Johnson continued, shaking his head.

"But I was out there on that gun raid, remember!"

"You were dying on the gun raid."

They had just gotten the tents a week before which was great and all, since the 82nd would be the ones using them. Two Soldiers from their advance party arrived at the base on the same movement I was on.

Everyone at the camp looked tired, not just in the physical sense, but mentally exhausted as well. More than 4,000 rounds fired, no true recovery period, pretty shitty living conditions, and exposure to the weather. Home was right around the corner, and everyone was missing it- or mentally preparing themselves for life when they got back.

I soon ran into Lt. Boroff, who gave me a greeting.

"What brings you up here!" She sounded livelier than everyone else, which was a pleasant surprise. I wondered if that was how we all looked in the first few months before the burnout started. It was funny, Capt. Rivas had told me back at Fort Campbell how the deployment cycle usually went: the first three months people were excited to be there and were trying to accomplish tasks with motivation. The next three months, they peaked.

The last three months, they burned out and started counting down the days until they could leave.

"NATGEO is coming up here for Christmas," my words to her as we caught up. "They're making a documentary and want you guys to be part of it.".

"That sounds cool! One of the guys in 1st Platoon is also getting a call from the President."

"Yep, just let me know the time, and I'll be there," my reply. "How have things been up here?"

"Pretty good; it's been pretty busy since the operation started. I've been trying to learn as much as I can from the guys --- this is an amazing experience. You're going to be with NATGEO?"

"Most likely." I pointed at my camera. "But just in case, I'll be ready to get some footage myself."

"Awesome!" she pointed towards the spots where 1st Platoon was located. "I'd love to see the guys highlighted. They're doing great work."

The saying that enthusiasm can be infectious rings true. I could tell that Boroff was humbled by the entire experience of getting to come to Iraq, and that she genuinely meant it when she said she wanted the Soldiers in the platoon covered.

"Glad to be here?" I asked.

"I'm honored, honestly. What they've done and are continuing to do is amazing, this is a dream come true. I'm glad to be a part of the team."

Who could blame her? For the battery's performance in Iraq, the U.S. Army would name C Battery the best one in the *entire force.*

Spc. Tristian Trammel cleaning his weapon in one of the bunkers, December, 2016. U.S. Army Photo by Daniel Johnson.

"Roads are closed down due to the weather. No one's coming to visit."

Sgt. 1st Class Young's words to me as we looked at the horizon. Fog, clouds, rain. Nothing was flying, and nothing was sure moving on the ground either.

"Guess that means no NATGEO." My response. "I guess I'll have to get the footage for them," It was par for the course. Somehow, I would be the only person to get video footage of them in action during the holidays. The last of the holiday packages had made it to the PAA before the weather rolled in: Christmas meat baskets, non-perishable goods, candy. Some of the bunkers even had stockings setup or small Christmas trees.

It didn't feel like the holiday seasons of yore, though.

"You've been all over the place, haven't you" Staff Sgt. Mont's words to me as we sat in one of the bunkers.

"Yeah."

I looked up at him. Exhaustion, stress --- he was only 28 years old but looked much older. We all did.

"Why'd you volunteer for this?" his question. A deeper one then, "how'd you get that job."

"The Army wouldn't be worth it to me if I didn't get to see what Soldiers have been up to."

"You could see that from home."

"I don't know- I just didn't want to get left behind while people I knew were risking their necks."

Wasn't that what officers were supposed to do? Share the conditions, make sure the Soldiers got the credit? At least that's what the old war movies my dad and I used to watch said. The reality was much different, something I had learned over those 8 months.

But then again, it's people's actions who led to the reality being very different from the ideals.

Mont regarded me with interest. It felt weird, someone trying to figure me out like I tried to do to others when I asked them why.

"We appreciate everything you've done for us." He continued, looking over towards me. "Other officers in your position might have just sent an enlisted guy out or have done the bare minimum."

Those words were worth more than any medal of accolade the Army could have given me.

Christmas Eve.

The Soldiers in Staff Sgt. Walker's section shivered as freezing rain continued to fall upon their position.

"Fire!" yelled Walker as he made a cutting motion through the rain with his hand. The round left the tube of the M777 with its trademark boom and smoke as the artillerymen began to move again, the soft sound of boots impacting the mud and gravel echoing through the gun pit.

It may have been the holiday season back home, but C Battery's war continued.

They were prepping Mosul for another assault. The Iraqis were in the city, bogged down in the house to house fighting. The east bank of the Tigris River was in sight, which meant that they were going to take it before 2BCT left the country.

If our leadership had any say, that is.

Cloud cover, low visibility. Enough to stop aircraft from flying, but all the M777s needed was the targeting data. They could and would work, rain or shine.

Boom, boom, boom.

The whole battery was in on it, six guns firing in succession, hitting targets. The tail end of the almost 4,000 rounds they had arrived since arriving in Iraq in May.

Loading a HE round on Christmas Eve, December, 2016. U.S. Army photo by Daniel Johnson.

The rain picked up, and a slight fog began to form in the distance as Walker's crew waited for their next command. Gone were their summer light-weight combat shirts, replaced by wearing multiple layers to stave off the wind-chill.

Down in Bartallah, Maj. Sanders and the AP were observing the first church service held by the Christians of the town since ISIL had taken it. NATGEO was there too, having to change their plans once the weather had prevented them from traveling to PAA 14. The whole event was nice, from what I understood. Some of our people got their photos in the papers.

"Fire mission at my command," came the transmission over the radio and the artillerymen sprang into action, beginning the crew drill to load artillery piece just as they had done for the past eight months. The Soldiers moved quickly through their tasks, and Walker gave the signal once more. Another boom reverberated in the pit.

More "presents" for ISIL. What says holiday cheer more than Christmas Eve raining down hell on the enemy?

Christmas Day

Being on an island in the clouds sure didn't help with the feeling of isolation. Visibility was down to a few feet in front of our faces, to the point where it seemed like the barrels of the M777s disappeared into nothingness.

Macaroni, ham, greens. A change of pace from what was usually served at the chow tent, and pretty good judging by the way everyone was digging in.

Like Thanksgiving at Q-West, chow was served by the company leadership, Berlin, Boroff, Frank, and others.

There wasn't a ton of conversation as we ate. Shoulders sagged, food into mouth. Finish up and then leave. Hope you could grab a couple of minutes on the MWR line. Let your family know you were ok, and that you would be home soon. Sometimes the voice on the other end's reaction wouldn't be as positive as the caller hoped.

Back in the tents, the Christmas meats were opened. Ham, cheese, turkey ham, it was kind of shocking that it didn't spoil on the way over, tasting almost as fresh as when you bought one at a local grocery store. The Soldiers sat on their cots as they ate; most of them lost in thought. Some light jokes, some ribbing, conversations about the reality that would be presenting itself in about ten days for some of them: life back home. The next day, the first group of them would leave. Gunny Joseph, Staff Sgt. Johnson, others among them.

The end of their adventure in Iraq. The end of mine too. It was a strange feeling, after everything, knowing that this was it. Not happy, not sad. Just there. Looking out into the fog, the thought that by next week I would be in Clarksville, Tennessee just felt so ...odd.

Like I didn't belong.

When we returned to Erbil, I made the usual pattern. Finish the story, upload the footage, submit it up. Unlike June, it was a quick turnaround --- less than half a day. On to DVIDs, for the last time in the country. As usual, featured news on Army.Mil. Defense Department Photo of the Day. Defense Department Video of the Day.

The punch line was the best part, however.

The BBC had started this wacky adventure in a way, so it fitted that they were the bookend of it. They ran the footage I took, almost in the entirety. They weren't the only ones; when some of the Soldiers got home, they got to see footage of themselves on the news.

Not bad for a neophyte, right?

Chapter Sixteen-The War at Home- 2017

Video footage of 1-320th in action at PAA 14, as shown on DVIDs and the BBC, December, 2016. U.S. Army image by Daniel Johnson.

The white light which heralded the sound of the 101st Airborne Division band playing at the edge of the hangar was like a portal into another world. It was surreal, like we had snapped into a different dimension, filled with cheering family members, people with bright clothes, little kids.

Reality at last.

We marched forward in a daze towards the spot designated in the hangar for us to stand in. To say Fort Campbell had a lot of practice with deployment and redeployment ceremonies would be the understatement of the century. Tallest guys up front, patrol caps on (even though it was the dead of winter and was snowing when we arrived, much colder than Iraq ever was), left-right, left-right. To the side, my mother was standing there, looking like she had aged much more than I had seen in the past 25 years. All the stress, and judging by a lot of the other family members standing nearby, she wasn't the only one who looked like they had gone through a stressful deployment. Then there were Vietnam veterans, standing among the gathering, stoically ---the welcome home ceremony they had never gotten, their presence there for the Soldiers who didn't have families waiting for them: *someone still cares.*

Maj. Gen. Volesky, on the stage, preparing to give a speech. This was his last coming home ceremony before switching out with the new commanding general. We stood there, awaiting his words.

"When you look at T.V., online," he began. Was this going to be a patriotism speech? This *was* the perfect place for one. "You see Strike Soldiers. They're the ones who are always on there."

I tilted my head, the rest of his words a blur. Was his tone, almost…*defeated?* I went to other ceremonies after that one, and his words still stick out to me as unique. What was he really trying to say? It didn't matter, I guess, because he kept the words short and sweet, releasing us to our families.

A tremendous yell as we all rushed the crowd. Photos, hugs. We went to turn in our weapons, and I happened to run into my old battalion X.O., the one who had told me ten months ago that I wouldn't be deploying to Iraq.

"Welcome back, Johnson," he said, looking confused. It was the oddest thing-, almost like he had never expected me to be standing there with a Screaming Eagle patch on both shoulders, a M4 that I had carried around for nine months in my hand.

To be honest, I was confused too. This whole thing still didn't make any sense.

I nodded towards him, running up the stairs to turn in my weapon, feeling an odd sense of emptiness once it left my hands. I felt…

Naked.

"See you guys Monday," the words from our company X.O. That was it. We were free, back into real life.

But of course, the Army being the Army, there was a mix-up with our bags on the planes and we had to stay an extra hour or two, walking around in the freezing cold to find our gear. The big show was on point, but the little details got us. They always do.

The same person at the McDonalds near my apartment was there from when I left nine months before. The first reminder that life hadn't changed, and how to navigate through it would be up to us. That weekend, I rode with a friend to Nashville to watch Star Wars, where we stopped at a pizza place before the film. It was off --- like I was watching a movie where I was a character. The colors, the people, the conversations, even the movie. It all felt---hollow. I had just gotten home, I told myself. Just got to readjust is all.

The post-deployment medical questionnaire, asking us about problems that wouldn't make themselves apparent until a couple of months later. As I looked down the list to mark what deployment I had been on, I noticed something missing. Operation Enduring Freedom, Operation Iraqi Freedom, and…. Other.

OIR didn't exist even on official army paperwork. We had participated in a nameless "other" conflict, one that no one even cared enough to *try* to name.

Still, we all felt great; we were home. No/no/no, N/A, a clean bill of health for all of us in the assessment. Post-Deployment briefings, finance, family life, moving forward. Most of us just sat there, waiting for them to end. But it had already started--- a Soldier's husband? Boyfriend? Came on base, into the briefing building, harassing her about…God knows what.

She had only been back in the country for 72 hours. A Captain eventually went out there and told him to beat feet as more and more of us turned towards the situation, postures growing more angrier. Marital problems abound, spouses and children used to doing things their own way for the past nine months. Soldiers coming back from deployment wanting things to go back to the status quo. All sides obstinate about how they deserved this, or that.

I found myself waking up at 3:00 A.M due to jet lag, unable to go back to sleep. I would eventually head to the gym at 5:30, just to do something, anything, but it wasn't healthy. I felt like a zombie through most of the days. Not that it felt like what we were doing workwise really mattered. since we were just treading water until the Brigade Commander returned.

There was an immediate clash between those who were on the deployment and those who weren't. To some of us, it felt like those on the rear detachment hadn't done *anything*. Which in hindsight, was a total misinterpretation. There was still training going on, intelligence Soldiers on base assisting with operations in Iraq, and supply personnel ensuring we were getting what we needed overseas. The whole deployment of the ready force in the summer and the fall was a testament that what they were doing worked.

But of course, we were still on our deployment "highs." Just a week, or a couple weeks before, some of us had been watching shells rain down on Mosul, or right outside Mosul, or clearing routes. Coming down from that wasn't exactly easy, especially since we couldn't go on leave as soon as we returned.

I was still wearing my Multicam and patrol cap for weeks, sun-bleached, and not to garrison standard. One day as I stood outside the Brigade HQ, a Major saw me. He furrowed his brow.

I looked, as the term was called, ate up.

"Where did you come from?" he asked, pausing at the door.

"I just came back from Iraq, sir." My reply, ready for the ass-chewing I was sure to receive. His face softened in immediate understanding.

"Welcome back." He patted me on the shoulder and walked inside. I was shocked.

Not that anyone else was going to give us a break. The unit was planning on going to Texas in the summer, where the Army fielded and tested new equipment. It was kind of odd. Usually, when a unit returns from a deployment, they didn't do a major exercise off the post for about a year. I would learn later that exercise didn't need the over 2,000 personnel from the Brigade who would participate. No one cared since the entire purpose was just to look like we were doing something, which added on to the overall stress.

My experiences in Iraq taught me to put very little faith in my leadership beyond Maj. Sanders. Maybe it was the *literal* jealousy that got me shut down for a month. Perhaps the fact that the standards shifted for rank, or failure on basic tasks such as battlefield circulation or ensuring that life support was adequate, the fact of covering up legitimate injuries suffered by Soldiers, or oh yeah, the fact that they had to be *begged* to give us 30 days of leave.

Then there were the dangers of life in the Clarksville area. In early February, Spc. Christopher Hoch, age 28, and who had been with 2-502 in Iraq, would be murdered, along with Spc. Priscilla East. East had come to the home of Hoch's fiancé to get away from an abusive husband. The husband tracked her down, and Hoch bravely attacked the man with a bat, unfortunately being fatally wounded in the process.

The big event was when the main body with the Brigade Commander came back. NATGEO's crew was there, after returning from Iraq. We escorted them onto the base and into the hangar. Their camera rigs were massive, worth tens of thousands of dollars. It was impressive. Alongside their footage, I decided to do a Facebook Live video, a practice started by Staff Sgt. Melendez when Soldiers had begun returning. We usually got into the thousands of viewers, a solid showing.

That night we got one million in 30 minutes. One million people, watching footage from my phone that had barely made it through Iraq.

The whole thing was a big deal. Local media organizations were wanting to talk to the Brigade Commander, NATGEO getting their high-definition footage. It was public relations to the maximum.

"Glad to have you back, Maj. Sanders," my words to her when she had some time after running around, ensuring the whole event went smoothly. It looked like a weight was off her shoulders since the last time I saw her. She was all business as always.

"I'm glad to be back," she paused. "There's so much work to do."

Something was off. I could feel it, but I didn't know what it was. It had been almost a month now, and that detached, nervous feeling wasn't going away. I couldn't sleep, and when I did, I was exhausted. I could feel my head hurting throughout the day.

Just adjusting, just adjusting, I told myself. It was a lie. Iraq was always on my mind. Sometimes I could literally *see* it. It was like everything before then was foggy, unreal. But Iraq was clear as day.

The adventure was over, and now the question arose- what happened to me? I was excess, in a position that didn't exist. The promotion board was coming up. How was Maj. Sanders going to rate me? Her gamble on me had paid off, at least.

I was the most viewed journalist in the United States Army. We had footage that was selected as the DoD photos and videos of the day. Multiple articles were highlighted by the U.S. Army or DoD as *the* featured news of the day. The footage I had taken was now on every major news channel in some way, shape, or form, sometimes in its *entirety*. Strike had been featured on the CENTCOM News Page, U.S. Army page, and even the Department of Defense home page. Our DVIDs page was and would be used for years as the source of imagery and video from Iraq, with media organizations contacting *us* for coverage opportunities.

We weren't just a good brigade PAO section; we were the *best*. When you're so good that the professionals check your stuff for updates, you've won.

Maj. Sanders' performance on the deployment would earn her a promotion to Lt. Col. In two years at Fort Campbell, she oversaw the best new journalist in the U.S. Army, and ostensibly the best journalist overall for the year.

"What do you want to do with your career L.T.?" her question in the office one day. "If you stick around here, you may not be promoted."

I waved my hands and shrugged. "So be it, ma'am," I picked up the Screaming Eagle magazine, which had one of my images on the cover. "I'll have this experience for a lifetime."

She shook her head.

Then she talked to the Brigade X.O. and made sure my OER had the right verbiage so I could get promoted to Captain.

She never explained why she cared, and never told why she gave me a shot.

The best I could get out of her when I said thanks was an odd look on her face that I took to be the closest thing to one of those feel-good moments you get in the movies.

I was looking forward to leave. A 30-day world tour, free from the Army and stress. Surely whatever difficulties I was having would dissipate as soon as I got on the road. I loved traveling, seeing new things, meeting new people. Every leave opportunity I got before we left for Iraq, I took, much to the chagrin of some people. Nothing had changed, I thought. Once February and March were through, I would leave Iraq in Iraq and get back to the "old" me.

Then I learned that you couldn't outrun your problems.

During my first few days in Australia, I didn't feel like doing much. It was odd, I never had a problem exploring. I eventually forced myself to go to some botanical gardens in Brisbane and explore the Gold Coast. It felt…different. I was going to meet my college friends in Tokyo after that, some of whom I had not seen in years. It would be great. And it was-

Or at least I told myself that.

We explored the city, sampling the fantastic food and ramen stands, walking through markets, playing in arcades, drinking alcohol. Every day we saw something new in the city, yet I felt like I was…detached. Not there. Nervous. *Out of place.* When the guys went out later at night, I decided to sleep in.

"This whole thing feels different," my words, as we drank in a bar in a picturesque district of Tokyo.

"What do you mean? You've never been here before, right?" one of the responses from my friends.

"I haven't," my reply, trying to grapple with what I was feeling. "I don't know, just decompressing from Iraq, I guess."

"Sounds like you need another beer." The reply.

So, I did. During that entire month I lived a hedonistic lifestyle, drinking, partying, eating, womanizing.

And yet it all felt empty, off, like it never happened. The happiness I used to feel doing those things were gone. I wasn't sad either.

I was just there.

When I returned to Fort Campbell, it got worse. Utter panic before a P.T. test, or while running, feeling like I was going crazy during a 12 miler, telling myself that I just wanted to go home and hide afterward.

So that's what I did after work. My life became work, go home, play video games. And then on the weekends, eat at the same 3 restaurants, sitting in the exact same spots. I didn't feel comfortable anywhere else.

The headaches presaged sudden mood changes I would have while driving, or sitting there at home, or eating. My distrust was getting worse.

I needed help. I had read about what happened in the years before --- Soldiers kicked out who had PTSD or TBIs because they were either misdiagnosed or were afraid to get treatment. Adjustment Disorder it was called, an easy way for the docs to process you out even if you did go in. All it took was one bad day, one trigger, and their careers were down the drain, with no medical record that would help them get treatment from the V.A.

An invisible wound of war that went untreated.

"You ok, sir?"

Staff Sgt. Mont's voice took me out of my head, sitting in the Burger King lost in thought.

"Hey Staff Sgt. Mont, how's it been?" my voice was cheery. My face wasn't. We caught up on what was going on. Mont was famous, as an Artilleryman goes. He would soon be leaving Fort Campbell onto the next duty assignment.

"And what about you, sir?"

His question, staring intently.

"I'm …here." My reply, the truth.

He looked concerned.

"Are you ok?"

Lack of good sleep, anxiety, anger, fear. I was falling apart, and he could tell.

"Not really, I guess." Admitting that something was different, that I needed help. The realization that my experience had affected me, as much as I didn't want them to. We spoke some more, him talking about how he was dealing with stress since he had been back. That talk with Staff Sgt. Mont convinced me to go seek help, and I'm forever thankful for it.

"If you ever want to talk sir, we'd love to have you over at the battery," He gave me a tap on the shoulder. "People do care."

I went to the Behavioral Health Clinic soon after that, deciding that if I didn't get help soon, then whatever was going on would eat me alive. It'd take a while for an appointment, they said.

The same answer for a mental program in Clarksville, it's location given to me by a fellow Soldier who warned me, "Be careful about going to behavioral health on base. They may try to fuck you."

Times had changed, though, right?

Summer approached, and with it, the Brigade Commander's change of command. The next stop, division chief of staff, another step on his way to a star. Most of the BDE staff would leave around the same time, including Maj. Sanders. No PAO Major was coming until next year, so she was leaving it in my hands.

1st Lt. Johnson, the 2nd Brigade Combat Team PAO. With no formal training at all.

I kept quiet about my problems. I didn't want to bother her with them --- no need to worry about me since she was leaving soon. *I'd be fine.*

The day before the change of command ceremony. The post photographer hadn't shown up to take the brigade photo, the commander's last one as part of 2BCT. He and Maj. Sanders were talking as I stood by. He walked over to me.

"So, I guess the photographer isn't here. Think you can get a photo?" I looked around. It was going to be hard since I didn't have the high ground or the right type of camera equipment.

"Why not wait until the photographer showed?" My thoughts.

"I can try, sir." My words.

He pointed to the roof of a building that was standing near the parade field. To get a photo from up there you had to climb a flimsy ladder and stand at the edge of the roof.

"So, it looks like you'll have to climb up there to take it." A question? A command? Either way, it sounded absurd.

"Are you kidding me?" I laughed in his face at the sheer goofiness. He paused, and for a few seconds, we stared at each other as if waiting for the other to flinch.

Neither of us did. I don't think anyone had the nerve to laugh at him like that, and to be honest, it wasn't even an intentional slight, just a reaction to something I thought was the dumbest thing I heard in a while. But then again, the guy had let his X.O. try to screw me over in Iraq, so I wasn't too thrown off.

Maj. Sanders looked shocked; I don't think she could believe it either. I wasn't moving to offer an explanation or say sorry, so-

"He meant to say he doesn't have the equipment." Her words, brokering a peace. The commander shook his head. I don't think he bought it, but Maj. Sanders motioned for me to flee so she could talk to him privately.

Adjustment Disorder was what they called it. My alarms went off immediately – adjustment disorder is what they diagnosed Soldiers with to medically discharge them out of the Army without having to diagnose them with PTSD.

Meds, and EMDR therapy. Though I didn't feel an immediate change, I started to process everything.

The training in Texas was coming up in July. I wasn't ready to go, and I told them that. I needed treatment, I said. It had to go to the company commander. No problem, whatever the decision was, I would take it. Be a good Soldier, don't fuck up, do the right thing. The leadership acquiesced, and I was held back for more sessions.

The training was a shit show. The Brigade brought more people than it needed, and Soldiers were literally sleeping in open fields for no reason at all than for the new Brigade Commander to show how "tough" his unit was. It was a toxic mindset.

It was the same line of thinking that had made itself very evident in Iraq.

The promotion board was coming up soon. I had already contacted my branch and sent in the paperwork. I was slated for the first class of the fiscal year and I had the leave days saved up to clear the installation by September. I informed my providers about this, and there seemed to be no issue.

I stayed busy, working with the Vietnam Veterans who were rededicating a memorial to their fallen on base, a fantastic project that refurbished the memorial stone. The veterans were the ones who pointed me in the right direction to ask about the Soldiers in Art Greenspon's "Help from Above" photo. The veterans' point of contact, a Vietnam veteran who had worked with Maj. Sanders and Strike for years, called me out immediately when he saw me.

"You have PTSD." His words, calm, measured, of a man who had been through it himself, and could recognize the same behaviors in others.

It was hard for me to admit that he was right.

On August 28th, Pfc. Jordan White, who had spent 5 months in Iraq with 1-75 Cav, was killed in a motorcycle accident in Clarksville.

I looked at treatment options at my next duty station to continue progress. Even if I couldn't do it on base due to scheduling conflicts, I was more than willing to pay for it off base, like I was already doing at Fort Campbell because I was leery of Army Behavioral Health. The promotion board results came in late August --- 98% rate for Lieutenants. My name was on it.

The same day, Spc. Albred Carroll-Horton took his own life. He had been on the deployment to Iraq from May-January with 2-502. Another two Soldiers from our deployment would die to mental health issues related to deployments in the next two years.

Suicide is the 2nd *leading* cause of death for service personnel in the United States military. The active-duty military suicide rate is higher than the U.S. population's and over 45,000 veterans and active-duty service members have committed suicide since 2013. Even further, research found that one in five veterans and Soldiers screened positive for either depressions, anxiety, or acute stress, but less than 50% sought treatment due to fear that *leaders would treat them negatively, peers would view them as weak and have less confidence, and that mental health treatment would negatively affect their career.*

Two weeks later, Sgt. Ryan A. Estridge from 1-502 entered the Cumberland River in Clarksville after allegedly getting into a scuffle with security guards and an unknown man. His body was found one week later; authorities couldn't ascertain whether Estridge had jumped into the river or fell. He had been on the deployment to Iraq too. I had a picture of him during the sling-load training in Taji that previous June.

Something was wrong.

I got my orders. I began to clear the installation. My company commander signed my PCS leave, and I signed out. Everything was right; I had notified the providers and everything.

I went to clear behavioral health.

"We just got a note on your file saying not to let you leave." The words from the installation clearing manager. They suggested I talk with my providers and commander. I did so.

My company commander, my provider and I walking into a meeting. Let's talk about my PCS, they had said.

Sure, no problem. Maybe I missed something, but we could clear this up.

The company commander was acting oddly before the meeting- in contrast to my previous dealings with her. Something was wrong.

My provider's and commander's main concerns were ensuring I had an adequate continuation of treatment. Based on our discussions, there seemed to be no issue with me departing Fort Campbell from the unit's standpoint when I had talked to the commander the day previous.

Twenty-four hours later, at our meeting with the provider, the tone of the conversation shifted.

"I don't think you're ready to go to Signal CCC," my commander's words.

"What?" My response. *We had talked about this.*

My provider agreed.

Just a week before, my leaving Fort Campbell hadn't been an issue. And now it was?

I decided to plead my case, bringing up the fact that there was treatment at the next duty station and that I was even willing to pay for sessions on my own.

"No, no, no," the commander's reply, sounding almost *rehearsed.* "You should stay here on Fort Campbell. If you're stressed, we can move you to a replacement unit."

I was confused. Both parties emphasized that I should continue to be treated with the installation. What I didn't understand was how I had gone from capable of incapable in the span of *24 hours.* Even stranger, my behavioral health provider was attached to the brigade. If I moved to another unit, wouldn't that mean I lost access to that provider?

I caught on quick.

I was being targeted for getting mental health treatment. Maybe it was the command, I thought to myself. The best way to get to the bottom of the issue, lest I seemed paranoid, was to talk to each person.

The next day I returned to speak to the provider and informed her that I had never been hospitalized, and I had never indicated any homicidal or suicidal intent, the critical indicators of danger to self or others. I even informed her of my previous negative experiences with the unit and that a change of pace would most likely be beneficial to my health and recovery, and how at Fort Campbell I felt isolated. My family was around the next duty station, why wouldn't I want to be nearer to them for once?

Another provider agreed and said he'd call the next duty station to see what was available. Everyone seemed very reasonable, and I even told them I'd continue to seek treatment off base if need be.

I returned to the commander.

"I spoke to the provider," my words. Maybe she was erring on the side of the medical professionals? Fair.

"I feel like I'd be ready to attend the course. Have I ever done or said anything dangerous?" I pushed the issue. "It's not like I'm a medical hold preventing me from PCSing."

"I don't think you're ready."

I tilted my head.

As far as I knew, she had studied mechanical something at West Point, not psychology. I knew the education at West Point was rightfully considered world class, but they also produced clinical psychologists out of every student no matter their major, and in *four* years?

And here I thought Appalachian State was overachieving with the School of Criminal Justice School of Journalism.

Maybe she had spent more time deployed than me. No, that wasn't it. We had both been deployed the same amount of time. Maybe at the time she had some insight that was gathered from the Captain's Career Course and staff time before garrison company command. After doing the Captain's Career Course and staff time, I can say that wasn't it either.

No, this was something personal.

"Why?"

"You're technically non-deployable since you were on profile a few months ago."

"There's no profile in the system. I checked. And why'd you sign my paperwork?"

"I thought about it." Then came the kicker. "I'm not comfortable with you, standing in front of a formation of Soldiers in six months."

Now we had it.

"You're not comfortable because?"

"You can't say what you've been saying about the command."

"You mean the people who screwed me over? Why does that matter?"

"You're not *supposed* to do that."

She was adamant about that point, and I saw what was going on. How dare I buck the system?

This whole thing was no different than with the Brigade X.O. I had never done anything negative, and the commander herself had said previously that the unit had never had any problems with me. Yet, this was her judgement?

"I've spoken with the battalion commander," she continued.

I'd never even met the guy. He had replaced the old battalion commander, the one who signed my orders to go to SCCC in the first place, obviously not displeased with my performance.

"He thinks that you should wait to attend SCCC, or perhaps just PCS there and be in a non-student status."

"So, I can't leave the unit to advance my career, but I can leave the unit to sit in a meaningless job?"

And there, the statement that the unit was worried about me and I should stay on Fort Campbell was rendered false; the commander was willing to send me to Fort Gordon but in a non-trainee status for an unknown period until I was "ready." She also spoke about sending me to another unit on Fort Campbell. Neither option was beneficial to continued career progression.

"I disagree, ma'am." My reply.

"It's not your decision."

"But I went in voluntarily, and it seems like I'm being punished for going to get the treatment the Army says it'll provide."

She looked at me coldly.

"Don't worry; *you'll* get over it."

I went back to the providers. They changed their tune to the tune the commander was singing. No matter what logical reasons I brought up, they disagreed.

"If I'm that unready to do my duties as a Captain in the United States Army, then please begin the process to medically discharge me. " My response, calling their bluff.

They were caught in a bind and demurred.

"Then what do I need to do to show progress?"

A vague answer, reassessment in 2-6 months.

My unit was the final decider, they said.

I went back to the commander.

She told me that the provider was the final decider.

Then she decided to talk to the new Brigade PAO, a Captain who was about to transfer to another branch, telling him that the command team was worried about me and I shouldn't PCS for now. It was utterly amazing; she was trying to turn the person I worked for against me for no reason at all. She was trying to use officer politics against me.

It failed because he knew my character from a place people couldn't hide what they were: Iraq. The acting PAO told me exactly what was going on.

"I don't know what her problem with you is," he said as we sat in his office. "She has to provide me some evidence of negative behavior if she's going to try to punish you."

He glanced at me with a half-smile. "I think it's because she knows you have a problem with authority."

"I don't, sir."

He laughed. "You do. People can tell. But it doesn't give them any right to try to punish you for seeking the help the Army provides."

I wish there were more officers like him.

My branch manager at the time called the commander, literally arguing on the phone with her about the whole situation. His words to me afterward, "I tried to convince her. However...I can't cancel your orders. You're still on them."

I knew exactly what that meant, and I told him I appreciated it. And therein lies the joke: the commander had let me stay on leave, telling me that it was just regular leave. However, I still had the document *she signed* saying it was PCS leave.

Do you know what you need to clear the installation? A copy of your orders and a signed PCS leave form.

I had *both*.

So, I continued clearing behind her back. I was plotting against my own commander as she conspired against me — what a fucking world.

The Soldier was different from the one I had seen in Iraq.

Tired, ragged.

Defeated.

"What's up, man!" I greeted him with a smile. "You PCSing?"

He shook his head.

"No, sir, I'm getting forced out."

"What?"

"I went in for treatment, and they decided to medically discharge me."

Anger in my body.

"They just beat you down around here, sir," continued, distraught. He was shaking slightly as he spoke. "Eventually, there's nothing you can do but give up."

In Iraq, he was a high performer, always on missions and setting the standards for Soldiers under him.

Now, he was getting kicked out for "Adjustment Disorder," thrown to the side without getting the full treatment.

How many other Soldiers were getting fucked? *Two Soldiers had just died*, most likely due to issues from the deployment. And the unit was intentionally targeting Soldiers for abuse or using paperwork trickery to force them out.

And no one was saying a word. What was happening to me was happening to God knows how many Soldiers? How many were going through it right at that moment? How many went through it before.

252

How many of them ended up dying? I could *already* count two.

The next day, the providers put me on a PTSD profile, dated in September. Bizarre, considering that the profile they said I should have been on was in *July*.

The last fucking straw.

It's the little things: not making sure Soldiers have adequate life support, not ensuring they get the awards they earned, hiding their injuries, running them into the dirt, not passing out the newer kit while you have yours, sending them to stand there and get shot at so you can say you were the first into Mosul --- all of its connected.

All those little things, encouraged by your bosses and peers, makes shit like targeting Soldiers for going in for mental health treatment too easy. They're *weak*; they're *faking*, they're *lose s----* all those stereotypes that make Soldiers afraid to go in and get help, even as their life starts to fall apart. Soldiers were dying- Soldiers would continue to die.

And the response was to make it harder for them to get the help they needed, while continuing to pile on stressors that would eventually lead to a breaking point.

I was told before I even started that going to B.H. on base may fuck me.

It happened.

I was supposed to sit there and just take it. I was supposed to just sit there and let it happen. I was supposed to let them scare me into silence. Because you don't rock the boat. No, you follow authority in the military.

Joke's on them, the officer oath they make us all say talks about faithfully discharging the duties of our office. Part of those duties is to ensure the health and welfare of the Soldiers under or command, authority, or power, to the best of our abilities.

That's the authority that I had to answer to. That's the authority Master Sgt. Wetmore, Capt. Rivas, Staff Sgt. Mont, Sgt. Owen, and all the others I had met and had helped me when they had no reason to would expect me to answer to.

My mother had emailed the office of our North Carolina Senator. He was on the Senate Armed Forces committee.

They got back to her within hours.

That night, I submitted the congressional inquiry into my situation.

Congressional Inquiries are the nuclear option of solving problems in the military. They are often misused, but when they aren't?

Targeting Soldiers for behavioral health issues while having multiple suicides. I didn't trust anyone at Fort Campbell to handle that one. Inspector Generals for divisions at the end of the day work for that division commander, and if they found nothing, you were done.

Congressional inquiries go directly from a Congressional representative to the Headquarters of the United States Army. You can't just cover it up--- and you sure can't cover it up when it's someone on the Armed Forces committee. The second an inquiry is started, a chain of events kicks off where everyone starts passing the buck. From HQDA, it goes down to the Combatant Command, then to the Corps Command, the Division Command, and finally, the Brigade Commander.

Army HQ expects a response in five days. I also named the battalion commander, company commander, and the provider in the letter, ensuring that their names would be seen at every level of the Army. I highlighted the fact that I had gone in myself, that I had shown progress, that there was treatment available at the next duty station, and the fact that the company commander had told me I wasn't fit to stand in front of Soldiers since I went for help. The profile magically appearing out of thin air was icing on the cake.

It's rare for an officer to go with this option, from my understanding. The second you do a congressional inquiry with allegations such as mine, everyone must drop what they're doing to respond. You can become public enemy number 1.

But Soldiers were literally dying because of what was going on. *Didn't anyone care?*

"Hey, what's up man," the call from a friend of mine down in Texas.

"How's it going down there?"

"Good, good." His voice was hushed. "What did you do man? I saw the legal officer writing a response with your name on it."

"They tried to fuck me, so I wrote my Senator."

"Jeez, man, that's crazy." He paused. "So, I guess this means you'll be gone when I get back?"

"Hopefully."

He laughed. "Good luck, man. It's not easy to escape this place."

I visited some friends, hung out, tried to relax. But I couldn't. The symptoms were getting worse; it was like I was back in Iraq. I was fighting a war with my chain of command, the people who were supposed to care about me. My trust in everything was gone.

Finally, the response from the Brigade Commander, sent up to the top. Generic stuff, except for one thing.

He blamed the providers, covering his own ass.

I had everything I needed.

I printed out a copy and immediately prepared to head into base.

I called my company commander.

"So, I got the response from the congressional back," my words, edgy.

"Why did you do that?" her reply. "You made people do a whole lot of extra work that they didn't have to do."

Or was it because I aired the dirty laundry?

"I have a right as a constituent of the state of North Carolina to contact my elected representative. It's not about extra work." Frustration rising, due to the response not dealing with the issue, but the fact that I had put the spotlight on the unit's behaviors.

"We could have talked about this."

"We did. You stonewalled me and told me I'd get over it. I'm going to talk to the providers and get this solved, then I'll be by your office."

I rushed in that morning, after calling my mother and telling her what I was about to do. She was worried that they would take me away to a padded cell. No, I was calm, I told her. I would handle this.

Into the behavioral health building, the document in my hand.

"I need to talk to the providers now."

They rushed out and brought me in.

"I got the response to the congressional back," I said, watching the reaction on their faces. I knew that they knew I had submitted it. More than a few people did by the looks I was getting from some other personnel.

"The unit's putting the blame on you," I pulled out a copy of the response, knowing that when it comes to self-preservation, alliances disappear quick. "Here, take it."

The provider read the letter. She was legitimately angry.

"They're putting the blame on us? They're the ones who told us to put the profile on you!"

Finally, a straight fucking answer from somebody.

All it took was a letter to a United States Senator. All of this because they wanted to screw a lieutenant in the United States Army from going to the Captain's Career Course.

I wish I could say I was shocked.

"Am I free to go." A question and statement. All I cared about.

The provider sighed.

"I'll release you from the medical hold."

"Finally."

One last stop. The building where this had all begun in April so long ago. I marched up the stairs to the commander's office, passing the first sergeant who just glared at me.

"The providers cleared me." My words to the company commander, immediately entering the office without knocking. No niceties, no respect- from either of us. "I'm going to bring my paperwork for you to sign. Unless you have some other reason."

She was angry.

"You didn't have to do all of this." Venom. "This is the stuff that makes other people not want to work with you."

For a moment, the utter absurdity of people not wanting to work with me being a bigger issue in my commander's mind then Soldiers getting targeted for getting mental health treatment threw me off.

But then, it all made sense.

I was supposed to let Soldiers who had served their country honorably get punished for trying to seek the mental health help the Army said it would give them. I was *supposed* to do nothing, to let them *die*, because my career was *more important.*

All because it'd make *my "leaders" look bad.*

I was supposed to be cowed by the threat of censure, exile, hatred, from my peers and leaders. I was supposed to sit there and take it, like a good little boy. Because that's how the Army worked. That's what other people would have done.

That's what my commander would have done.

But then, how could you consider yourself an officer in one of the most trusted institutions in the nation if you did that? You were supposed to be setting the standard. How could you talk about honor, integrity, selfless service, and all that other stuff people with rank gave lip service to, if you weren't trying to do it yourself?

It was the difference between internal and external motivations, what Master Sgt. Wetmore, Capt. Rivas, and others in my life had been trying to teach me. It was what Maj. Sanders had seen in me when I had volunteered the year before.

It was about trying to do the right thing, no matter your position, your wealth, your title, and whether people liked you or hated you. Because at the end of the day, when all of that was gone, when the opinions of people who may or may not want to work with you no longer matters, when all that's left is *you,* what are you?

Who are you?

The people who know the answer to that question usually die happy, because that's something even death can't take away.

That's why I made some of them nervous; they could tell that I really didn't care about them or their opinions, and if that was the case?

What power over me did they really have?

To think, I was supposed to be more afraid of *them, her,* than I was the enemy in Iraq.

Looking down at my commander, I pitied her. And not in the "I felt sorry for making her upset way," but more in the existential.

I knew who *I* was.

Did she?

Could you ever know if you lived your life basing your standards on how other people would react?

"Is there something else?" I continued, looking down at her.

Her eyes were red. Furious.

"Some reason I can't stand in front of Soldiers?"

Egging, my frustration getting the better of me.

"Some reason I'm not fit to be a leader?"

The frustration was causing her to tear up.

"Is there anything else."

I wish I could say I was just angry at her, but there was more than that.

I wanted to know why. Why even choose to serve your country if this was the outcome?

"I'll sign it."

"Good."

A pause.

"You'll get over it," I said as I shrugged at her and walked out.

I changed into my uniform and brought my paperwork in for her to sign, even managing to put on a little smirk as I watched her do it with a scowl on her face.

Funny how people who tried to screw you over behave when you flip the tables on them.

My next stop was the out-processing center. A cheery civilian greeted me at the desk, making sure my paperwork was good. She stamped it.

"Thank you for your service at Fort Campbell!"

"No, thank you!" I smiled at her.

I didn't even look back as I left the base. By the time Monday came, I was a couple of states away.

Epilogue-Korea – 2018

Mosul would be fully seized in July of 2017, after over 9 months of fighting around and in the city. CJFLCC-OIR closed in April of the next year, it's mission "complete". Victory over ISIL would be declared in May of 2019, and the coalition presence at Qayarrah West would be completely removed by March of 2020.

ISIL wasn't fully defeated, however, with intelligence later on in 2020 indicating that they still had a very sizeable presence and power structure. The Iranian government practically taking over the Iraqi government during the conflict would lead to protests throughout the country against Tehran's influence, the rampant militias, and government corruption. The very same conditions that led to fertile ground for ISIL in the first place, caused by our invasion and then mishandling of the situation in the country back in 2003.

The worthiness or worthlessness of our nameless Iraq conflict hung over me as the Major regarded me from his desk, looking over my file. Another Army doc, another person I couldn't trust, another day halfway across the world. One year after getting home from Iraq, I was now in South Korea, due to the leader of our country sabre rattling on Twitter.

No one was looking out for my interests, or anyone else's. Not the president, not my "leaders", and especially not high-ranking officers in the military. They'd all sell me out for the next rank- I was sure of it. Fort Campbell had taught me not to trust anyone, to stay alert, to always be prepared to get screwed.

If even people in the military, the "most trusted institution in America", couldn't be trusted, who could I trust? I was powerless, each day waiting for everyone else to prove me right.

The Major continued reading my treatment notes. All part of the same song and dance you had to do with every new Army Behavioral health doc- all of it transient and temporary. As he looked through my file, he paused.

"Your parents were in the military?" he asked.

"My father was."

"What'd he do in the Army?"

"He was an infantryman." I sighed, shaking my head. "I guess I wanted to be just like him."

"Did your dad do any deployments?"

"He was in the Gulf War in 1991 in Northern Iraq, the same place I was in." I chuckled at the irony of it all. "Don't think he ever thought his son would end up there too. He said he saw some rough stuff that had been done to the Kurds, and how one of their Soldiers-"

"Lars Chew." He interrupted me, suddenly.

I stopped, surprised, looking at the Major.

"He was killed by a mine in Northern Iraq. He was just a kid. I was there too." He looked closer at me, recognition on his face.

"What rank was your father?"

"He was a Staff Sgt. at the time." The Major's face changed, like he had seen a ghost, but then again, didn't I find myself in this predicament because of things that had happened before I was born?

"I was a private back then, just arrived in Vicenza before we went to Iraq." He continued. "The good old Blue Falcons of 3/325 Parachute Infantry." He chuckled. "Did he tell you about how none of us got CIBs for Operation Provide Comfort, while the guys who volunteered to do nothing but drive trucks in Desert Storm did?"

"He still does."

"I bet, the guys on Facebook still complain about it all the time." He laughed again for a moment and then looked over at me seriously. "The notes say you have problems with trust."

"I can't trust these people," my response. "They lie, they change the standards, they don't care about the Soldiers' well-being. They don't deserve to wear the uniform."

"That's pretty black and white." He looked at me sadly. "You don't trust anyone higher ranking?"

"I can't, sir. They have the power to order me into a situation that can lead to my death, and I can't trust them with that. I don't have any control of what happens to me. Nothing I do matters- no one even knows the point."

"You have more control than you think."

I breathed in, gathering my thoughts. "I'm sorry, but I don't believe you. Nothing I do matters. If I try to do the right thing, the next person will just do the wrong thing. If I try to treat Soldiers with respect, the 'leaders' at their next unit could still destroy their lives. I'm in Korea right now because of someone's *tweets*."

"You don't have to believe me. It doesn't mean it's not true."

"Why do you care? Why did you decide to do this?"

"I was trying to understand why an 18-year-old kid died on some hillside in Iraq. I was trying to understand why in Africa me and my fellow Soldiers watched civilians get slaughtered right in front of us, and we couldn't do anything. I was trying to understand everything that I saw, and then I realized that I could try to help my fellow Soldiers try to understand too."

I wanted to think that what he was saying wasn't true.

I couldn't.

I'm not a religious man, or one who believes in fate, but the more I spoke with the Major during treatment, and how it was the death of Lars Chew that started him down the path to hopefully help Soldiers in their mental health treatment, I began to look back at my life and all the moments, chances, coincidences that got me to where I am today.

As always, it was someone else who saved me from myself.

He was the best provider I ever worked with in the military, legitimately caring about my well-being. He gave me Viktor Frankl's most famous book, "Man's Search for Meaning". I didn't want to read it at first- but when I finally did, I realized what everyone had been telling me all that time.

I had to create meaning. In the face of what I thought was wrong, if I let that destroy me, then I was the very thing I hated. Then I had failed. I couldn't allow that to happen. In the absence of everything else, who was I?

I wish there were more people like that Major who served with my father. Even though I had a deep mistrust of senior officers, he was the first person to show me that my all or nothing thinking was warped, was wrong.

He got me the help I needed, getting me sent to the Warrior Transition Battalion, which is a unit for Soldiers with medical conditions that prevent them from serving in their assigned duties, temporarily or permanently, at Fort Bragg, North Carolina. For the first time in years, I had time to think, process, and get treatment.

With all of the free time, I started to finish writing this book, mostly on my cellphone while waiting for- or in-between appointments. I had started at Fort Campbell but had stopped a quarter of the way through. I didn't want to think about Iraq. I wanted to forget it; I didn't want to confront my experiences.

But they weren't just my experiences. They were everyone's. People may argue over the definition of the word combat, or how their deployment was worse, better, more consequential. True perhaps, but also irrelevant- the world is made up of billions of people, whose stories are no more or no less important than the other. Every person who was out there, every person who had to deal with the aftermath, every person who tried to get help but *couldn't,* had an experience that *mattered.* With all the crazy stories out there about things as mundane as teenage drama or working in a cubicle or the drama of the stock market, these Soldiers' stories deserve to be heard just as much as anyone else's. Hopefully, someone can learn from this and can gain a better understanding of what these men and women went through and will continue to go through.

I don't know what to make of my military service, whether to be proud or cynical. I may never know. What I do know, looking back at all of this, is I'm the outcome of people caring about me, even when they didn't have to; even when they shouldn't have had to.

It was Master Sgt. Wetmore deciding to give me a chance when I didn't deserve it; my professors in college who took the time to try to teach me even when I didn't want to listen- my parents encouraging me to learn when I was a child; the Soldiers in the brigade and battalion who looked out for me even when I was a joke; Capt. Rivas continuing to do the right thing even as his time in service ran out.

It was Maj. Sanders deciding to take a chance on some kid with nothing going for him, because she thought I deserved a shot. Untold amounts of people, who at no benefit to themselves chose to take time out of their lives to pour into mine.

My goal is to become a teacher and spend the rest of my days in the same cheesy sweater and thick glasses, sometimes talking fondly of my young days as some kid in the back doses off, like I did all those years ago in Dr. Simon's Criminal Law class at Appalachian State. If this writing and journalism stuff is something I'm good at, or at least proficient at, why not use it to try to affect the world in a positive way?

To not do so would be insulting to the people who poured themselves into my life. I may not have been able to do it while in the military. I may not be able to do it in the future either. But I can try to do my part right? Live up to the Appalachian State Criminal Justice Program School of Journalism? Why not?

Someone did it for me.

THIS PAGE INTENTIONALLY LEFT BLANK

ACKNOWLEDGEMENTS

I thank the dozens of military personnel who took time out of their schedules, in sometimes very rough conditions, to speak with me or allow me to observe them in action. Most of the content in this book is from conversations or footage of Soldiers, who were the most important reason the stories we published in Iraq were successful.

Thanks goes to Ireka Sanders and Nathan Hoskins, for reviewing my stories and images in Iraq and taking the time to develop my skills as a journalist. Thanks also goes to Sierra Melendez, who assisted in our preparation at Fort Campbell before we deployed and has continued to provide helpful feedback after.

I am grateful to Chalk Wetmore, Ryan Rivas, Richard Bumgardner, Sgt 1st Class. Mac, and many others who took the time out of their lives to help me in my career or personal life, with no expectation of benefit for themselves. I will never forget their lessons.

I wish to thank the Appalachian State University Criminal Justice Department, especially Dr. Simon who taught Criminal Law, for the outstanding instruction they provided during my undergraduate years. I also thank University of North Carolina at Chapel Hill and the professors there for providing and continuing to provide excellent instruction and feedback as I embark on my academic career.

I wish to thank my friends, both in the service and out, who have always been there for me, in particular Jensen Sales, Walter Archie, John Manzano, Austin Albers, and their families.

Finally, I would like to thank my family, especially my mother and father who spent my childhood and afterwards encouraging me to read, write, and learn, and who have supported me in all of my endeavors.

About the author:

A North Carolina native, Daniel Johnson attended Appalachian State University for his undergraduate education. He is a retired Army officer who served in the military for five years as an infantry officer, journalist, public relations officer, signal officer, and finally, social media administrator for the Army Reserve.

He is currently a Park Fellow in the Hussman School of Media and Journalism's MA program at UNC Chapel Hill.

Made in the USA
Las Vegas, NV
20 July 2022